SAHL IBN BISHR

THE INTRODUCTION TO THE SCIENCE OF THE JUDGMENTS OF THE STARS

Translated from the Twelfth Century Latin Version

By

JAMES HERSCHEL HOLDEN, M.A.

Fellow of the American Federation of Astrologers

Copyright 2008 by James Herschel Holden

No part of this book may be reproduced or transcribed in any form or by any means, electronic or mechanical, including photocopying or recording, or by any information storage and retrieval system without written permission from the author and publisher, except in the case of brief quotations embodied in critical reviews and articles. requests and inquiries may be mailed to: American Federation of Astrologers, Inc., 6535 S. Rural Road, Tempe AZ 85283-9760.

First printing 2008

ISBN-10: 0-86690-581-2
ISBN-13: 978-0-86690-581-7

Cover Design: Jack Cipolla

Published by:
American Federation of Astrologers, Inc.
6535 S. Rural Road
Tempe, AZ 85283

www.astrologers.com

Printed in the United States of America

Contents

Translator's Preface	xi
Book I Introduction	3
The Essential Signification of the Circle	3
The Accidental signification of the Circle	6
The Ascending House and whatever is in it is about Questions, and the rest of theTwelve Signs	6
Angles, Succedents, and Cadents	9
Difference in Strength of the Houses	9
Aspects	11
The 16 Modes that Signify Perfection and Destruction	12
The Knowledge of the Light or the Orb of the Seven Planets.	13
Separation	14
The Conjunction of Light	15
Prohibition	15
Reception	17
Minor Reception	18
A Planet not Received	19
Void of Course	19
Return	20
Giving Virtue	20
Giving Disposition and Nature	21
The Strength of the Planets	21
The Debility of the Planets	23
The Defects of the Moon	24
Explanation of Besieging	26
Hays	26
Testimony	27
The Joys of the Planets	27

Book II The Fifty Precepts	29
Book III Questions or The Book of Judgments of the Arabs	28
General Rules	43
A Chapter on the Conjunction of the ASC	49
The Second House on Matters of Substance	50
The Third House on the Matter of Brothers	52
The Fourth House on Matters of Heredity	52
The Fifth House on Matters Relating to Children and First about One Child	55
Whether a Child will be Born to Him or Not	55
Whether a Woman is Pregnant or Not, and Whether she will Bear a Child or Not	56
Whether a Pregnancy is True or False	57
Whether or not a Pregnant Woman will Bear Twins	57
Whether She will Bear a Male or a Female	57
The Sixth House on the Matter of Infirmity	58
Something on the Matter of Slaves and Freedmen	61
Buying a Slave-girl	63
The Relicts of a Dead Slave	63
Possession of the Same	63
The Seventh House on Matters of Marriage	64
The Impediment to the Marriage	65
Whether a Woman who has fled from her Husband will Return	66
Whether a Woman is a Virgin or not	66
Whether or not a Woman will bear a Child	67
Whether a Woman is Pregnant from Fornication	67
Whether a Woman has a Man she loves, or One who loves her	68
Which of Two will win a Competition	68
What will be the Action in Buying and Selling	71
Whether a Fugitive or Property or something	72

else that is lost will be found or not	
The Place of the Fugitive or the Robber	73
Whether it is better to Flee or to Return	74
Whether or not the Querent will get back what was Stolen	74
A Question about something lost—will it be found or not	76
A Question about the Robber—is he a Foreigner?	77
The Place of the Stolen Items	80
Whether the number of the Stolen Items is One or More	80
The Suspicion of the Robber	81
On the Same Subject	81
What Sort of Thing was Stolen	81
The Thing Stolen or Pilfered, What it is and the Type of Thing	84
A Question about the Robber, Whether it is a Male or a Female or an *Imbrio*	87
A Question about Association and its Outcome	90
A Question about a General going to War	90
The Cause of Wars	97
The Quality of the Army	98
The Eighth House in Connection with an Absent Person	100
The Ninth House on the Matter of Travel	101
The Entrance of a Traveler into a City	104
The Journeys of Princes and Kings	105
What Land Would be Better for the Querent	106
Whether it Would be Good for the Querent to Set Out on a Journey	106
Release from Captivity	106
The Return of Someone Absent	109
The Tenth House, About a Kingdom	110
Question about Anything, Whether He will get it or not	112
Royal Expenditures	115

A Question about Someone's condition put by a Representative	117
Where is the Ruler of the Kingdom	117
A Question about His Taking His Seat	118
The Current Condition of a Kingdom	122
A Person or a King Absent from a Kingdom	124
Will he remain in his Kingdom or not	126
The Eleventh House, About Hopes	126
The Relationship Between Two Persons	127
The Realization of Something Hoped For	127
The Twelfth House, On the Matter of Animals	127
The Condition of the Animal	128
A Question about the Age of the Animal	129
Enemies	129
Letters	130
Another Chapter on Letters	132
Whether the Letter is Good or Evil	132
What will be the Response to the Letter	133
Whether the Letter is Delivered or not	133
Whether the Letter is Signed or not	133
The Man who is Sending the Latter	134
Whether a Letter has Reached the King or not	134
Rumors	134
A Question about Something that is Feared	136
If a Slain Person will be Avenged or not	137
Whether Anything is True or False	138
Many things	138
More Things	139
Hunting on the Land	139
The Quantity of Hunting	140
A Banquet to Which You have been Invited	141
The Cause of the Banquet	144

The Significations of the Planetary Hours in Questions	146
Book IV Elections	149
The Ascendant and What is in it of Elections in the Knowledge of the Natures of the Signs, the First of which are the Mobile Signs	151
The Fixed Signs	152
The Common Signs	152
An Election for the Beginning of any Work, and the Ten Impediments of the Moon	154
The Second Sign or the Second House with its Elections, and First about Receiving and Allocating Money	157
An Election for Sharing Money or Some Kind of Work with Someone	158
An Election for Investing Money in Order to Profit from it	158
An Election for Buying or Selling	159
An Election for Alchemical Operations	160
The Third Sign or the Third House and its Elections	160
The Fourth Sign or the Fourth House and Whatever Kind of Elections are in it, and First for Building a House	160
An Election for Tearing Down a House	161
An Election for Buying Land or for Leasing it, so that You may Receive a Return from it	161
An Election for Diverting a River or for Digging a Well	162
An Election for Planting Trees	162
An election for Sowing Seed	163
The Fifth Sign or the Fifth House with its Elections, and First about Begetting a Male or Female Child	163
An Election for Removing a Dead Fetus from the Womb	164
An Election if you Want to Enroll a Son in a Course of Instruction or Send him to a Place in which he may be Taught some Trade	164
The Sixth Sign or the Sixth House with its Elections,	164

and First about Expelling Devils and Ghosts from any Place	
An Election for Taking Medicine or Applying a Plaster or Any Other Kind of Medication to Any Part of the Body	165
When Remedies for the Belly Should be Administered	165
The Head	165
The Body	166
Cures for Diseases	166
The Eyes	167
An Election for Shaving the Head with Medicine	169
An Election for Buying Slaves	169
An Election for Giving Freedom	170
The Seventh Sign or the Seventh House with its Elections and First for Marriage	170
An Election for Going to War	171
An Election for Buying or Mutually Accepting or Returning Instruments of War, or for Destroying any Place or any Instrument	174
The Eighth Sign or the Eighth House with its Elections	174
The Ninth Sign or the Ninth House with its Elections, and First for Travels	175
An Election for the Entrance of a Traveler into a Region or a City	178
The Tenth Sign or the Tenth House with its Elections, and First about Going with the King to a Region that he Rules	180
An Election for Elevation to a Kingdom	180
An Election for Putting the King on the Seat of Empire	180
An Election for Putting Someone in Charge of a Restoration	181
An Election for Strengthening a Rulership	181
An Election for being Inimical to a King	182

An Election for Mollifying a King who is Angry with You	182
The Eleventh Sign or the Eleventh House, and First for Making Friendship	182
An election for Seeking Something from Someone	182
The Twelfth Sign or the Twelfth House with its Elections, and First for Buying Animals	183
An Election for Going out to Hunt	184
An Election for Taking Flight, or for Whatever you Wish to do Secretly	185
An Election for Finding a Fugitive	185
An Election for Writing a Letter	185
Book V The Book of Times	**187**
The Principal Knowledge of the Times	189
Finding the Significator of the Time	189
The Life of a Man in the Ascendant	192
The House of Substance	193
The Times of the Third and Fourth Houses	193
The House of Children	193
The House of Illness	194
The 7th Sign for the Times or Hours of War from the Sayings of Theophilus	194
Remarks on the Eighth House	196
The 9th Sign on Travels from the Sayings of the Ancients	196
The Return of a Traveler	197
A Letter and Rumors	197
The 10th Sign in Connection with a King from the Sayings of Mâshâʾallâh	198
Appendix, a 9th House Question	**205**
A Question about a Vision or a Dream	205
Index of Persons	209
Bibliography	211

Translator's Preface

The Arabian astrologer known in the West as Zahel (or Zael) was actually Sahl ibn Bishr (1st half of the 9th cent.), a Jew, who served as court astrologer to the governor of Khurasan in the period 820-822 A.D. and later to al-Hasan ibn Sahl (d. 850/851), the vizier of Baghdad during the reign of the Caliph al-Ma'mûn (reigned 813-833). Al-Nadîm, the author of the *Fihrist*,[1] says that Sahl was "learned and distinguished," and he lists the titles of eighteen books that Sahl had written in Arabic. Among these are five that were translated into Latin by the 12th century translators. These are apparently those mentioned in the *Fihrist* as "the small book" *Introduction, The Keys of Judgment*, "the large book" *Questions, Choices*, and *The Times (Periods)*.

Some of the example charts discussed in Sahl's books can be dated to the 820s and evidently reflect his activity as a professional astrologer during that time.

Sahl's books are frequently cited in both versions of *The Book of Nine Judges*,[2] two anonymous compilations that were perhaps made in Arabic in the late ninth or tenth century and translated into Latin in the twelfth century.

Judging from the Latin translations of his five books, Sahl was a master of Horary and Electional astrology. He is very often cited by later astrologers writing in Latin or in modern languages as Zael or Zahel. His five short treatises, *Introduction to Astrology, The 50 Precepts, Judgments of Questions, Elections*, and *The Book of Times* appear to be the principal medieval source of rules for

---

[1] The priceless catalogue of Arabic literature written at the end of the 10th century by Muḥammad ibn Isḥâq al-Nadîm. I have used the English translation of Bayard Dodge, *The Fihrist of al-Nadîm* (New York: Columbia University Press, 1970. 2 vols.).

[2] See Francis J. Carmody, *Arabic Astronomical and Astrological Sciences in Latin Translation* (Berkeley and Los Angeles: California University Press, 1956), pp. 103-112.

Horary Astrology and Elections.[1] They constitute a corpus of instruction consisting of five books on these two branches of astrology.

The present English translation is from the first printed edition of the Latin text. So far as I am aware, Sahl's books have not previously been translated into English in their entirety. However, there is a modern Spanish translation[2] made from the early printed version.

Book I. Introduction to Astrology.

The first treatise defines the principal terms used in Horary and Electional Astrology and contains a chapter entitled "The 16 Modes that Signify the Accomplishment or Destruction [of the Question]." These are the particular aspects or configurations that give the main indications in Horary and Electional Astrology. They are: Perfection, Deterioration, Conjunction, Separation, Translation [of Light], Collection, Prohibition, Reception, Non-Reception, Void of Course, Return, Giving Virtue, Giving Disposition, Fortitude, Debility, and the Conditions of the Moon. This is followed by separate chapters defining each of these configurations in detail.

Writing a century after Sahl's treatises became available in Latin translation, the Italian master astrologer Guido Bonatti (c.1210-c.1295), in his *Book of Introduction to the Judgments of the Stars*,[3] lists these configurations (along with their badly corrupted Arabic names) in the 4th of his "146 Considerations."[4] Abraham Ibn Ezra (1089?-1167) discusses some of them in detail

---

[1] First printed together by Bonatus Locatellus at Venice in 1493/1494 in an omnibus edition, along with books by six other astrological authors.
[2] *Textos astrológicos Zahel-Hermes-Bethen-Almanzor* trans. by Demetrio Santos (Spain: Teorema, 1996?).
[3] I have used a photocopy of the first complete edition (Augsburg: Erhard Ratdolt, 1491).
[4] He also uses one of Sahl's charts (set for 5 July 824) as an example in Treatise 6, First House, Chapt. 4.

in Chapt, 7 of his book, *The Beginning of Wisdom*.[1] And the great modern master of Horary Astrology, William Lilly (1602-1681), explains those that he considers most important: Application, Separation, Prohibition (and Refrenation), Translation of Light, Reception, Void of Course, Frustration, Hayz, Combust, and Collection.[2]

Book II The Fifty Precepts.

The second treatise contains 50 Precepts of Horary Astrology. Most of these are paraphrased by Bonatti, *op. cit.*, Treatise V, the section containing the "146 Considerations," in Considerations, Nos. 17-77, where he often comments on or illustrates Sahl's precepts in his customary discursive style.[3]

Book III The Book of the Judgments of the Arabs.

The third treatise is devoted to Horary Astrology. It sets forth general rules for judging a horary chart followed by specific rules and examples for questions that pertain to each of the twelve houses, an arrangement that was followed by many subsequent writers.

Book IV Elections.

The fourth treatise explains the rules that are necessary for making Elections for various undertakings. The elections are listed in the order of the twelve houses to which they pertain.

Book V The Book of Times.

The fifth treatise is another shorter book on Elections that gives additional advice on choosing times for certain actions.

---

[1] *The Beginning of Wisdom* ed. by Raphael Levy and Francisco Cantera (Baltimore: The Johns Hopkins Press, 1939).
[2] *Christian Astrology* (London: Partridge & Blunden, 1647), p. 107 ff.
[3] See the English translation by Henry Coley, *A Guide for Astrologers* (London: B. Harris, 1676). That book is available in a modern edition from the A.F.A. (but erroneously attributed to William Lilly as author). The reader who is curious about Bonatti's version of the precepts can compare Coley's rendering of them with the translation of Sahl's original given herein.

Horary and Electional Astrology

Horary Astrology is the branch of astrology that deals with answering questions put at a definite time or with judging events that occurred at a known time. Electional Astrology is a related branch of astrology that seeks to determine the best possible moment to initiate a particular action within a specified time period. These two related arts were dealt with as a single branch of astrology by the classical Greek astrologers under the name *Katarchic Astrology* or the Astrology of Initiatives.

The earliest astrologer known to have written a book on the subject was Dorotheus of Sidon (first century A.D.). His book, the *Pentateuch*,[1] has unfortunately not come down to us in the original Greek, although many excerpts from it are found in Book III of the *Apotelesmatics* of the Egyptian astrologer, Hephaestio of Thebes (b. 380 A.D.),[2] and a few shorter citations by other writers remain from the end of the classical period. The earliest medieval treatises were written by Theophilus of Edessa (c.695-785), a Greek astrologer who lived in Baghdad and served as court astrologer to the Caliph al-Mahdî (reigned 775-785); Theophilus wrote on Elections; his books are extant in Greek but have not yet been published in a modern edition[3] or translated. In Book V, *The Book of Times*, Sahl mentions him as a source of rules for military Elections.

In the last years of the eighth century and the first years of the

---

[1]The *Pentateuch* was translated into Pahlavi (Middle Persian) in the fourth century and that version was subsequently translated into Arabic c.800 A.D. David Pingree has published an edition of the remains of the Arabic version along with the Greek and Latin excerpts and an English translation of the Arabic version, *Dorothevs Sidonivs/ Carmen Astrologicum* (Leipzig: B.G. Teubner, 1976). Some excerpts from Pingree's translation are published in my book, *A History of Horoscopic Astrology* (Tempe, Az.: A.F.A., Inc., 1996), pp. 32-41.
[2]See the edition of the Greek text by David Pingree, *Hephaestio Thebanus/Apotelesmatica* (Leipzig: B.G. Teubner, 1973-74. 2 vols.)
[3]Some short excerpts have been edited in the *Catalogus Codicum Astrologorum Graecorum* (Brussels, 1898-1953), V. 1. See also my book *A History of Horoscopic Astrology* (Tempe, Az.: A.F.A., Inc., 1996), pp. 100-103.

ninth century, the famous Jewish astrologer Mâshâ'allâh (c.740-c.815) wrote some short tracts in Arabic on Horary Astrology and Elections, among them is the tract entitled the *Reception of the Planets or Interrogations*, which was translated into Latin in the twelfth century and is available in modern Spanish and English translations. Sahl had certainly read those books, and in his youth he may possibly have even known Mâshâ'allâh personally.

But the principal font to which most later works on Horary and Elections can be traced is the book of Guido Bonatti mentioned above. Bonatti had evidently read everything available in Latin and was also an experienced professional astrologer. He mentions Haly[1] and other astrologers frequently, but he also relied heavily on Sahl's books. It is, therefore, useful to return to Sahl's books and read his explanation of and instructions for Horary and Electional Astrology.

Some Special Features of Sahl's Techniques

Many special planetary configurations are carefully noted by Sahl. Most of them will be unfamiliar to the modern astrologer. They are all explained in his text or in my footnotes.

The careful reader will note that Sahl used the original classical system of house division, the one that I have termed Sign-House.[2] This was the system devised by the inventors of horoscopic astrology in Alexandria, Egypt, in the second century B.C. It was the principal system used in classical antiquity. It passed to the Arabs in the eighth century, and before that to the Hindus (who still use it) when they too learned horoscopic astrology from Greek books.

---

[1] 'Alî ibn abî al-Rijâl (d. after 1037), a court astrologer to the Prince of Tunis, known to later astrologers as Haly Abenragel or Albohazen Haly or simply Haly. He was the author of an extensive general treatise on astrology called *The Outstanding* (or, *The Complete*) *Book on the Judgments of the Stars*. It was first printed by Erhard Ratdolt (Venice, 1485). I have not read the entire text, but I do not recall having seen Sahl's name mentioned among the many authorities that Haly cites.

[2] See my paper "Ancient House Division" in the A.F.A. *Journal of Research* 1, no. 1 (1982): 19-28, and my book, *A History of Horoscopic Astrology*, p.90, etc.

Sign-House works like this: the rising sign—all of it—constitutes the first house or Ascendant, regardless of which degree of it is rising; the next sign (again, all of it) is the 2nd house, the next sign after that is the 3rd house, etc. The tenth sign is the MC. Thus, Sahl, like the classical astrologers before him, often speaks of the "6th sign" or the "11th sign," where we would speak of the "6th house" or the "11th house." The ASC degree is mentioned from time to time, but it was not considered to be a "cusp" in the modern sense. And the astronomical MC degree is seldom or never mentioned. References to the MC are to the 10th sign from the ASC, not to a specific degree. In short, there are no "house cusps" in the modern sense of the word, or, if you like, they are all at the 1st degree of the sign that constitutes the house.

The ancients were accustomed for special purposes to count subsidiary houses from a planet's sign (especially from the Moon sign) or from the sign of the Lot of Fortune. But the primary set of houses was always the set counted from the ASC sign; hence, to make this clear, Sahl (like the classical astrologers) often adds "from the ASC" to a house number, as "the 9th house from the ASC."

Since the ASC sign was the primary house of the horoscope, a planet in the 12th sign was termed "cadent from the ASC." And this same term was also applied to planets in the 3rd, 6th, and 9th signs (houses). Moderns would merely say of a planet in the 3rd, 6th, 9th, or 12th house that it was "cadent," but the original term was "cadent from the ASC," which served to remind the astrologer that he was using houses counted from the ASC.

Two features of Sahl's text that will strike the modern reader are the continual and consistent use of house rulers as significators and the treatment of Mars and Saturn as malefics. Contrary to modern usage, Sahl called a spade a spade—the planets Venus and Jupiter are consistently called *fortuni* 'fortunes', which I have translated as 'benefics', and the planets Mars and Saturn are equally consistently called *mali* 'evils', which I have translated as 'malefics'.

The Moon is usually treated as a co-significator of the querent, but aside from that Sahl treats the house and the house ruler as the principal significators. In particular, the ASC sign and its planetary ruler are the principal significators of the querent, while the appropriate house sign and its ruler are the principal significators of the thing asked about. And since Sahl wrote in the ninth century, Scorpio was ruled by Mars, and Aquarius and Pisces by Saturn and Jupiter respectively.

When speaking of aspects, Sahl constantly uses the terms "conjoined with" and "joined to," both of which mean "in aspect with," and this can be either bodily (by conjunction) or by visual aspect. He also often uses the phrase "joined to such-and-such a planet in one sign." This apparently is done to exclude close approaches of two planets in which one is at the end of a sign and the other is at the beginning of the next sign. Modern astrologers would consider two planets thus situated to be in conjunction, but Sahl did not—the change of sign was considered to be a barrier between them. (However, he does record that Mâshâ'allâh would allow such a pair of planets to be in conjunction if they were within orbs, but he would not extend this to visual aspects, since he considered the aspects to be a function of the *signs* that the planets are in, not of the degree positions of the planets within the signs.)

In translating the Latin version of Sahl's treatises, I have generally rendered *locus* 'place' as "house," and *domus* 'house' as "domicile," which means the same thing, but is more frequently used than *signum* 'sign'. I have used some old terms such as "afflicted" and "impedited," which mean badly placed by house, badly aspected, or "under the Sun beams." The latter term is similar but not quite identical to the modern term "combust." I have also retained the now obsolete term "testimony," which refers to a planet's rulership in the sign in which it is posited in connection with an aspect that it makes. And occasionally I have used the convenient old term "fortunated," which means "placed in a fortunate position" and is thus similar to the more familiar term "fortified." The opposite of this is the term "vitiated," i.e. "debilitated." Some other terms are explained in the footnotes.

I have also sometimes referred to the Moon or Venus as "she" or "her" and to a planet as "he" or "him" for the sake of clarity in a sentence that would otherwise have several "it's" whose individual referents would be uncertain.

Some Reflections on the Changes in Society

Some of the significations of the houses and planets given by Sahl are no longer appropriate for most modern societies. For example, the 10th house is frequently assigned to "the king." But few modern societies have kings. We must then understand these references to refer to "the chief of state," "the prime minister," "the president," or some similar modern head of government. On a lower level of society, it can refer simply to "the boss." In general, it refers to that individual who is dominant and in a position to order or command the querent and to exact penalties for non-compliance with his directives.

Similarly, slaves are assigned to the 6th house. But slavery has been abolished in most modern societies. Hence, the 6th house now signifies those who are social inferiors of the querent. These may include hired servants or employees of the querent, or his management subordinates. In the rare cases where the querent has a title of nobility or aristocracy, it may in some instances simply refer to those common or untitled people with whom he is associated.

Marriages were most often arranged in the ninth century. Today they are generally contracted by the individuals themselves. Hence, there are fewer "go-betweens" taking part in marriage arrangements. And of course, the occasional references to multiple marriages must nowadays generally refer in the Western world to successive marriages rather than to polygamous ones.

A bothersome term used in connection with the 2nd house and its questions and elections is the Latin word *substantia* 'substance'. This is a term that encompasses the querent's total assets, large or small, including valuable possessions both fixed and moveable, monetary assets, and current income. It could be translated as "wealth," but that implies riches. The legal term "estate" covers possessions, but to most people other than lawyers that term implies merely lands and buildings and does not include monetary and moveable possessions. And the word "assets" does not usually include income. I have, therefore, sometimes translated *substantia* one way and sometimes another. The reader may wish to substitute another term that he finds more appropriate in a particular instance.

The technological marvels of the current age—electronic devices, automobiles, airplanes, etc.—are of course not mentioned. Consequently, the reader must decide for himself which house they belong to and which planets are most analogous to them.

The Basis of the Translation

The present English translation is based upon the early printed editions of the Latin version with additions from my unpublished edition of the Latin text, made mainly from a microfilm copy of the 13th century Latin MS 16204 in the Bibliothèque Nationale in Paris (cited in the notes as **P**) and from the early printed editions. I have used a photocopy of the incunabula edition (Venice: Bonatus Locatellus, 1493), which I have cited in the notes as **v**.

There are a number of places in the text of the printed versions where words are found that are not present in MS **P**. In some cases these are obviously due to accidental omissions by the copyist of **P** (attributable to homoeoteleuton, etc.), but in other places they may be insertions by the editors of **v** and **b**; and as such, they are not part of the original text. Nevertheless, I have usually treated them as if they were parts of the original text accidentally omitted by MS **P**. There are also places where the opposite occurs and **v** (or **b**) omits words that are present in **P**; this probably reflects accidental omissions in the unidentified MSS used by the editors of the early printed editions.

In some places where the Latin text seemed to be faulty, I have compared similar passages in Guido Bonatti's book. Bonatti sometimes cites the Latin version of Sahl verbatim, but more often he paraphrases it. Still, he usually retains the sense of the original, which is helpful in restoring corrupt or defective passages in Sahl's text. The reader who does not know Latin can compare parts of the present translation of Book II of Sahl's work with the corresponding passages in Henry Coley's translation of Bonatti's "146 Considerations" (available from the A.F.A. Book Department as William Lilly, *The Astrologer's Guide*). There is also an edition of extracts from the Greek version that was independently translated from the Arabic in *Catalogus Codicum Astrologorum Graecorum* V. 3. I have cited a few passages from it. And in a few places I have found something useful in the Arabic excerpts (and their German translation) published in Viktor Stegemann's *Dorotheos von Sidon und das sogennante Introductorium des Sahl ibn Bishr* (Prague, 1942), which compares the Arabic text of Sahl's Book I with the Latin and Greek versions.

The Latin translation from the Arabic was fairly faithful, although somewhat paraphrased. And, judging from Stegemann's citation of the Arabic text, the Latin translator appears to have appended some explanatory remarks to his translation. The present English translation is a fairly literal translation of the Latin version. However, the reader will find some places where the translation is confusing or does not seem to make any sense. In most cases these are places where one of three things has happened: (1) the copy of the Arabic text used by the twelfth century Latin translator was faulty; (2) the Latin translation itself was faulty; or (3) my edition of the Latin text is not helpful. In rare instances, the Latin text may be sound, but I have failed to understand it. However, I do not believe that this has happened very often because most of the text is straightforward and easy to understand. Generally, where I have found difficulty in understanding it, it seemed plain that the Latin text itself was faulty. Also, in some places, I have judged that one or more words are missing from the Latin text; in those places I have usually called attention to the omission in a footnote; and in some such places I have supplied a missing word or words in square brackets (or in angle brackets in a footnote). In addition, I have also used brackets to enclose words that I have added to the translation to clarify its meaning for the reader.

Some characteristics of the translated text reflect the language of the original Arabic version. The most obvious example is the ubiquitous 'and'. Arabic, like Hebrew, most frequently ties clauses together with the coordinating conjunction *wa* (Hebr. *waw*) 'and', where other languages would use 'but' or 'or', thus making its sentences rather like the speech of a child, "I went outside, and I sat down on the grass, and I saw a bird, and the cat chased it, and the bird flew away, and I watched it go . . . ." In the translation I have sometimes changed 'and' to 'but' and rarely to 'or', but the reader will see other places where this could have been done. And I have sometimes broken up long strings of clauses into two or more sentences, but more often I have merely separated them by semicolons.

Since the present edition is based upon the first complete printed edition (printed at Venice in 1493) and a single MS of the 13th century, it is conflated to some unknown extent. An improved Latin text of all five of Sahl's treatises could be made by collating additional MSS, establishing their mutual relations, and by reference to the Arabic text, which is preserved in a few MSS in European libraries, but I leave that task to others.

SAHL IBN BISHR

THE INTRODUCTION TO THE SCIENCE OF THE JUDGMENTS OF THE STARS.

2/Sahl Ibn Bishr

(p.433a) Here begins the book of Zahel the Jew, *The Introduction to the Science of the Judgments of the Stars in Questions.*[1]

Book I.

The Essential Signification of the Circle.

In the name of God, the Pious and Merciful!

Sahl ibn Bishr, the Israelite, said: Know that there are twelve signs; of these, six are masculine and six feminine. Aries, therefore, is a masculine sign of the diurnal signs and Taurus a feminine one of the nocturnal signs; and similarly, masculine follows feminine and feminine masculine down to the end of the signs. And of these, there are six signs ascending *directly*, i.e. they have a direct ascension, and another six ascending *crookedly*, i.e. they have a crooked ascension. And the directly ascending ones are those from the beginning of Cancer down to the end of Sagittarius because the latitude[2] of each of these is more than its length, and it ascends in more than two equal hours; on account of this, they are called "ascending directly." And those ascending crookedly are the ones from the beginning of Capricorn down to the end of Gemini because the latitude of each of these is less than its length, and it ascends in less than two equal hours; on account of this, they are called "ascending crookedly."

And four of these are called *mobile*, i.e. Aries, Cancer, Libra, and Capricorn; and they are called mobile for this reason— because when

---

[1] This is the *incipit* of the Parisian MS that I have designated as **P**. Note that the Latin spelling of the author's name, Zahel, probably reflects the Spanish custom of writing an initial *s* as *z* (which was pronounced like an *s*). The number and letter in the parentheses refer to the page and column number in the MS.
[2] Here, and in the next sentence, the word *latitudo* 'latitude' does not refer to celestial latitude but rather to the length of time it takes a sign to rise.

the Sun enters into the beginnings of these signs, the season changes to the nature of the following season. And four of them are *fixed*, i.e. Taurus, Leo, Scorpio, and Aquarius; and they are called fixed for this reason—because when the Sun enters into their beginnings, the season is fixed in its own essence and is not changed, i.e. if it is hot it will stay hot, and if it is cold it will stay cold, and if it is spring it will stay spring, and if it is autumn it will stay autumn.

And four of these are said to be *common*, which in the Arabic language is called *dhawat al-jasadayn*, i.e. *bicorporeal*; which are Gemini, Virgo, Sagittarius, and Pisces; and they are called common for this reason—because when the Sun has come to the middle of these, the seasons are mingled, and the first half of it is hot and the second half cold, or the first half is cold and the second half hot.

And some of these are called *quadrupedal*, i.e. Aries, Taurus, Leo, Capricorn, and the end of Sagittarius.

Also, some of these signs are *fiery*, i.e. Aries, Leo, and Sagittarius; and that is the first *triplicity*. And the second triplicity is *earthy*, and it signifies whatever is in the earth and is born from it, i.e. Taurus, Virgo, and Capricorn. And the third triplicity is *airy*, and it signifies men and winds and whatever is in the air, i.e. Gemini, Libra, and Aquarius. The fourth is *watery*, i.e. it signifies waters and whatever is in the waters, i.e. Cancer, Scorpio, and Pisces.

And some of the signs are said to be *dark*, i.e. Libra and Capricorn. And there is a certain place in the signs that is called *combust*,[1] and it is the end of Libra and the beginning of Scorpio.

And some of these signs have only a *half voice*, i.e. Virgo, Capricorn, and Aquarius. And some of them have [*full*] *voices*, i.e. Aries, Taurus, Gemini, Leo, Libra, and Sagittarius. And some of them *do not have voices*[2], i.e. Cancer, Scorpio, and Pisces.

---

[1] More often called *the combust way*.
[2] Usually called *mute*.

And some of them in the generation of children are half or common, i.e. *not entirely sterile*, i.e. Taurus, Gemini, and Aquarius; and some *have many children*, i.e. Cancer, Scorpio, and Pisces; while some are *sterile*, i.e. Aries Leo, Virgo, Sagittarius, and Capricorn.

And some of these signify mountains and rough country, i.e. Aries, Leo, Sagittarius, and Capricorn. And some signify habitable and flat country, i.e. rural areas and those that are cultivated, i.e. Taurus, Virgo, and Capricorn. But some signify sandy country, i.e. Gemini, Libra, and Aquarius. Some too signify wet and watery areas or those which are next to water, i.e. Cancer, Scorpio, and Pisces. Therefore, the *fire signs* signify unknown things and every substance that pertains to God or is made by Him. And the *signs of seed* signify the earth and all its culture and everything made from it. The *human signs* signify men and winds and everything that is elevated above the earth. And the *water signs* signify wet lands and everything that is made from wetness; and the signs generating more children signify groups of men.

The Aries triplicity, therefore, is hot and dry; of the natures, it has the *red choler*, and of the parts of the world, the east. The *rulers* of this triplicity are the Sun by day and Jupiter by night; and their *partner* by day and by night is Saturn. The Taurus triplicity is cold and dry; of the natures, it has the *black choler*, and of the parts of the world, the south. Its rulers are Venus by day and the Moon by night; their partner by day and by night is Mars. The Gemini triplicity is hot and wet; of the natures, it has the *blood*, and of the parts of the world, the west. And the rulers of this triplicity are Saturn by day and Mercury by night; and their partner by day and by night is Jupiter. The Cancer triplicity is cold and wet; of the natures, it has the *phlegm*, and of the parts of the world, the north. And the rulers of this triplicity are Venus by day and Mars by night; whose partner by day and by night is the Moon.

The Accidental Signification of the Circle.

2. The Chapter of the Substance of the Twelve Signs and what every Sign Signifies.[1]

Know that for every *querent* or for every *thing* asked about, we have found a signification that signifies whatever of good or evil there is in the question [resulting] from the several modes that the wise men have expounded with regard to the signification of questions and of things [asked about] from the inherent qualities of the twelve signs and from the natures of the seven planets; and we shall, according as God wills, endeavor to state the houses from which things [of significance] are received, just like the planets, from their natures and significations.

The Ascending House and whatever is in it is about Questions, and the rest of the twelve Signs.[2]

The *first house* is the one whose beginning arises or ascends in the east in the hour of the question or of the nativity or of the beginning of any work; and it signifies death and life because it is the ascending of that life which precedes its life when it leaves the womb of its mother. For this sign ascends from the lower part of the earth to the upper part of it and, as it were, from darkness into light[3]; and similarly, the native goes out of the darkness of the womb into the light of this age and from the narrowness of the womb to the broadness of the air; and it shows the querent asking his question from the secret of his own heart, and it brings into the light and then discloses what was hidden. Therefore, it signifies bodies and life and the beginning and the motions of the body and whatever will come from some occurrence and the starting up or taking place of whatever thing, and everything mobile or rational, and the beginnings of all things.

---

[1] A chapter heading in MS **P**.
[2] This is a chapter subtitle in MS **P**.
[3] This same statement is made by Paul of Alexandria, *Introduction to Astrology*, Chapter 2, in connection with the rising times of each of the twelve signs.

The *second house* from the ASC does not aspect the ascending sign[1]; it signifies the gathering of substance and the maintenance of life and things aiding that and receipts and gifts.

The *third house* is cadent from the ASC; it signifies brothers and sisters, neighbors and relations, and their activities, also patience and advice, faith and religion, and contention among sects, letters, delegations and delegates, travels, and dreams.

The *fourth house* is called the *angle of the earth*; it signifies fathers and their condition, i.e. the parental origin and stock, and prisons, lands and country property, and country places and communities, and every kind of building, and everything that is covered and concealed, or hidden treasures, and death, and what will happen after death, i.e. what will happen to the deceased, viz. from [the time of] his burial, and whether the deceased will be dug up or cremated or put in a pillory or in some other place, and other things that will happen to deceased persons; and it signifies the end of things, and houses and lands, i.e. inherited property, and everything that is buried under the earth.

The *fifth house* succeeds[2] the angle of the earth; and it is the house of love because it is of the triplicity of the ASC and it is the house of the *joy* of Venus,[3] and it signifies children and everything in which there is trust, delegates[4] and gifts of lands[5] and seeking for women, friendships and friends, communities and communal affairs, and the fruits of heredities.[6]

---

[1]The ancient and medieval astrologers did not recognize semi-sextiles and quincunxes as aspects, but only the conjunction, sextile, square, trine, and opposition. Hence, from their point of view, the second house is not in aspect with the first house.
[2]That is, it 'follows' or rises *after* the fourth house. In modern terminology, it is a *succedent* house.
[3]'the joy of the ASC' in both **P** and **v**, but I have written 'Venus' for 'ASC'. Each planet is said to have its *joy* in a particular house; this is discussed in a later chapter.
[4]Ambassadors and other go-betweens.
[5]Reading *donationes *terrarum* 'gifts of lands' rather than *donationes herrem* with MS **P**. or *donationes honorem* 'gifts honor' with **v**. Probably an early scribal error.
[6]Because it is the 2nd house from the 4th.

The *sixth house* is cadent from the ASC; it does not aspect it; and it is a malign house; it signifies infirmities, both curable and incurable, and the causes of infirmities, also male slaves and female slaves, injustices, and changes from place to place.

The *seventh house* is the *angle of the west*; it signifies marriages and matters relating to women, battles, and contentions and contrarities, and [especially] contentions that are between two people, also the one who asks the question and the one asked about, such as fugitives and thieves, and persons lost, and other things similar to these, travel and losses of things and matters relating to them. And this sign[1] is an enemy of the ASC, and every planet that is in it is opposed to the ASC.

The *eighth house* succeeds the *angle of the west*; it signifies death and killing and lethal poison and fear, and whatever is inherited from the dead, and everything that dies, toil and sorrow, wars also and contentions, attendants and assistants of adversaries and contemners[2] and things entrusted, i.e. handed over to be preserved, and estate management, laziness, and talents.

The *ninth house* is cadent from the ASC; it signifies travels and journeys, and the worship of divinity and all houses of religion, philosophy, and the foreknowledge[3] of things, knowledge of the stars and divinations, letters, and delegates and delegations or commissions, dreams, faith, and divine knowledge, and sanctity and religion, and all things past and receding [in time], and a man deprived of honor or his own work, and things of a future time and foreknowledge of the future.

The *tenth house* is called the *angle of heaven*; it signifies the king or kingdom, eminence and supreme authority, glory and re-

---

[1] Sahl used the Sign-House system of house division, so the word "sign" here is also equivalent to "house."
[2] Because it is the 2nd house from the 7th—hence it rules the *assets* of opponents.
[3] Reading *prescientiam* 'foreknowledge' (with **Bonatus**, ii.3, f. e2, and h) instead of *presentiam* 'presence' with MS **P**.

membrance or the praise of voice; mothers too; and substance stolen or taken away; judges, princes and prelates; work and every profession.

The *eleventh house* succeeds the angle of heaven; it signifies friends, faith and good fortune, the substance of the king and his return or tribute,[1] and his soldiers and attendants, and the man who succeeds the king or the first prince; and it signifies praises and children.

The *twelfth house* is cadent from the ASC, and it does not aspect it; it signifies enemies and labors, lamentations and sadnesses, sorrowful sighs, and hatreds, and malevolent craftinesses, travels, and all [kinds of] malice, hard work, prisons, and animals.

Angles, Succedents, and Cadents.

Moreover, the [houses] that are more worthy and more praiseworthy than all the other houses of the circle that are succeeding them in power in turn are thus distinguished. The circle is divided into 12 signs, of which 4 are named *angles*, i.e. the sign ascending, and the fourth, the seventh, and the tenth. These signs are just like angles of heaven, which signify everything that is present and in which it is, i.e. the presence of things and their strength in everything; and four of these houses are called *succedents* or "following the angles," i.e. those rising after them, i.e. the second, the fifth, the eighth, and the eleventh. These signify everything that will be and that follows, and whatever there is and that follows from things. And the remaining four are said to be *cadent* from the angles, i.e. those that have receded and fallen from the angles—these are the third, sixth, ninth, and twelfth. And these signify whatever has receded and gone away from things, by the will of God.

Difference in Strength of the Houses.

The ASC is stronger than all the other houses of the circle. And this sign is worthier than all the other signs, and a planet that

---

[1] Namely, his assets and revenue.

is in it is stronger than all the other planets, and especially if that same planet is in its own domicile¹ or its exaltation or its triplicity or in its own terms or face.² The one that follows next in strength is the MC, then the angle of the west, i.e. the seventh from the ASC, then follows the angle of the earth, i.e. the fourth from the ASC. Then the eleventh house from the ASC follows that house next in strength; and the fifth house follows it, then the ninth. These seven houses are praiseworthy and strong. The first of them is better than the second, and the second is better than the third, etc. And after these, from the signs that are chosen as being good, is the third sign from the ASC because it is the house of the *joy*³ of the Moon. Then the second house from the ASC because it ascends next after the ASC. But in the eighth sign from the ASC there is impediment and great evil because it is the house of death, and it does not aspect the ASC.

The rest of the signs of the circle, i.e. the sixth and the twelfth, are worse than all the other houses and inferior to them. And every planet that is in [either of] those two houses will be of no use because the 6th sign from the ASC is the house of infirmities and bodily defects and every kind of illness, curable or incurable; it is cadent from the ASC and does not aspect it, and it is the house of the *joy* of Mars. And the twelfth from the ASC is the house of enemies and hard work and sadness; and it is cadent from the ASC and it does not aspect it, and it is the house of the *joy* of Saturn. For Saturn rejoices in lamentation and the expression of sadness and distress.

<And note that each sign aspects the third before it, and the third after it, which is the eleventh; and this aspect is called the *sextile*, because it comprises a sixth part of the circle, i.e. 60 degrees of the 360 degrees of the whole circle; e.g. a planet that was in the beginning of Aries aspects the one that was before it in Gemini, and the fourth after it, i.e. the tenth; and that aspect is

---

¹The sign that it rules.
²Face is another name for decan.
³Each planet is said to have its *joy* in a particular house. These are enumerated individually in a later chapter.

called the quartile because it comprises a 4th part of the circle, i.e. 90 degrees. It also aspects the 5th before it and the 5th after it; and that aspect is called the *trine* because it comprises a third part of the circle, i.e. 120 degrees. It also aspects the 7th [sign] by *opposition*; and that is an aspect that is one of enmity; and if there were planets in these signs, they are said to be in aspect.>[1]

Aspects

3. A Chapter on the Knowledge of the Aspects of the Planets.[2]

There are seven[3] *aspects* of the planets, i.e. conjunction, sextile and square, trine and opposition. For the conjunction is when two planets are joined *in the same sign* and there are [not more than] 15 degrees between them, and thus this is the limit[4] of the conjunction. The sextile aspect is from the third sign and the eleventh.[5] (p. 436a) The square aspect is from the fourth sign and the tenth. The trine aspect is from the fifth sign [and the ninth]. But the opposition is from the seventh sign.

Therefore, of these aspects, the strongest ones are the conjunction and the opposition. And these are [aspects] of stronger action and enmity. And these aspects signify enemies that are openly harmful; and they signify contrariety and divisions.[6] And the square aspect is medium, i.e. it does not disclose its enmities. And the second sextile aspect is stronger than the first sextile aspect. And the second square aspect is stronger than the first square as-

---

[1]This passage on the aspects is in the printed book **v** but not in MS **P**; hence, it may be either an accidental omission in **P** or an interpolation inserted by the editor of **v**.
[2]A chapter heading in MS **P**.
[3]*Seven*, rather than eight, because properly speaking the conjunction is not an aspect but a position, and there are two each of the sextile, square, and trine, and one opposition, thus making a total of seven "aspects."
[4]That is, its "orb."
[5]Counting both ends, as we do with the houses.
[6]The Latin word *participationes* 'participations' refers to sharing something among two or more. But here it must imply a division of either ownership or action that is discordant, so I have translated it as 'divisions'.

pect. And of the trine aspects, the second is stronger than the first. And this aspect is called "elevation."

Moreover, the signs that do not aspect each other and in which a planet in one of them does not aspect a planet in the other are these: the second sign, the sixth, the eighth, and the twelfth. Aside from these four, the others aspect each other.

The 16 Modes that Signify Perfection and Destruction.[1]

4. A Chapter Explaining the Perfection of Things and their Destruction.[2]

Know that everything that the stars signify is done or not done in one of 16 *modes*, i.e. *alichel* in Arabic that Latin dubs "perfection"; *alicher*, i.e. "deterioration"; *alitisal*, i.e. "conjunction"; *alitiuctraf*, i.e. the "separation" or disjunction of the planets from their conjunction; *anualac*, i.e. "translation"; *algemee*, i.e. congregation, or "collection", which sounds better; *almane*, i.e. forbidding or "prohibition"; *alchobol*, i.e. "reception"; *gattalchobol*, i.e. "non-reception"; *halaaceir*, i.e. that is "void of course"; *atrad*, i.e. "return"; *defaalchota*, i.e. that is "giving[3] virtue"; *defaatesbir*, i.e. "giving disposition" and nature; *alchoe*, i.e. "virtue" or strength; *adoef*, i.e. "debility"; *lalcoa*, i.e. "virtue" or strength; *wah wel alchamar*, i.e. "condition of the Moon".[4]

---

[1] Cf. Bonatti, *Liber astronomicus*, Treatise 5, the 4th Consideration, p. k 6. The spelling of the Arabic terms is badly corrupted.

[2] A chapter heading in MS **P**.

[3] In this and in the next mode, the Latin text has *pulsatio* 'striking', which is an incorrect choice of the possible meanings of the Arabic verb *dafaʿa*, which can mean 'to shove away' but also 'to hand over'; here, it should be understood as "giving," and I have so translated it. Likewise in a few other places below. Cf. Wright, *The Book of Instruction...* by al-Biruni, p. 303 n.1. Also, the independent Greek version (ed. by I. Heeg in CCAG V.3, p.107) translates the Arabic word correctly as *paradosis* 'handing over'.

[4] The words in italics are the corrupted Latin transliterations of Arabic words as they appear in MS **P** (I have omitted the corresponding transliterations in the printed book **v**, which are sometimes better and sometimes worse than those in MS **P**). The original Arabic words are these: *al-iqbâl* 'progress'; *al-idbâr* 'deterioration'; *al-ittiṣâl* 'conjunction'; *al-jamʿ* 'collection'; *al-manʿ* 'prohibition';

Explanation of *alichel*. *Alichel* is when a planet is in an angle or in the house following an angle.

Alicher is when a planet is cadent from the angles.

Alittisal is when a planet that is light and swift goes to the conjunction of another planet that is slower and heavier, and the lighter planet has fewer degrees than the slower one, so long as it will go to it until it is joined to it and is in such a minute by aspect. *Mutathil*,[1] i.e. "conjunction" or "bonding,"[2] is said until it is separated from it by the space of one degree, and then it is called *musarif*,[3] i.e. "separated from it." But if the planets are conjunct in the same sign, a planet is not said to be separated from another until it goes past it by the space of half of its orb, i.e. of its light, because each planet has an orb of light and individual degrees, half of which degrees are before the planet and the other half after it, and when another planet has passed through that space it is called "separated" from it.

The Knowledge of the Light or the Orb of the Seven Planets.

Know that the *orb* of the light of the Sun is 30 degrees, of which half is before it and the other half after it, i.e. 15 degrees before the Sun itself and 15 behind. Whenever there is from 1 to 15 degrees between the Sun and another planet, then its light is projected upon it, and it is conjoined to it. And the light of the Moon is 12 degrees

---

al-qabûl 'reception'; *ghayr al-qabûl* 'non-reception'; *khalâ> al-sayr* 'empty course'; *al-radd* 'return'; *dafᶜ al-quwwa* 'giving virtue or power'; *dafᶜ al-tadbîr* 'giving disposition'; *al-quwwa* 'virtue' or 'strength'; *al-uᶜf* 'debility'; *al-quwwa* 'virtue' or 'strength'; *wa aḥwâl al-qamar* 'and conditions of the Moon'. I have enclosed the English terms most frequently used in double quotes.

[1] Probably from the Arabic *muttaṣil* "adjacent'.
[2] The term *bonding* for a close conjunction or aspect (within 1 degree) is an earlier term used to designate a conjunction or aspect with an orb of 1 degree or less. It is thus the ancestor of the term *partile*, although in modern usage 'partile' usually designates two planets in aspect that are in the same numbered degree of their respective signs, which is not quite the same thing.
[3] Probably from the Arabic *inṣirâf* 'departure', with the letters scrambled by the Latin copyists.

before and behind. The light of both Venus and Mercury is 7 degrees before and behind, by this amount of light each of them is conjoined to another planet. The light of both Saturn and Jupiter is 9 degrees before and behind. And the light of Mars is 8 degrees before and behind.

Whenever one planet aspects another and within its own light strikes the degree of that other, it is said to be conjoined to it; and if it does not strike it within its own light, it is not said to be conjoined but rather "going to conjunction" until it begins to be [actually] conjoined to it. And if there was a planet at the end of a sign, joined to none, and it strikes another within its light, [then] whichever one of the planets that was more worthy within its own light will be conjoined to it, even thought the planet that was in the first sign does not see it.[1]

Separation.

The explanation of the recession or *separation* of the planets is that a lighter planet overtakes another heavier one and [then] begins to have more degrees [than it] either by aspect or by conjunction. For an aspect is from one sign to another, while a conjunction is said to be from one degree to another. This is the opinion of Messahalla (i.e. "the one whom God wished to be great").[2]

Translation of light from one planet to another is when a lighter planet is separated from another that is heavier and is joined to still another; then it "conjoins" them as it were and carries the nature of the first to the other one to which it is conjoined. An example of which is when Virgo was ascending and there was a question about marriage, and the Moon was in the 10th degree of the sign

---

[1] This seems to say that if a planet was at the end of a sign but within the light (orb) of another planet in the next sign, it will be in conjunction with it, although technically the two are not in aspect, since adjacent signs are disjunct.

[2] The famous Jewish astrologer Mâshâ'allâh (c.740-c.815). Sahl (or perhaps the 12th century translator) has tried to explain his Muslim name (it actually means "What God wills"). His original Jewish name was either Jethro or Manassaeh (the authorities differ).

Gemini and Mercury in the 8th degree of Leo and Jupiter in the 13th degree of Pisces. And Mercury, which was the ruler of the ASC, which was the significator of the querent, was not aspecting Jupiter, which is the ruler of the marriage, because it was in the eighth sign from it. I therefore looked at the Moon, which I found in the 10th degree of Gemini, viz. separated from Mercury and joined to Jupiter, for it was carrying the light between the two of them; and this signified the completion of the thing, i.e. the attainment of the woman through the hands of go-betweens and those running back and forth between the two [parties].[1]

The Conjunction of Light.

The *conjunction of light* is when the ruler of the ASC and the ruler of the thing quesited are both joined to a heavier planet, which conjoins their strength and light and receives their natures. For example, a certain question was about a king, whether he would acquire a kingdom or not. And the sign Libra was ascending, whose ruler is Venus, who was significator of the querent in the 10th degree of the sign Aries. And the Moon, ruler of the royal house that signified the kingdom was in the 12th degree of the sign Taurus; and the two were not aspecting each other. And Jupiter was in the 15th degree of the sign Cancer in the angle of heaven (the MC), viz. in a royal house; and the Moon and Venus were joined to him. Jupiter, therefore, conjoined the light, i.e. the rays, of both of them in the house of the thing quesited, i.e. in the house of the kingdom. This signified the acquisition of the kingdom through the hands of some judge or bishop or through the hands of some chosen man to whom both planets freely gave their assent.

Prohibition.

Almane, i.e. *prohibition*, is made in three modes, of which one is said to be "the *abscission of light*." And this is when between the ruler of the ASC and the ruler of the thing quesited there is some planet in fewer degrees than one of them, and there will be a con-

---

[1] It seems to me that this is the chart of an actual case.

junction with that one before the conjunction with the ruler of the thing can be made. An example of which is when Virgo was ascending, and a question was made about marriage, and Mercury was the ruler of the ASC, which is the significator of the querent, [and it] was in the 10th degree of the sign Cancer, and Jupiter, ruler of the 7th house, which is the significator of the bride-to-be, in the 15th degree of the sign Pisces, and Mars was in the 13th degree of Aries. Mars, therefore, cut off the light of Mercury from Jupiter. And Mars was in the 8th sign from the ASC, namely in the sign of the woman's property. It was signified, therefore, that the destruction of this thing would be from a description of the dowry.

The second mode is when a light planet and another heavier planet are in the same sign and there is a third one between them in the same sign moving to a conjunction with the heavier one; that one takes away the conjunction of the first one. An example of which is when Cancer was ascending, and the question was about marriage,[1] and the Moon was in the 8th degree of Gemini and Mars in the 10th degree of the aforesaid sign, but Saturn was in the 12th degree of the same before[2] Mars. Therefore, Mars separates the Moon and Saturn; it takes away their conjunction and destroys the matter.

The third mode is when a light planet is joined to another heavier planet in the same sign, and there is [still] another, which is below the lighter one in degrees (i.e. having fewer degrees), that is joined to that same heavier one by aspect. Therefore, the light planet that is with the heavy one in the same sign prohibits the conjunction of the third one that is in aspect; whenever it transits, the conjunction will be true. And this mode similarly prohibits matters and renders them just like the other preceding ones.

An example of which is when Cancer was ascending, and it was a question about marriage, and the Moon, ruler of the ASC, which

---

[1] The positions given in this example can be dated approximately to 22 August 824 at about 2 AM–seemingly an odd time for a question to be put in the ninth century.
[2] We would say "after" Mars.

is the significator of the querent, was in the 15th degree of Scorpio, and Mars in the 10th degree of Taurus, and Saturn in the 23rd degree of that same Taurus.[1] And Mars was below the degrees of the Moon, i.e. less in degrees, and consequently it was cutting off the aspect between the Moon and Saturn and prohibiting their conjunction because Mars was being joined to Saturn in the same sign, and a conjunction of that sort is stronger than a conjunction by aspect. For an aspect does not destroy a conjunction, but a conjunction does destroy an aspect. And an aspect does not cut off an aspect, but it does prohibit the matter. But a conjunction does in fact cut off an aspect.

And when one planet is joined to another, but before it comes to it, it is joined to a third; and when it has been joined to that one, the conjunction itself is destroyed. Similarly, if a planet is joined to another planet in the same sign, and it commits its own disposition to [still] another, i.e. it is joined to [still] another, which is in another sign, and after its conjunction with that one it comes by aspect to the one that is with it in the same sign and is joined to it, the judgment will be according to the second planet that is with it in the same sign.

An example of which is when the Moon was in the 10th degree of Taurus and Mars in the 20th degree of that same Taurus, and the Moon would be joined to Venus by aspect before it would be joined to Mars, and Venus was in the 15th degree of Cancer, even though Venus was less in degrees, nevertheless, the judgment would be referred to Mars because it was [actually] with the Moon in the same sign. And a conjunction of this sort is, as we have said, stronger than an aspect.

Reception.

The *reception* of the planets is when a planet is joined to [an-

---

[1] This could be dated to 13 December 822 at about 6 PM, but at that time the Moon was nearly opposite Saturn. A better fit to the stated positions would be 4 February 853 at about 2 PM, but this may be too late for Sahl.

other] planet by its own domicile or its own exaltation; then it receives it in a good spirit and in a *perfect reception*.¹ There is also another reception that is below this, i.e. less than that [kind], viz. when a planet is joined to the ruler of its own triplicity and terms or to the ruler of the terms and the face, i.e. when it is joined to a planet that has in its own place two or more of those *minor dignities*; and then it will be a true reception. But if it has only one, there will not be a reception there; and he says this because something different was transferred from them, and by a skilled astrologer it is said to be of no importance.²

An example of which is when the Moon was in Aries and is joined to Mars, who is the ruler of Aries, then Mars would receive her because she is in his domicile or when she is joined to the Sun, who is the ruler of his exaltation [in that sign]. Or she was in Taurus and was joined to Venus, or in Gemini and joined to Mercury. That is a perfect reception.

Minor Reception.

The *reception by triplicity* is when the Moon is in Virgo in the *terms* of Venus and is joined to that same Venus, and Venus was ruler of the *triplicity* of the Moon and ruler of *its terms*, or if the Moon is in Gemini in the terms of Saturn and is joined to Saturn, and Saturn would receive her, because he is the ruler of the triplicity and the terms. And whenever the Moon or a planet is in such a situation, it will be received. This is the opinion of Messehallah on the reception by triplicity and terms.

And if the Moon in such a situation was joined to any planet, and that planet was joined to the ruler of the *domicile* or the exaltation in which the Moon is, or to the ruler of its exaltation, the Moon will be received. And if the Moon was *void of course*, but after that

---

¹ That is, a planet that is in the domicile or exaltation of another planet is *received* by it.
²The latter part of this sentence is awkward. The Arabic (as translated by Stegemann) reads: "...then the astrologer recognizes [it] not, and he knows it not, and accepts it not, and looks at it as not significant for an issue."

Book I Introduction/19

she crossed into another sign and was conjoined [there] to the ruler of the first sign or to the ruler of its exaltation, the Moon will be received. And if she was joined to a planet that is not the ruler of the first sign or the ruler of its exaltation, it *impedites* her.

A Planet not Received.

But there are places in which there is *no reception* and no conjunction. When the Moon or the ruler of the ASC was joined to a planet that does not have any *testimony* in the place of the Moon or the ruler of the ASC, i.e. it does not have any *dignity*, [then] it does not recognize it and it does not *receive* it. Similarly, if the Moon or the ruler of the ASC is joined to a planet in its own fall, it will be like someone who comes to him from the house of his enemies—it does not receive it nor esteem it.

An example of which is when the Moon is in Aries, and it is joined to Saturn, or it is in Capricorn and joined to Jupiter, or in Cancer and joined to Mars, or in Virgo and joined to Venus, or in Libra and joined to the Sun, or in Pisces and joined to Mercury. And if any significator was in its own fall and was joined to a planet that does not have in the place of that significator <any> power, namely of domicile or exaltation, it will see him for nothing, as if an unknown garment should be given to anyone asking; and if there was a planet joined to another planet in its own fall, or that planet descends giving disposition, it makes him to descend, and it diminishes what will come to him from this.

Void of Course.

The explanation of *void of course* is when the Moon and its orb or that of a planet is empty, that planet will be like one who is exiled; then it is said to be "void of course"; this is when it is not joined to any planet or when no planet is joined to it.[1]

---

[1] The reader should note that this definition of "void of course" is entirely differerent from the usual modern definition, which is that no aspect is formed before the Moon leaves the sign that it is in.

Return.

The explanation of *return* is when a planet or the Moon is joined to another planet that is *retrograde* or *under the Sun beams*, and it returns to it whatever it receives from it, and it destroys the matter. There is also another mode of *return* and judgment and destruction when a planet that is *giving disposition* is joined, i.e. a light planet that is cadent from the ASC is joined to a heavier cadent planet; and it also returns to him what it receives from him; and it destroys his *disposition*. And this signifies that that question has no beginning and no end. An example of which is when Cancer is ascending and the Moon is in Sagittarius in the sixth, namely cadent from the ASC, and is joined to Mars; and Mars itself was cadent from the ASC in Gemini in the twelfth. And it denotes destruction of the beginning of the question and [also] of its end.

There is still another mode of *return*, when there is a light planet that is joined in an angle and is joined to a planet that is cadent from the ASC; then there will be a beginning of the matter because the one that is joined which signifies the beginning of the thing was in an angle, but it will not have an ending because its receiver, which signifies the end of the thing, was cadent, and the one that is joined is light, and the beginning of the thing is from it; and the receiver is the one that is heavier, and it is termed the receiver of the disposition, and the light one is called the *giver* of the disposition.

Giving Virtue.

The explanation of this thing is when a planet is joined to another from its own domicile or from its triplicity or from its own exaltation under such an example, namely, as when the Moon was in Cancer or in Taurus, and it was joined to Jupiter or to another of the planets, and it *gives its virtue* to him because it has given it, i.e. it has committed its disposition to him from its domicile or from its own exaltation. Similarly, the rest of the planets will do this when they have given their *disposition* from their domiciles or their own exaltations.

Giving Disposition and Nature.

Giving disposition and nature is when a planet is joined with another planet, and it gives its own *disposition* or *nature* to it. Of which an example is when the Moon or another planet was in Aries and was joined to Mars, or it was in Gemini and was joined to Mercury. And when the Moon is in Taurus or in Cancer, she gives both, i.e. her virtue and her disposition; and when she is not in those two signs, she only gives her disposition.[1]

The Strength of the Planets.

The explanation of *the strength of the planets* is to which of them will there be missing an opportunity or an impediment to completing a matter when they have received and promised it. This is done in 11 modes, of which the first is when there is a planet in a good house from the ASC, i.e. in angles and the succedents of the angles, viz. from those houses that aspect the ASC.

The second is when there is a planet in some of its own particular places or *dignities*; that is, in its own domicile or exaltation or triplicity or terms or its own face or its own joy.

The third is when it is *direct*.

---

[1] This definition is not clear. The Arabic text says simply, "And what [the] explanation [of] giving the disposition is. This occurs when the planet from its own domicile or its exaltation joins itself with another and delivers *disposition* and *nature* to it." The Byzantine Greek version says, "The handing over of rulership is when one star that is a significator on some basis joins together with another star and *delivers its rulership* to it." Ibn Ezra says, "The *communication of two natures* occurs in two ways. One is when the star is in a sign in which it possesses dignity, or is joined to another star which possesses dignity in the sign, or forms a visual angle with it, as, for instance, Venus with Jupiter in Pisces...." Unfortunately, Bonatti, who would probably have explained this in more detail, omits it altogether. All this seems to refer to the case where a planet is in aspect with its *dispositor*. The statement about the Moon in Taurus or Cancer seems to mean that if the Moon is in Taurus and is in aspect with Venus or is in Cancer and is in aspect with Jupiter, then she gives both her virtue (by being in the sign of her exaltation or rulership) and her disposition (by being disposed by the ruler of the domicile or exaltation) to the planet. But this is what was defined above as "a perfect reception."

The fourth is when there is no *malefic* with it, i.e. in the same sign in which it is, and to which it is joined, or that aspects it by opposition or by square aspect.

The fifth is when it is not joined to a star that is *cadent* from the ASC,[1] or to a planet that is in its own *fall*, or when it itself is not in its own *fall*.

The sixth is when it is *received*.

The seventh is when the higher masculine planets, which are Saturn, Jupiter, and Mars, are *oriental*, i.e. when they appear in the morning going out from under the Sun beams; and the feminine planets, i.e. Venus, Mercury, and the Moon, when they are *occidental*, i.e. appearing in the evening.

The eighth is when the planets are *in their own light*, i.e. when the masculine planets [are visible] by day and the feminine by night.[2]

The ninth is when the planets are in *fixed* signs.

The tenth is when the planets are *in the heart of the Sun*,[3] i.e. with the Sun in one degree, because then the fortunes increase good fortune and their good, but the malefics both increase and greatly strengthen their evil.

The eleventh is when the masculine planets are in the masculine quarters of the particular parts of the ASC of the circle; that is, from the MC to the ASC and from the fourth to the seventh, direct; and the feminine planets in the feminine quarters, i.e. from the 7th to the MC and from the ASC to the 4th, direct; and when the masculine planets are in masculine signs, and the feminine planets in feminine signs.

---

[1] A planet in any one of the four cadent houses (i.e., the 3rd, 6th, 9th, or 12th) is called "cadent from the ASC" by the older astrologers.

[2] The Greek astrologers called this "in sect." The Arabic term is *in hays*. See the chapter on that subject below.

[3] Often called *in cazimi*, but other astrologers reduce the maximum separation to 17 minutes of arc (which they took to be the semi-diameter of the Sun).

These are the *testimonies* by which the planets are greatly strengthened (and they do not have an opportunity that might harm them) for completing the matter when they have received and allowed.

The Debility of the Planets.

And the *debility of the planets* and their *impediment* in nativities and questions is in 10 modes. Of which modes, one is when a planet is *cadent* from the angles and does not aspect the ASC, i.e. when it is in the sixth or in the twelfth.

The second is when a planet is *retrograde*.

The third is when it is *under the Sun beams*.

The fourth is when it is *joined to the malefic planets* by conjunction or opposition, i.e. when it is with one in the same sign or in the seventh from it, or by square aspect, i.e. from the fourth sign.

The fifth is when it is *besieged between two malefics*, i.e when it is separated from one malefic and joined to the other.

The sixth is when a planet is in its own *fall* or is joined to a planet that is in its own *fall*.

The seventh is when it is joined to a planet that is cadent from the ASC or is separated from a planet that was receiving it.

The eighth is when a planet is in a domicile in which it has no *testimony*, i.e. no *dignity*, i.e. it is when it is not in its own domicile or in its own exaltation or in its own triplicity, etc., and when it is *peregrine* and already being pursued by the Sun, i.e. when it is before the Sun.

The ninth is when a planet is with the Head or the Tail [of the Dragon], if it has no latitude.

The tenth is when planets *impedite* themselves, i.e. when they are in opposition to their own domiciles, which is a sort of an *impediment* to them.

These then are the chapters in which is [described] the *impediment* or *detriment* of the planets that is made in nativities and questions and in other [astrological] works. Therefore, follow these modes that we have set forth with regard to the planet that receives the *disposition* and the one that promises the matter.

The Defects of the Moon.

The *defects of the Moon* and its own bad condition by which it makes *detriments* of things in every question and in every initiative are made in 10 modes. And the first is when the Moon is *combust* under the Sun beams, not yet having passed through the 12 degrees [before it], and similarly those after it, but that is less serious.

The second is when it is in the degrees of its own *fall* or when it is joined to a planet that is in its own *fall*.

The third is when it is in *opposition to the Sun* within less than 12 degrees, but it has not yet come to the degree of the opposition.

The fourth is when it is *joined to the malefics* or when they aspect it by square aspect or by opposition, or when it is *besieged between the two malefics*, viz. when it is separated from one and joined to the other.

The fifth is when it is in the Head or the Tail [of the Dragon] in the same sign, and there is less than 12 degrees between them.

The sixth is when it is in the twelfth sign from its own domicile, which is the sign Gemini, or when it is in the end of the degrees [of one] of the signs, which is the *terms of the malefics*.[1]

---

[1] In the Egyptian terms, the last degrees of each sign are assigned either to Mars or Saturn.

The seventh is when it is *cadent* from the angles or when it is joined to a planet that is *cadent* from the angles.

The eighth is when it is in the *Via Combusta*, which is the end of Libra and the beginning of Scorpio.

The ninth is when it is *feral*[1] or *void of course*.

The tenth is when it is *slower* in its course, i.e. when the equation is being diminished from it,[2] or when its *light is being diminished*, which is at the end of the lunar month.

These are the aforesaid *defects of the Moon and its impediments* during which no work should be begun, i.e. while the Moon is so [*debilitated*], no work should be begun; and it is not praiseworthy in a nativity [either,] or in travel.

Know too that the condition of the Moon is [discernible] in the *augment of its light* and in the *diminution of it*, i.e. when it *waxes* and when it *wanes*, because when the Moon is *augmented*, i.e. when it is *waxing*, if Mars aspects it from the fourth sign or from the seventh or is with it in the same sign, Mars *impedites* it because it will then be hot. But on the contrary, if Saturn is conjoined with it or aspects it by a square aspect or by opposition, it *impedites* it because when the Moon has more light, i.e. in the beginning of the month,[3] and it is *hot*, Saturn does not *impedite* it because it is *cold*; but Mars does *impedite* it because it is hot; and when it has less light, i.e. at the end of the month,[4] it will be cold—then, Mars does not *impedite* it because it is *hot*; but Saturn *impedites* it because it is *cold*.

And know that in diurnal nativities and in questions that are

---

[1] Here the term *feral* (from the late Latin *feralis* 'like a wild beast') is used as a synonym of *void of course*.
[2] This refers to one of the numbers used in calculating its position from lunar tables.
[3] By "the beginning of the month" Sahl evidently means "in the first half of the month" when the Moon is waxing.
[4] By "the end of the month" Sahl evidently means "in the last half of the month" when the Moon is waning.

asked during the day and in the beginning of the month and in masculine signs Saturn *impedites* less; but by night and in the end of the month and in feminine signs it *impedites* more. And a planet is not called *impedited*, nor is the Moon or a sign so called, unless there are malefics with it or unless they are aspecting it from the fourth sign or from the seventh or from the tenth. And a planet is not called *fortunate*, nor is the ASC, unless there are benefics in the angles of that same planet or in the angles of the ASC.

Explanation of Besieging.

The explanation of the *besieging* of a planet is when there is a planet between the two *malefics*, separated from one of them and joined to the other without the projection of the rays of another planet between them, i.e. when no other planet projects its rays between them. And this is stronger and worse if the separation and conjunction is by 7 degrees or less. An example of which is when Mars is in the 10th degree of Cancer and Saturn in the 18th degree of Aries and the Moon in the 13th degree of Libra, and the Moon is separated from a second square aspect[1] to Mars and joined to Saturn by opposition; then the Moon is *besieged* because it is separated from the light of Mars and joined to the light of Saturn.

Hays.[2]

And this is the explanation of a planet illuminated by its own light. A planet is said to be *in its own light*,[3] such as Mars by night, since it is a nocturnal [planet]. And Saturn is said to be in its *own light* by day, since it is a diurnal [planet].

---

[1] A "second square aspect" is another name for a "dexter square."
[2] Sometimes spelled 'Hayz'. From the Arabic *al-hayyiz* 'field' or 'domain', the equivalent of the Greek term *hairesis* 'sect'. The idea is that a diurnal planet is more fortunate above the earth than below it, and conversely for the nocturnal planets. The Greek astrologers designated a planet in such a position as being 'in sect' or 'out of sect'. But this distinction is unknown to modern astrologers.
[3] The classical astrologers used the term 'in sect.' See the previous note.

Testimony.

And [here is] also the explanation of those things that are said of planets because they have *testimonies* or parts or *dignities*. If a planet is in its own domicile or is in its exaltation or triplicity or terms or its own face, it is perfecting [the matter], since it is in a sign in which it has *testimony*.

The Joys of the Planets.

But the explanation of the *joy* of a planet is in 4 modes.

And their first *joy* is from the circle [of houses] because Mercury *rejoices* in the ASC, and the Moon *rejoices* in the third [house], and Venus *rejoices* in the fifth, and Mars *rejoices* in the sixth, and the Sun *rejoices* in the ninth, and Jupiter *rejoices* in the eleventh, [and Saturn *rejoices* in the twelfth].[1]

And secondly they may in fact have their *joy* from their strength in their own domiciles. For Saturn *rejoices* in Aquarius because it is a masculine sign; and Jupiter *rejoices* in Sagittarius and Mars in Scorpio and the Sun in Leo and Venus in Taurus and Mercury in Virgo, and the Moon *rejoices* in Cancer.

Thirdly, because the *diurnal* planets *rejoice* when they are in the *orient*, that is, when they arise in the morning. And the *nocturnal* planets *rejoice* when they appear in the evening in the *occidental* hemisphere.

And there is a fourth mode of *joy*, because Saturn and Jupiter and Mars *rejoice* when they are in a masculine part of the circle, which is from the MC down to the ASC and from the fourth sign to the seventh. But the Moon and Venus *rejoice* when they are in a feminine part, viz. from the seventh up to the MC and from the ASC to the *angle of earth*, which is the fourth sign. But Mercury *rejoices* in both parts; i.e., when it is with masculine planets, it *re-*

---

[1] The joy of Saturn is omitted in the Latin translation, but it is mentioned elsewhere in Sahl's book, so I have added it here.

joices in a masculine part, and when it is with feminine planets, it *rejoices* in a feminine part, on account of the diversity of these planets and their domiciles.

Book II.

The Fifty Precepts.

First Chapter. Know that the *significator*, i.e. the Moon, whose circle is nearer the earth than the circles of all the other planets, is, before all the other planets, the one most like the things of the earth. Do you not see that a man begins by being small and then increases until he attains full growth? The Moon does the same thing. Therefore, take it to have the signification of all things, because its good state is the good state of every thing, and its bad state is the bad state of every thing. And it gives,[1] that is it commits, its *disposition* to that one on which it casts its rays, and to that one of the planets to which it is joined, and it sends its light to that same planet, and that planet is termed the receiver of the disposition because it receives that which was committed to it. Therefore, the Moon itself is the informer of these planets; and she pacifies them, and carries [influence] from some of them to others.

Second. The evil planets signify a *bad state* and *evil* on account of *excess* or superfluity. The force of cold or heat in them is overcoming and *impediting*. But if there is a good planet in the domicile of a malefic or in its exaltation, the malefic receives it and restrains its own evil from it. Or if there is an aspect of the malefics by trine or by sextile aspect, it is restrained, and by the fact that it is an aspect of friendship without indeed any enmity to good fortune, because they are of a temperate nature and an equable configuration;[2] that is, because they are tempered by heat and cold, they al-

---

[1] The Latin text of the MSS and the first edition has *pulsat* 'strikes', which is a mistranslation from the Arabic. I have emended it to read **donat* 'gives', but the later writers in Latin preserved *pulsat*.

[2] The Greek version (CCAG V.3 pp. 98 ff.) has "And the malefics show the destruction of affairs and the greatest evil through their excess of heat and cold. And if any star is in the domicile of a malefic or in its exaltation, and is joined to it by an inharmonious configuration, i.e. by square or opposition, the malefic receives it and the impediment of the malefic is restrained by this same reception. And if

ways help and advance [the matter], whether they receive another planet or not. But *reception* between them is more useful and better.

Third. The stars have two modes: namely *good* and *evil*. Wherever, therefore, you see *malefics*, i.e. evil planets, pronounce *evil*; and wherever you see the *benefics*, pronounce *good*.

Fourth. And a planet is not declared to be *impedited* until a malefic projects its rays over its light according to the quantity of their orbs which I have said to you. And when it has passed the limit of the [orbs of the] malefics, it is called "seeing the evil," and it will not be able to be *impedited*; and when the malefic has passed a planet by one complete degree, it sends fear without *impediment* of body; and the malefic cannot do more because it is separated from it. Similarly, when a planet passes a benefic and has separated from it by a whole degree, it hopes for but cannot perfect the thing; because every malefic that is *impeding*, when it is cadent from the ASC, sends fear, but it does not *impede*. Similarly, a fortune, when it is cadent from the ASC, *hopes for* but does not *perfect* the thing.

Fifth. A planet, when it is in the *angles of the malefics*, i.e. when it is with it or in the fourth [sign] from it or in the seventh or in the tenth, will be just like one who is fighting for himself in the trouble and evil that descends upon him. And when it has passed him and is separated from him by a whole degree, just as I have already said to you, he has already escaped the impediment of that malefic, and the malefic can do nothing more than send fear.

Save these chapters because they are from the secrets of interrogations!

Sixth. The Moon, when it is void of course, i.e. joined to none of the planets, signifies inaction and annihilation from the same

---

their configuration arises from a harmonious configuration, i.e. a trine or sextile, again their impediment is restrained because the harmonious configurations are friendly."

cause and the impediment of that same cause.

Seventh. The *conjunction*[1] of the Moon signifies what is going to be and what things are hoped for according to the quantity of the nature of the planet that receives the disposition of the Moon; i.e. good if it is a benefic, and evil if it is a malefic.

Eighth. The *separation* of the Moon from a planet signifies what has transpired and what has already gone by according to the quantity of the nature of that planet from which the Moon is separated.

Ninth. A planet, when it is in its own *fall*, i.e. when it is in the domicile in which it falls, signifies sadness, imprisonment, and want.

Tenth. A *retrograde* planet signifies disobedience and contradiction and retraction and reversion and diversity or discord.

Eleventh. A planet in its *station* signifies evil and what has already become still.

Twelfth. The *malefics* signify difficulty and pressure and frustration in the work.

Thirteenth. When a planet is slow and when it moves slowly, it postpones its number[2] or its promise, i.e. it makes procrastination in the number or in its promise, both in good and in evil. It acts similarly when it is in the domiciles of Saturn or Jupiter; but in the domiciles of the lighter planets it hurries.

Fourteenth. When the Moon is joined to any planet and has completed its conjunction, i.e. when it was with it in one minute,[3] look for what will come of this question from the planet with which the Moon is joined after that.

---
[1] Here he actually means the *application* of the Moon by conjunction or by aspect.
[2] The "number" refers to the degree number of the planet, and consequently to its rate of motion.
[3] That is, when it is in exact conjunction.

Fifteenth. When a planet is in the last degree of a sign, its strength has already departed from that sign, and its strength will be in the second sign; and it is like a man who has put his own foot on the threshold of a door, wishing to go out, but if the house then falls down, it will not impede him. But if a planet is in the twenty-ninth[1] degree, the strength of that planet will be in that same sign because for each planet there are three degrees in which the virtue of that degree spreads out, viz. the one in which it is and the degree before and behind it.[2]

Sixteenth. Sometimes a planet seeks a conjunction but does not attain it in its own sign until that planet is sent onward by its own swiftness. And when it has pursued it into the second sign and it is not joined to another, the matter will be accomplished; but if it is joined to another or configured with it, and afterwards it is joined to the first planet, the matter will not be accomplished because it was configured with the light of the other planet.

Seventeenth. A planet is wishing to join with a planet in the same sign but is unable to overtake it until it has moved out into another sign, and if it reaches it in that other sign, the matter will be perfected then unless it is first joined to another. But also, if it is joined to another by aspect, that fact does not impede it, according

---

[1] MS **P** has *xxviii* '28th' but the first printed edition has *29th*, as do Ibn Ezra and Bonatti.

[2] This statement has confused many readers. (But Ibn Ezra understood it; see his *The Beginning of Wisdom*, Chapter viii, Prognostic 35. Likewise Bonatti; see the 30th of "The 146 Considerations.") The ancients had no zero, and they usually truncated degrees and minutes by retaining the degree number and dropping the minutes. But they knew that a sign has 30 degrees in it, so a calculated longitude of say 30°45' was said to be in "the 30th degree of **Aries**." (Those modern astrologers who follow this illogical practice of degree numbering would say it was in the 0th degree of **Taurus**.) Consequently, by "the 29th degree" Sahl means a position from 29°00' - 29°59', and, by "the last degree," he means a position from 30°00' - 30°59' of a sign, which is of course in the next sign. Hence, as he puts it, when it is in the "29th degree" its influence extends from the "28th degree" to the "30th degree," so it remains in the sign, but when it is in what he calls "the last degree" of a sign, its influence extends from the "29th degree" of the previous sign to the "1st degree" of the following sign, so it has definitely "put its foot in the door" of the next sign. And in fact it is actually in the next sign, as he says.

to what I have said to you, because a conjunction¹ that is made by aspect does not annul a conjunction that is made by body in the same sign; and this conjunction [by body] annuls the matter that is made by the aspect; and one aspect does not cut off another aspect, but it does prohibit the matter. But a bodily conjunction does cut off an aspect.

Eighteenth. When a malefic planet is *oriental*,² i.e. when it appears in the morning in the east in its own domicile or in its own exaltation, and it is not joined to [another] malefic that impedes it, it is better and more worthy than a retrograde benefic [that] may impede.

Nineteenth. When the *malefics* are rulers of the matters, and the ruler of the ASC or the Moon is joined to them by square aspect or by opposition, i.e. from the fourth sign or the seventh sign, they will accomplish the matter, but they will destroy it in the end. And if those that are conjoined are *malefic*, it will be better than when they are themselves *receiving* the *disposition*, i.e. when the malefics strike³ and are joined to them.

Twentieth. A *malefic* when it is in the ASC in its own domicile or in its exaltation is restrained from *evil*, unless it is *retrograde* in the ASC. But if it is *retrograde* in the ASC, its *evil* is greatly strengthened, and its diversity and variation is multiplied.

Twenty-first. When a planet is in its own character and likeness from the signs, it will be appropriate for it, i.e. if Saturn is in its own domicile or in its own exaltation or in a frigid sign; and if Mars, just as I have said to you, is also in a hot sign, it will be *good*. But if it was [in a sign] contrary to its own nature, it will be *evil* for it, like water and oil that do not mix and are not combined; and if it is in a sign similar to itself, it is mixed and combined, like water and milk.

---

¹By "conjunction" here he means a configuration between the planets.
²When it is behind the Sun in the zodiac and rises before it in the morning.
³That is "give their disposition" ('strike' is a mistranslation from the Arabic as noted earlier).

Twenty-second. When *benefics* aspect *malefics*, they reduce their *impediment*.

Twenty-third. When the *malefics* aspect the *benefics* by a square or opposition aspect, they lessen their *good fortune*.

Twenty-fourth. When the *benefics* are *cadent* from the ASC or *retrograde*, they will be *impedited* [and] similar to the *malefics*.

Twenty-fifth. When planets are received in the domicile or exaltation of another, and when those planets are *benefics*, it will be a stronger [*good*] for them; and if they are *malefics*, their *impediment* will be stronger.

Twenty-sixth. When *malefic* planets are in a sign in which they are *peregrine*, i.e. when they are not in their own domiciles or in their exaltation or in their triplicity, they increase their *evil*, and their *impediment* is magnified. And when they are in signs in which they have *testimony*, they are restrained from *evil*, and there will be no *impediment* at all.

Twenty-seventh. When *malefics* that are rulers of things are in their own domiciles or in their exaltations or triplicities or in their own terms, and in angles or in [the houses] following the angles, they will be strong just as the *benefics* are strong [in similar circumstances]. **Understand what I have said!**

Twenty-eighth. When the *benefics* are in a sign in which they do not have *testimony*, their *good fortune* and *good* is diminished; and when they are in a sign in which they do have *testimony*, i.e. in their domiciles or in their exaltations or triplicities or their own terms, their *good fortune* is magnified; and the thing is accomplished, and their *good* is increased.

Twenty-Ninth. When there are both *benefics* and *malefics* in a *malign* sign, i.e. in some other one of the signs that I have mentioned, or if they are *combust* under the Sun beams, they signify petty and despicable things; and the planets cannot signify *good* or *evil* because of the *debility* that is in them, because when a planet *is combust* under the Sun beams or *in opposition* to the Sun, it will be *weak*, because in that place there is nothing useful nor anything *good* for the *good planets*, nor anything *evil* for the *evil ones*, because the *benefics* signify just a little *good* when they are *under the Sun beams*; and similarly, when the *malefics* are *under the Sun beams* their *impediment* will be less.

Thirtieth. And for every planet, *benefic* or *malefic*, when it is in its own domicile or in its exaltation or in its own triplicity, etc., whatever *evil* there is in it is converted into *good*. **Admire, therefore, what I have said to you, and accept it as a rule for judgment!**

Thirty-first. When the *malefics* are in an angle of the ASC and are *impeding* by a square aspect or by opposition, they will be *evil* and strongly harmful; and their *affliction* will be greater, and especially and properly if they are stronger than the planet which they oppress or *impedite*, i.e. if they are in a stronger place, i.e. if they have some *dignity*, but if they aspect by a trine or a sextile aspect, they are restrained from *evil*, and their *impediment* is diminished.

Thirty-second. A *benefic* does not always signify only *good fortune*, and a *malefic* does not always signify only *evil* on account of the superfluity of its nature and the malignity of its complexion. Therefore, one ought to look at the houses of the planets, i.e. their houses with respect to the ASC and the signs in which they are posited, because even though a planet is *evil*, nevertheless if it is in its own similitude or *in its own light* or in its own domicile or exaltation or triplicity or in a good house with respect to the ASC, it signifies *good*.

Thirty-third. If a benefic is not *in its own light*, i.e. if it is one of the *nocturnal* planets and it is the *significator* by day, or if it were one of the diurnal planets and it is the *significator* by night, or if it is *peregrine* in the sign where it is, or *cadent* from the ASC, or *under the Sunbeams*, it impedes and does not *accomplish* [the matter].

Thirty-fourth. When Jupiter aspects a *malefic*, it turns its nature into *good*. And Venus cannot change anything important, i.e. the *evil* of Saturn, unless it aspects Jupiter. For Jupiter releases what Saturn snags up, i.e. if Jupiter is configured with Saturn, [for] it breaks down its *malice* and changes it. And Venus releases what Mars snags up.

Thirty-fifth. When a *malefic* strikes, i.e. when it is joined to, a *malefic*, one *evil* is turned, i.e. is changed, into another *evil*. And if a *malefic* is joined to a *benefic*, the *evil* is converted into *good*. But if a *benefic* is joined to a *benefic*, *good* is converted into *good*. And if a *benefic* is joined to a *malefic*, there will be *evil* after *good*. **Combine things in that manner!**

Thirty-sixth. When the Moon or the ruler of the ASC is *impedited* by a conjunction or by a square aspect or by an opposition of the malefics, if then *benefics* are joined to it by trine or sextile aspect, whatever venom it finds will be freed from destruction by the *benefics* and released by them. Similarly, if they are joined to malefics by a square aspect, and the *benefics* aspect by a square aspect, that man will escape from what happens to him from that destruction, and [then] he will fall into another.

Thirty-seventh. When a planet is not in its domicile or in its exaltation or its own triplicity and is not in its own terms or in its *joy* and is *cadent* from the angles, that will be an *evil* sign without any utility, and there is no good in that planet.

Thirty-eighth. When a planet is *under the Sun beams* towards the west, i.e. when it arises in the evening, its strength will be *weak*—as is said of the superior planets. For there will be no *strength* to it or to its light, and its *impediment* will be less if it is a *malefic*. And if it is *retrograde*, it will be *slow* in all things.

Thirty-ninth. When the planets are *under the Sun beams*, they will be *weak* in all things. This is the case if there are less than 12 degrees between them and the Sun, unless the planet is in the degree of the Sun because then it will be *strong*.

Fortieth. And when a planet is further than 12 degrees from the Sun in the morning and in the east, it will be strong in every initiative and in every work; and when it is made apparent, and if it is 15 degrees from it, then it will be stronger, i.e. then it will have greater strength than it would otherwise have. And if there is a planet before the Sun on the western side, i.e. if it rises as an evening star in the west, and there is [a distance of] from 15 to 8 degrees between it and the Sun, then it will begin to be weakened; [and] from the 7th degree until it is in the heart of the Sun,[1] the planet will be still weaker. And when it is in the heart of the Sun, it will be strong. By "heart of the Sun" should be understood "when it is in the same degree as the Sun."

Forty-first.[2] When a planet is *peregrine*, i.e. when it is not in any of its own *dignities*, such as exaltation, face, etc., its disposition and its nature is crafty; and if it is not in its own domicile or in its exaltation, but it is *direct* and in a good place with respect to the ASC, or in the MC, or in the 11th house, it will be *good*.

Forty-second. When the *receiver* of the *disposition* is *occidental*, i.e. before the Sun by 12 degrees or less, it will be *weak* and broken, and it will not *accomplish* what it indicates. And if it is *occidental*, it will be *strong* and indicative, *perfect* in its indication, because an *impeded* planet is like a building that when it falls down and is rebuilt, is improved, and is made *good*.[3]

Forty-third. When a planet is in the eighth house from the ASC and is a *benefic*, it does not produce either *good* or *evil*; but when the *malefics* are there, their *evil* is magnified.

---

[1]Sometimes called *cazimi* in the translations. Wright says this term is probably from the Arabic words *ka samîm* 'as the heart'.

[2]The Greek version has: "When the star is in the sign of another, its nature is *impeded* if it is not yet in the ASC or in the MC or in the eighteenth [*sic*!] house."Bonatti has (the 55th Consideration, in part): ". . .the one whose significator it is will be crafty, astute, and malicious, for he will know how to do good or evil. . .nevertheless, his intention will be more towards evil than to good. . . . And if it is in any of its major dignities, viz. in its domicile or exaltation, and it is direct, and it is in any good house from the ASC, in the tenth, or in the eleventh. . ."

[3]The Latin text (and hence, the translation) is incomplete. Cf. Bonatti's 56th Consideration.

Forty-fourth.[1] When a planet is in the beginning of a sign, it will be *weak* until it is firmly placed in it and has traversed 5 degrees in it. And a planet is not *cadent* from the angles until after 5 degrees. For example, if the angle is 10 degrees of Aries, every planet that is in less than 5 degrees of Aries is *cadent* and is not considered to be in the angle.[2]

Forty-fifth. And every planet that is 15 degrees past the angle will be just like one that is in the angle, and if it increases its degrees, it will have no *strength*. For example, if the angle were 10 degrees of the sign Aries, then every planet that was from that same 10 degrees up to 25 degrees of that same Aries would be considered to be in that same angle; but if it added on more than 25 degrees, it would not be in the angle.[3] But Ptolemy says that the planet would be in the angle up to 25 degrees after the angle.

Forty-sixth. When planets are in *fixed* signs, they signify a "fixing," that is firmness and stability of the things that the question is about. And when they are in *common* signs, they signify the loosening of things and their repetition, and a different thing or something of that sort will apply to that [matter]. And when they are in *mobile* signs, they signify speed of the conversion or changing of things, either into good or evil.

---

[1] The Greek version has: "Every star that is in the beginning of a sign is weak in the [first] five degrees of that sign; and also when the star does not at any other time decline from the angle, or when it declines five degrees; for if it is more than five degrees of the degrees of the angle, it is not in the angle but rather in the following degrees; if the star is within fifteen degrees, it is in the angle, but if outside of fifteen, it does not have power in the angle." This version seems to be either confused or incomplete.

[2] This refers to that famous doctrine of Ptolemy (*Tetrabiblos*, iii. 10), which holds that a house begins 5 degrees before the cusp and extends for 25 degrees after the cusp, which is based upon the Equal House system of house division. But elsewhere in his books Sahl uses the Sign-House system, so this entire instruction would appear to be inappropriate.

[3] And here we have a reference to still another house system, in which the cusp was considered to be the center of the house, with the house extending for 15 degrees before and after the cusp (as in some Hindu charts). But again, in the rest of his books, Sahl never mentions this system. Thus, this and the previous Precept probably reflect Sahl's reading of books that mentioned these systems, although in his own practice he did not use them.

Forty-seventh. A *fixed* sign signifies a "fixing," i.e. firmness in the things that the question is about, and every thing that is *fixed* and absolutely constant and stable; and this is a good help in questions. And the *common* signs signify things that cannot be done and everything that is done twice. And a *mobile* sign signifies the quick change of one thing into another.

Forty-eighth. When a planet becomes *static retrograde*, i.e. when it is in its *first station*, it signifies the dissolution of the matter and disobedience; and when it becomes *static direct*, i.e. when it is in its *second station*, it signifies the forward motion of the thing after tardiness or endurance; and every planet that is a significator and is going to be *direct*, i.e. if it is in its second station, signifies the renewal of things and their suitability and strength or directness; and if it is in its *first station*, wanting to *retrograde*, it signifies their destruction and tardiness and dissolution.

Forty-ninth. Know that on the day on which the Moon is *impedited*, everything that is asked about on that day will be *impedited*, unless the *malefic* that is *impediting* it is *cadent* from the ASC and *weak*, and the Moon then does not hold a part of the ASC, because when a *malefic* impedes her and is *cadent* from the ASC, it stirs up fear and anxiety; and when it is in [one of] the angles or in [one of the houses] following the angles, it thrusts fear into the [querent's] body.

Fiftieth. Know that the planet to which the Moon is *joined* signifies *what is going to be* and the result of things; and if it is joined to *benefics*, it signifies a *good* result, and if it is joined to a malefic, it signifies an *evil* result! And know that the ruler of the ASC or the Moon in opposition to its own domicile, i.e. in its own seventh[1] house, the ruler of the question will be shrinking from the matter about which he is asking, for it will be oppressive to him![2] Know all this!

---

[1] The seventh house counted from the planet or the Moon is of course the sign opposite the sign it is in.
[2] The Greek version has "When the ruler of the ASC and the Moon are in [signs] opposite to them, they show the querent rejecting the question." Bonatti (Consideration 77) says "...the Lords of the Question abhor the business; nor does he love it should it be accomplished, but is rather against it." (Coley's translation)

40 / Sahl Ibn Bishr

Book III.

Questions or the Book of Judgments of the Arabs.

When you have been asked about any question, you will begin to look just as I have said to you before. For I have already established for you for every thing the manner in which the thing ought to be looked at. Therefore, you shall not seek to deviate to another [manner], nor should you change the matter about which you were asked into another matter about which you were not asked; nor should you change that commixture yourself, like the one who asks about marriage, and when you have looked at this, he will ask you about some other thing that just then came to his mind.

Moreover, if you have been moderate before considering different things, it is just and proper for you to accept one particular thing from its chapter. And it is not permissible for anyone to ask in one interrogation about two things that are not of the same kind.

And you should [not] look [at a chart] except for him who has come to you hoping, or out of necessity, or who is sad and for that reason concerned, and who has come to you with effort. For the one who has come to you knowingly as a crafty person and as a tempter, you should not look for him, because the thing will turn out in accordance with the amount of concern the Querent has for the thing about which he asks.

Beware, therefore, of [using] these chapters; for then the question will be better when the man has asked about his own self or when he has sent someone who will ask on behalf of the one who is concerned about a thing of his.

Know, therefore, the intentions of men, because the consideration and the work is done in accordance with the concern and the intention of the Querent. For whoever has asked [a question], and his intention was unlike the question in its own actual time, the places of the planets and the hour of the question signify his own true state of being at that very time. Similarly, if his intention shall have been to ask about any thing in its own year or month or day or whatever, it will be thus.

Understand, therefore, their intention before [giving it your] consideration, because no Querent asks [a question] unless it is about that which is prevailing in him from the nature of the circle, together with his own condition, about which he asks because of the combination of the circle namely with his own condition, concerning some good fortune or some evil. For there are branches and parts.

Therefore, the one for whom it happens by chance that a benefic is the ruler of the ASC and the Moon is rendered fortunate; and the one for whom their impediment is appropriate is impeded, because he does not ask in the condition of the impediment of the significator, that is of the Moon and the ruler of the ASC in the hour of the question or the nativity, unless he is a man who is impeded and evil and troubled, or an impeded man, whom evil things ought to find.

Similarly, in the case of good fortune, no one asks about it unless he is fortunate, and is a man who ought to have fortune. And you shall not beware if you been asked about different questions under one ASC, since the things were different, so if many of them agree in one essential condition, that is in evil or in good, they will experience that good fortune or misfortune, for we see some of them made fortunate and others just like them, unfortunate.[1]

---

[1] The Latin text has *...fortunatos et alios consimiles fortunatos*. 'fortunates and others just like them fortunate', which is inconsistent with the previous clause. I have therefore assumed that the last *fortunatos* 'fortunate' should read *infortunatos* 'unfortunate'.

General rules.

Moreover, if you have been asked about any thing that ought to go forward and improve and be stable, look at the conjunction of the ruler of the ASC with the ruler of the thing and the reception of the receiving planet, namely the planet that receives the disposition, whether it was the ruler of the thing or the ruler of the ASC, namely the one that was weightier, and look at its freedom from those impediments of the planets that I have already mentioned to you.

And if the question was about the instability of a thing, or about its motion, such as travel or change, or about the release of an incarcerated person, or the escape of anyone from trouble and sorrow, look for those things from a place of instability, i.e. from the [houses] cadent from the angles and from recession.

And if you have been asked about any thing of those things that are in the 12 signs,[1] give the ASC and its ruler and the Moon as the significators of that man who asks you; and give the sign[2] of the thing and its ruler to the thing asked about.

After that, look at the ruler of the ASC and the Moon, and the stronger of them, the one namely that is in an angle and that aspects the ASC, and begin with that one. But if any one of them was joined to the ruler of the thing, that thing will be perfected by the action of the Querent. And if you have found the ruler of the thing joined to the ruler of the ASC, that thing will be perfected with ease and by the application of the Querent without his action and without any difficulty.

And if you have found the ruler of the ASC or the Moon in the place of the thing, or if you have found the ruler of the thing in the ASC, that thing will be perfected unless the ASC is impeded and

---

[1] That is, the twelve houses.
[2] Again, by "sign" he means "house," since he is using the Sign-House system of house division.

its ruler is in its own fall or is combust in it, in which case it will not be perfected. This same thing should be understood about the ruler of the ASC [when it is] in the domicile of the ruler of the thing.

And if you have found the ruler of the ASC or the Moon joined to any planet in the house of the matter, or if you have found the ruler of the matter joined to any planet in the ASC, and that planet has testimony in it [by being in its own] domicile or exaltation or triplicity, etc., [then] it will be perfected.

And if there is not any one of all those things that we have said, then look at the *translation of light* by the Moon or by any of the light planets, which if you have found it separated from the ruler of the ASC and joined to the ruler of the thing, or separated from the ruler of the thing and joined to the ruler of the ASC, the thing is perfected through the hands of go-betweens and those who run back and forth between the two of them; and if you have not found a planet between them that carries the light of one of them to its companion, then look at the *collection of light*. Because if you have found the ruler of the thing and the ruler of the ASC, both of them namely, joined to a weightier planet, and that planet aspects the place of the thing, or was in the ASC or in the MC, the thing will be perfected through the hands of a judge or some man to whom it is committed. The effects of all things are made by these three modes:

First, from the conjunction of the ruler of the ASC and the Moon and the ruler of the thing.

Second, when any planet carries its light between them, i.e. it is separated from one of them and is joined to another, then the thing is done through the hands of go-betweens.

Third, from the collection of light, i.e. when both are joined to another planet, namely one that is weightier, which conjoins their light, receiving the strength of both, and its judgment will be acceptable between them, or through some man who will help in that same thing. Effects of things are made from these three chapters.

Book III Questions / 45

After that, look, just as I have told you, at the receiver of the disposition of any of those, which is a weightier planet, or the ruler of the ASC or the ruler of the thing and at the planet that collects their light; if it is free from the malefics, in [one of] the angles or the succedents of the angles, and is not retrograde or combust or cadent from the angles, [then] that thing will be perfected after its attainment; and if it is impedited, it will be destroyed; and if the receiver is retrograde, it will be dissolved; after he thought that it had been attained. And if you have been asked whether he will attain it, and then whether it will be with ease or difficulty, look to see if the ruler of the ASC and the ruler of the thing were joined by trine or sextile aspect; [if so], it will be attained with ease; and if they were joined by a square aspect or by opposition, it will be attained after harshness and difficulty and delay.

And if you have been asked whether [the Querent] will attain it by his action, or whether it will come to him without any action on his part, look at the ruler of the ASC and the Moon; if it is joined to the ruler of the thing, this will be with his action. And if the ruler of the thing is joined to the ruler of the ASC, it will come of its own accord. Also, if the ruler of the ASC or the Moon was in the place of the thing, it will be with the action and the effort of the Querent, i.e. with his own hard work, etc. But if the ruler of the matter is in the ASC, men above him will support him in this thing, and it will be given to him spontaneously.

But if a question has been asked about the receipt of any honor—will it come to him unasked, and will he not come to the doors of kings on account of this?[1] And if there has been an accomplishment of the thing by the translation of light, it will be through go-betweens and those who run back and forth between them; and if the Moon was separated from the ruler of the ASC and joined to the ruler of the thing, the use of go-betweens will be initiated by the Querent. But if the Moon is separated from the ruler of the

---

[1] Perhaps this means, "will he not have to make a formal request of the king to obtain the honor."

thing and conjoined to the ruler of the ASC, a go-between will come to him and he will work over him in this; and if there is an attainment of the thing from the collection of light, the attainment of the thing will be through some judge who goes in over them, or through a man who involves himself in the thing until its attainment is accomplished.

And know that if the ruler of the ASC and the Moon are joined to a planet from the fall of that planet, it signifies the destruction of the thing, as if for instance it was joined to Mars from Cancer or to Jupiter from Capricorn. For these [positions] destroy things and they do not make progress. Similarly, if planets were joined that were in the falls of those who do not receive them, it signifies an evil disposition of the ruler of the interrogation in those things that he wishes to accomplish and that the thing will not be perfected.

Of which an example is when the Moon is joined to any planet that is in the 3rd degree of Scorpio, which is the fall of that same Moon, or if Mars, the ruler of the ASC, is joined to a planet that is in the end of Cancer, which is its fall.

And know that an evil planet, if it was the ruler of the thing, and the ruler of the ASC or the Moon was joined to it by square aspect or by opposition, and it does not receive them, the Querent may lose, so that that thing is not done because of the evils or troubles or hard work that enter into that thing over him; and if the ruler of the ASC or the ruler of the thing is the same planet, i.e. if the same one is both the ruler of the ASC and the ruler of the thing, and it is received, that is it is joined to the ruler of its domicile or its own exaltation, and if it was free from the evil planets, the thing will be perfected; but if otherwise, it will be destroyed. Similarly if the Moon was joined to it, and if she was safe from debilities, it will be accomplished.

And know what the testimonies of the signs are in the accomplishment of things, as let the ASC be a fixed or a common sign and the angles stable, i.e. the 10th sign, the MC, and the angle of earth, the 4th sign, and do not let the MC fall in the 9th sign or the angle of the earth in the 3rd sign.¹

This is an exposition of the stable angles; and the testimonies of the stars on their effects on the earth are three, from which things are sought, i.e. the ruler of the ASC and the Moon and the ruler of the thing; if two of them shall have been free from the aforesaid evils, i.e. the ruler of the ASC and the ruler of the thing, two parts of the thing will be perfected; [and] i.e. if one of them is safe, a third part of that thing which was wanted will be perfected.

That is, if there is one testimony, he will have a third part; and if there are two testimonies, he will attain two parts of those things that he has sought; and if all the testimonies are conjoined, and if the ruler of the ASC and the ruler of the thing and the Moon are safe from retrogradation and combustion, safe from the evil planets, and safe from fall or cadency, he will attain everything that was sought; and if they are received with their own testimonies, and the one that receives them is also received, it will increase the good of it.

Know, therefore, those questions that are conjoined and that agree in all things! An example of which thing is a certain question that was made about a kingdom, whether he would acquire it or not. The ASC was 20 degrees of the sign Gemini and the MC the 1st degree of Pisces, and the Sun in 12 degrees of Cancer, and the Moon in Virgo with Caput in 19 degrees, and Mercury in 27 degrees of Gemini, Mars in 8 degrees of Taurus,² and Venus in 3 degrees of Leo, and Jupiter in Pisces with Cauda³ in 20 degrees in its first station about to turn retrograde, and Saturn in 6 degrees of Gemini.⁴ In this question, there-

---

¹Here, Sahl is speaking of the Sign-House system of house division, since the astronomical MC degree can fall in either the 10th or the 9th house.
²"Mars in Taurus" is the reading in the printed book **v**, and that is the true sign position of Mars. However, MS **P** has "Mars in Cancer," and that position, although wrong, may have been where Sahl thought it was. See the note on the next page.
³The Moon's South Node.
⁴From the planetary positions, we can determine that Sahl received this question on 5 July 824 at about 3:00 A.M. LAT in latitude approximately 33 N—seemingly an unlikely hour for a query.

fore, I looked at the ASC sign and its ruler and the Moon, which are the significators of the Querent, and at the sign of the MC and its ruler, which are the significators of the kingdom that was in question; and the ASC was the sign of Gemini, and Mercury was in the ASC but at the end of the sign, and at Jupiter, which was the ruler of the thing, in the MC in 20 degrees of Pisces.

And I found the ruler of the ASC separated from the ruler of the thing. I looked, therefore, at the Moon, which I found in the angle of earth[1] joined to Jupiter by opposition; and it was signifying attainment of the thing through acquisition and difficulty, since they were joined by opposition; but if it had been joined by sextile or trine aspect, the attainment would have been made with ease; and it was the Moon that was joined to the ruler of the thing, signifying that it would be done through the action and the effort of the Querent; and if it would have been the ruler of the thing that was joined [to the Moon], the attainment of the thing would have been with ease through the initiative of someone who would have arranged it, and that without any action or question on the part of the Querent.

I also looked at Jupiter, who was the receiver of the disposition; I found him in the MC in his first station about to turn retrograde, signifying the resolution of the thing which I have said; and its destruction would be quicker; and that will be on the part of the king on account of Jupiter, who was ruler of the tenth house, which is the house of kingdom, and which also was signifying the king; and if the ruler of the ASC had been the receiver of the disposition and he had been impeded, I would have said that the destruction would be made by the Querent and by his very own action, because the ruler of the ASC will be changed from its own domicile into the house of substance,[2] which signifies the swiftness of the change of the Querent and of his things for the finding of substance

---

[1] The 4th house.
[2] The 2nd house, here evidently counted from Gemini, the sign that Mercury was in at the time of the question.

at the place in which he would make his sojourn, and he would not receive it, because when he would go out from his own sign he would be joined to Mars,[1] and he would not receive him; and so this signified that he would make such an action in his own exit, that through it loss and sadness would come upon him; and because Mars was the ruler of the sixth from the ASC, which is the house of slaves and illnesses and persons of low degree, it was signifying that which I have said concerning slaves and persons of low degree and infirmity.

And because Jupiter, who was the ruler of the thing, was about to retrograde and because it was with Cauda, it was signifying the dissolution that would come upon the man by whom the thing was being queried and [also] much confusion; and the separation of Mercury from the ruler of the thing, that the Querent will be before that very day, i.e. before that very time [of the question] in hopes [of attaining] that thing, i.e. he will hope that it would be perfected for him, and since it was separating from the ruler of the thing, he will lose hope of [attaining] it. Similarly in things in general.

{A Chapter on the Conjunction of the ASC.}[2]

{And this should not be neglected by him in nativities and similarly in questions; and indeed this very thing corrupts questions and corrupts the life of the native. Mâshâʾ allâh indeed is cutting off secret things from this; and it is as if you are looking at a star that is shining and dominating in nativities and in questions and a star with which the ruler of the ASC or the ruler of the thing is con-

---

[1]This may indicate that the reading "Mars in Cancer" in MS **P** is where Sahl thought Mars was (see the note on the preceding page), in which case Mercury would come to a bodily conjunction with Mars. However, "Mars in Taurus" may be correct, and Sahl may have meant that when Mercury moved into Cancer, it would be "joined to" Mars in Taurus *by sextile*.

[2]This chapter is found in the printed book **v** but not in MS **P**. Its wording seems incompatible with the rest of the text of Sahl's books, so I am inclined to think that it is not a part of the text and should probably be omitted. However, since it is in the printed versions of Sahl's books, it was taken to be part of his text by the renaissance and early modern astrologers. Therefore, I have included it, but with this warning to the reader.

joined, or with which the Moon is conjoined when the Moon is a joint ruler with the ruler of the ASC, or when it is shining or dominating over the ASC and its ruler and the ruler of the thing in a question.

Consider, therefore, the star conjoined to it with what [other star] it is conjoined. For if it is conjoined with a malefic that does not receive it, or with a star that is retrograde, or with one that is cadent, or with a star that is combust, or with a star that is made unfortunate by the abscission of light, it corrupts the thing. And if it is conjoined with a star, and that star is safe [from affliction], and there is a conjunction to that star, we look at the star with which that star is conjoined until the conjunctions are diminished; then we look at the conjunctions with it; and if there is abscission of it, in accordance with what we have related previously, the thing will be corrupted after [having been] made right. And if there is no abscission, then the question is completed [satisfactorily]. And if it is conjoined in the beginning of the thing with a malefic, it suffers abscission with corruption; but if the malefic is [in] reception without a square or opposition and without pairing (?), the thing will be completed when there is not an opposition or square.

And if it is conjoined in the beginning with a benefic and it has no conjunction with a malefic, the thing will be completed; and if a star transfers the light between them, and the star to which the light is transferred is a malefic that is not received, it corrupts the thing. And if the light of two stars is combined and the combination between the two is afflicted, the thing is corrupted. And if there is [a star] receiving one of them and not receiving the other, it is corrupted.}

The Second House on Matters of Substance.

When you have been asked about any substance[1] that is hoped for, [i.e.] whether he who has asked you about substance will find it or not, look at the ruler of the ASC and the Moon, which are the

---
[1] Money or other valuable assets of any kind

significators of the Querent, and the sign of substance[1] and its ruler, which are the significators of substance; if the ruler of the ASC and the Moon are joined to the ruler of the house of substance, or if the ruler of the house of substance is joined to the ruler of the ASC, or whether you have found the Moon going from the ruler of the house of substance to the ruler of the ASC or from the ruler of the ASC to the ruler of the house of substance; [if so], he gets the substance. Similarly, if it was Jupiter or Venus, which are benefics,[2] in the house of substance, he will find the substance.

And if there is none of those [configurations] that I have said, he will find nothing. But if there were malefics in the house of substance, which is the second from the ASC, it signifies loss in substance. And if the Moon was then [the significator of] the Querent, he will not cease to experience loss, and that condition will not cease until he dies.

But if the question was by what means there will be gain, look at the receiver of the disposition, whether it was the ruler of the ASC or the ruler of the thing itself, namely which of them was weightier, which if it was in the ASC or in the second, he will find and acquire it by the work of his own hands; and if it was in the third, from brothers and friends; and if it was in the fourth, from his father and his parents and from lands, i.e. from inheritances; and if it was in the fifth, from his children; and if it was in the sixth, from infirmity and from slaves and from persons of low degree; and if it was in the seventh, from women if it was a feminine sign, or from war or contention; and if it was in the eighth, from the relics of the dead; and if it was in the ninth, from travel and from sects or cults; and if it was in the tenth, from kings or magistrates; and if it was in the eleventh, from friends and business[3]; and if it was in the twelfth, from enemies; and if the sign was [quadrupedal], from

---

[1] The 'second sign' in the sign-House system is of course the 'second house'.
[2] That is, *benefic planets*.
[3] Because the eleventh house is the second from the tenth.

quadrupeds or wild beasts; and if it was one of the signs of humans, from prisons and their inhabitants.

These are the natures of the twelve signs; and however often you have found a benefic, the acquisition is from the substance of that sign; and however often you have found malefics, judge that there will be loss and confusion. And look thus in every case, so that you may know in what manner there will be ease and in what manner there will be dispersion.

The Third House on the Matter of Brothers.

When you have been asked about the condition of a brother, look at the third sign, which is the sign of brothers, and its ruler and the aspect of the fortunate and the malefic planets to it. If you have found the ruler of the third from the ASC in the sixth, which is the house of infirmity, or joined to the ruler of the sixth, say that his brother will be infirm.

Similarly, he will be [infirm] if the ruler of the sixth is in the third; and if you have found the ruler of the third in the fifth or in the eleventh, his brother will be absent; and if it was impedited in the twelfth, his brother will have infirmity or sorrow; and if it is going into combustion, he will not escape from that.

Similarly, you will announce from the substance of the signs; and if he has asked you about his own father or about his mother, [you will announce it] from the fourth; and about his child, from the fifth; and about his slaves, from the sixth; and about his wife from the seventh; [and so forth], just as I have said to you, if God is willing.

The Fourth House on Matters of Heredity.

When you have been asked about land or about a house or about a heredity that someone has sought—whether or not he will get it—look at the ruler of the ASC or the Moon, which are the significators of the Querent, and the sign of the fourth and its ruler, which are the significators of the land.

If the ruler of the ASC or the Moon is joined to the ruler of the fourth, or if the ruler of the fourth is joined to the ruler of the ASC, or if the ruler of the ASC or the Moon is in the fourth, or the ruler of the fourth in the ASC, he will get it. But if the Moon carries the light from one of them to the other, he will get it through the hands of go-betweens.

And if you were asked about any inheritance that he may get—what is its condition and the condition of the building and whatever is in it—you will take the hour of the ASC in which you were asked about it, and you will put [the ASC] as the significator of those farm workers,[1] namely those farm workers who work on the place; and the sign of the fourth signifies the land and what [sort of land] it is; and the sign of the seventh signifies whatever was in it by way of crops that are [grown] under the trees; and from the MC, whatever is in it by way of trees.

And if a malefic was in the ASC, those farm workers will be robbers or those who carry off things; and if that malefic was direct, they will remain on the land, but if it was retrograde, they will run away from it. And if a benefic was in the ASC, the farm workers will be honest and faithful; and if that benefic was direct, they will not go away from the land, but if it was retrograde, they will go away.

And if the benefic was in the MC, it signifies a multitude of trees; and if it was direct, its trees will be strong and abounding in fruit. But if it was retrograde, they will experience loss, and the buyer will find that out and will sell all the fruit from the trees. But if there was a malefic in the MC, it signifies a scarcity of fruit from

---

[1] Some words seem to have fallen out of the text. *Cf.* Bonatti, *Book of Introduction*, Treatise VI, Fourth House, "If the Querent has asked...whether...the workers are good and faithful or not, look at this similarly from the ASC and its ruler, since then the ASC and its ruler signify the workers of the land or the vineyard and those dwelling in the wooded area and the inhabitants of the house." The logic seems to be that since the 4th house represents (among other things) the residence of whoever is represented by the ASC, then the inhabitants of the house and the workers who live around it must be represented by the ASC.

the trees; and if it was retrograde, what has remained on them will be sold; and if there was no planet in the MC, look at the ruler of the MC; and if it aspects the MC, there will be trees in it; and if it was oriental, they will be newly planted; but if it was occidental, those trees will be from an old planting; and if it was direct, they will remain; but if it was retrograde, they will not remain because they will be destroyed. And if the ruler of the MC does not aspect its own domicile, i.e. if it was in the second from it or in the sixth or in the eighth or in the twelfth, the land will be devoid of trees.

After these things, look at the sign of the seventh for the substance of the land, just as I told you in [the case of] the MC; and look at the fourth sign from the ASC; if it was Aries, Leo, or Sagittarius, that land will be dead and hard to cultivate, i.e. unworthy of much cultivation; and if it was Taurus, or Virgo, or Capricorn, it will be flat land; and if it was Gemini or Libra or Aquarius, it will be of two kinds, i.e., mountains and fields; and if it was Cancer or Scorpio or Pisces, it will be wet or close to water; and if the fourth sign was common, i.e. Gemini or Virgo, Sagittarius or Pisces, the land will be of two kinds, that is there will be mountains and fields in that land.

And when you want to take a lease on land or parts of it or you want to lease it out or do anything of that sort, look at the matter of the seller from the ASC and the buyer from the seventh, and the end of his action and its cause from the MC, and from the sign of the fourth the end of that thing; and if a benefic is in the ASC, he himself will be a ready seller, and he will be willing; and if a malefic is in it, he will regret his having sold, and he will withdraw himself from that [sale], or he will have wanted to sell it with craftiness, and it will not profit him; and if there was a malefic in the seventh, the buyer himself will renege, i.e. he will regret [his offer], and he will not pay him; and if he does pay, he will enter into dispute and into deprecation, and it will not profit him; and if a benefic is in it, the buyer himself will be ready and willing.

And if you have found a malefic in the MC or if it aspects it with an inimical aspect, the end [of the matter] will be a very great evil; and if it was a benefic, there will be a good end [to the matter] and a praiseworthy one, if God is willing.

The Fifth House on Matters Relating to Children, and First about One Child.

If any man has asked you whether he will have a child from this particular woman or not, look at the ruler of the ASC and the Moon [to see] if she is joined to the ruler of the house of children, or if the ruler of the house of children is joined to the ruler of the ASC, or if the ruler of the house of children is in the ASC, or if the ruler of the ASC or the Moon is in the house of children, or if you have found a planet that transfers the light between the ruler of the ASC and the ruler of the house of children, [then] there will be a child for him; and if there was a return of light, there will be a delay in this.

After that, look at the receiver of the disposition, which is a weighty planet, and if it was free from the malefics, i.e. if it was not joined to them and they were not joined to it, and it was not cadent from the ASC[1] nor combust, the child will live; and if it was retrograde or combust or cadent from the angles, after this it will happen that it will die; and if you have found Jupiter in a good place from the ASC, and it was not impedited nor under the Sun beams, it signifies pregnancy; and if there was a malefic with Venus, it does not signify pregnancy.

But if the Moon was joined to a malefic. know that she will not become pregnant; and if you have found a benefic in the fifth, which is the house of children, the woman will become pregnant; and if there were malefics in it or if they aspect it by opposition or by square aspect, it does not signify pregnancy.

Whether a Child will be Born to Him or Not.

And if a man or a woman has asked whether or not he or she will have a child, look at the ASC; if there were benefics in it, or if

---

[1] He actually means 'cadent from any angle', i.e. in the 3rd, 6th, 9th, or 12th.

the ruler of the ASC was in the ASC or in the tenth or in the eleventh or in the 5th, and Jupiter was in the best house from the ASC, a child will be born to him; and if the ruler of the ASC was in the ASC or in the 4th or in the 7th and Jupiter was in a good place from the ASC, a child will be born to him with some delay after [the time of] his own question.

But if you have found a malefic in the ASC or if it aspects it by opposition or by square aspect, and the ruler of the ASC was in a bad place, and Jupiter was cadent or in the house of death or under the Sun beams, it signifies few children, and they will live only a short time if there are any.

And you should not fail to look at the 5th from the ASC, which is the sign of children; in which, if there were benefics, a child will be born to him quickly; and if there were malefics in it and you have seen anything good in the question, there will be a child, but he will see its quick death. If you have found Jupiter oriental in an angle, a child will be born to him quickly. But if it was occidental in an angle, i.e. if it has appeared in the evening in the west, and if the ruler of the ASC was in the best place, it will be born to him or to her tardily and after some delay.

Whether a Woman is Pregnant or Not, and Whether she will Bear a Child or Not.

And if the question was about some woman, whether or not she is pregnant and whether or not she will bear a child or whether it would be fortunate for her or not, look at the ruler of the ASC and the Moon, which are the significators of children. If you have found the ruler of the ASC and the Moon in the House of Children, and if the ruler of the House of Children is in the ASC free from the malefics, say that she is pregnant; and if the ruler of the ASC and the Moon have *given, i.e. if they have committed*, their own disposition to any planet in an angle, there will be a pregnancy, and all the more so if it was received; and if they were joined to a planet cadent from the ASC, it signifies loss, and the pregnancy is in vain;

and even more so if the ASC was a mobile sign or if there was a malefic in an angle, or if the Moon was joined to a malefic, because all of these signify loss.

Moreover, the receiver of the disposition, i.e. a weightier planet which receives the disposition from the ruler of the ASC or from the Moon, when it is free from the malefics, i.e. if it was not joined to them, and the malefics were not joined to it, and it was in a good place, the pregnancy will be perfected.

Whether a Pregnancy is True or False.

And if [the Querent] has asked about a pregnancy, whether it is true, i.e. whether it will come to delivery or will be frustrated, look at the ruler of the ASC, which if it was joined to a planet cadent from the ASC and not receiving, it signifies loss; similarly, if it is joined to a retrograde planet, unless the Moon was received or the ruler was in a good place from the ASC, because then it will signify pregnancy.

Whether or Not a Pregnant Woman Will Bear Twins.

And if you have been asked about a pregnant woman whether or not she will bear twins, look at the ASC in the hour in which the question was put, [to see] whether it was a common sign or whether there were two fortunate planets in the ASC or in the house of children; [if so], she will be pregnant with twins, i.e. she is carrying twins. Similarly, if you have found the Sun and the Moon in common signs, and if neither the ASC nor the sign of children was a common sign, nor was there in them any of the planets which I have mentioned, nor were the Lights in common signs, she is carrying [only] one child.

Whether She Will Bear a Male or a Female.

And if you have been asked whether she will bear a male or a female, look at the ruler of the ASC and the ruler of the house of children; if they were in masculine signs, there will be a male in her belly; and if they were in feminine signs, there will be a female in her belly; and if one of them was in a masculine sign and the other one was in a feminine sign, look at the Moon's sign and at the planet to which the Moon is joined; if the Moon was in a masculine sign and was joined to a masculine planet, she will bear a male, but if the Moon was in a feminine sign or was joined to a feminine planet, she will bear a female. And know that Mercury, when it is oriental, i.e. when it is behind the Sun, will be feminine, if God wills!

The Sixth House on the Matter of Infirmity.

But if you have been asked about a sick person, whether he will get well or die, look at the ASC; for the ASC signifies the physician, and the MC signifies the sick person, and the seventh sign signifies the infirmity; but the fourth sign signifies the medicine. If a malefic was in the ASC, the medicine [given by] the physicians and their care will not help him; and if there was a malefic in the MC, the sick person will not help himself, but he will get more excited over his infirmity, and this is because the sick person will be inobedient to the instructions of the physician.

But if there was a benefic in the tenth, the sick person will cure himself with those things that are helpful to him; and if a malefic was in the seventh, he will be turned from one infirmity into another infirmity; and if there were also benefics there over it, health will come without any curation by which he can be cured; and if there was a malefic in the fourth sign, the medicine will increase the gravity of his condition, that is the medicine will make him worse; and if there was a benefic there [instead], it will help him.

After that, look at the ruler of the ASC and the Moon; and begin with the one that was in an angle and that aspected the ASC, if it was free from the malefics and was not in aspect with the ruler of the House of Death, which is the eighth sign from the ASC, and especially in the square or in the seventh aspect,[1] and it was not un-

---

[1] The opposition (because the sign opposite is the seventh sign from the starting sign), counting both ends of the interval as was the old custom.

der the Sun beams, it signifies health; and if it was joined to a benefic, it signifies health.

But if that benefic is retrograde, it signifies a prolongation of the infirmity; and if the Moon was not above the earth, but it was joined to a planet that is above the earth, it signifies health unless the planet that is the receiver of the disposition should enter combustion, because then it signifies death.

And if the Moon is joined to the ruler of the ASC and that planet was increased in its light and course, it signifies the swiftness of his [return to] health and the improvement of his body; and if the ruler of the ASC is under the earth and the Moon is joined to a planet in the ninth from the ASC going to be cadent, it signifies death; and if the ruler of the ASC was joined to the ruler of the house of death and the Moon was impeded, it must be feared that that is bad; and if it was received, the infirmity will be prolonged.

But if the ruler of the first is joined to the ruler of the eighth by a trine aspect, and if the ruler of the ASC is in an angle when the ruler of the House of Death comes to the degree of the ASC sign, it will signify death; and if any planet returns the light of the ruler of the ASC to the ruler of the eighth, and if the ruler of the ASC was cadent, and the ruler of the eighth in an angle, it signifies death; and if the ruler of the House of Death is in the ASC, and the ruler of the ASC or the Moon is impeded, it signifies death; and if the ruler of the ASC was in the eighth, which is the House of Death, and a malefic has aspected it or the Moon is impeded, he will die.

And if the receiver of the disposition is impeded, it signifies breaking down, i.e. a relapse of sickness, i.e. relapsing after [a period of] health; [and] with the presence also of the ruler of the eighth in an angle, it is bad.

And if the ruler of the ASC is above the earth and was joined to the ruler of the eighth in the fourth or in the House of Death, it signifies death; and if the ruler of the eighth did not aspect the ruler of the ASC but some other planet returns the light of these and the ruler of the ASC was cadent and the ruler of the eighth in an angle, it signifies death; and if the ruler of the ASC is entering into combustion and there was less than 12 degrees between it and the Sun, he will die. Similarly, if it was combust and not received. But if a planet did not give its disposition, i.e. if there was a planet not receiving and it was free from combustion and the Moon was safe, it signifies a going out [from illness]; and if the sign of the house of infirmity was mobile, the sick person will be comforted by some change, and he will be made worse by another; and if it was a fixed sign, he will continue in one condition.

And if the Moon was separated from an oriental planet, i.e. one arising in the east in the morning, it will be a new infirmity, i.e. a recent one; and if the Moon was separated from an occidental planet, the infirmity will be prolonged; and if it was joined to an oriental planet, it signifies the swiftness of convalescence, and it will be better if a benefic aspected the ruler of the ASC and that planet was in a good place from the ASC, and the aspect of the malefics to it will be quicker if it was by square aspect or by opposition, or if the malefic was with it in one sign, and if the Moon was joined to a retrograde planet, [then] it signifies a worsening and renders his [condition] doubtful.

Know also the place of the Moon on the seventh day from the beginning of his infirmity and his question about it, and on the fourteenth and twenty-first and the twenty-eighth day! For the Moon, on that day on which it comes to the malefics or to the ruler of the house of infirmity, the sick person will worsen on that same day; and when it has come to the benefics or they have aspected it, health will transpire for him and a respite from his infirmity; and to know the condition of the sick person on the seventh day, add 90 degrees to the place of the Moon, and you should look at the degree of the Moon to which it has come, [for] there will be the Moon on the seventh day[1];

---

[1] The Moon's mean daily motion in 7 days is a little over 92 degrees, or roughly 90 degrees. Sahl is merely giving an approximation to the future place of the

but for the 14th day, add to its [original] place 180 degrees, and this is the opposition of that place in which it was on the day on which the infirmity began or the query [was made]; also for the 21st day, add 270 degrees.

But on the 28th day the Moon returns to its own place, i.e. to the sign and the degree in which it was [placed] at the beginning of the infirmity or the query; and however many times the Moon will have been joined to any benefic on these days, that same number of times the sick person finds repose and improvement; and however many times it was joined to a malefic, his pain will be increased and made more severe.

And if you have been asked about anyone, whether he is infirm or not, look at the ruler of the ASC and the Moon, namely the one of them that was the stronger, that is the one that was in an angle or in a succedent to an angle; which, if it was in the 6th from the ASC, which is the house of infirmity, or joined to the ruler of the 6th, or if it was in its own fall or was combust under the Sun beams, say that he is sick; but if otherwise, that he is not.

Something on the Matter of Slaves and Freedmen.

And if a slave has asked whether he will be freed from servitude or not, look at the ruler of the ASC and the Moon; and if you have found either one of them separated from the ruler of the MC, because the Sun and the MC signify the master. And the malefics signify the affliction and toil with which the slave is afflicted, either by the Sun or by the malefics; and if it was not joined to any of those that I have mentioned, say that he will be free; but if otherwise, not.

And if a slave has asked, "Will I go out from the hands of my master to another one or not?" Look in this case at the ruler of the ASC. If it was in the MC angle and not joined to a planet that was cadent from

---

Moon. It would, of course, be better to get the Moon's position from an ephemeris or by actual computation.

the ASC, he will not go out of his hands; and if it was joined to any planet in the ninth or the third, it will signify his departure.

But if the ruler of the ASC was in an angle, impedited by an opposition or a conjunction or by a square aspect or is entering combustion, he will die before he departs from his own master.

And if a slave has asked you saying, "Is he better for me, [to be with] my master with whom I am [at present], or the one to whom I want to go?" Look at the ruler of the ASC; if it was received in the sign in which it is [posited], i.e. if it was joined to the ruler of its domicile or exaltation,[1] his master with whom he is [at present] is better for him; but if the ruler of the seventh was received, the one to whom he wishes to go will be better for him.

Then look at the planet from which the Moon is separated and the one to which it is joined; if the one from which the Moon is separated was a benefic, his master with whom he is will be better for him; and if the one to which the Moon is joined did not receive her, the one that he seeks will be better for him; and if it is not joined to it, look at the ruler of the ASC and the Moon; if either of them was received in the sign in which it is [posited], or if the sign in which it is was its domicile or exaltation or triplicity, then[2] his master with whom he is is better for him. But if it was received in the second, then that one to whom he goes will be suitable for him, [i.e.] he will be better than his own master, and it is better to change.

It will be judged similarly for a man traveling, [when the question is] about his [condition] in the land in which he is or about that land to which he is going to go, i.e. when he has asked which is better for him. Similarly, look at a revolution, that is in the change of everything, namely when he ought to be changed from one house to another, and then the condition of one house [as compared] to another, and one land to another, and from one [kind of] work to another kind.

---

[1] He means, either the sign ruler or the exaltation ruler (if the sign is the exaltation of a planet).
[2] Reading *tum* 'then' instead of *cum* 'when'.

Whenever you have been asked about buying a slave, whether his purchase would go through or not, look at the ruler of the ASC and the Moon; and if they are joined to the ruler of the seventh from the ASC, while the ruler of the sixth from the ASC was joined to the ruler of the ASC, or if you have found a planet transferring light between the ruler of the ASC and the ruler of the sixth, he gets that which he asked about.

Buying a Slave-girl.

And if you have been asked about a man who wants [to get] a slave-girl from someone, the ASC and its ruler will be for the Querent, and the seventh and its ruler for what he is asking about. If in fact the twelfth from the ASC will be for the slave-girl, look therefore [to see if there is] a conjunction of the ruler of the ASC and the Moon with it, or the translation of light between them by any planet, just as I have already told you in this chapter.

The Relicts of a Dead Slave.

And if you have been asked about the relicts of a dead slave, whether his master will get them or not, look at the ruler of the ASC and the Moon; if they were joined to the ruler of the seventh from the ASC, which is the second from the House of Slaves, he will get them. Similarly, if the ruler of the seventh is joined to the ruler of the ASC, or if the ruler of the seventh, or if the ruler of the seventh from the ASC or the ruler of the ASC or the Moon [is in] the seventh, or if you have found a planet transferring the light from one of these to its associate, he will get them.

Possession of the Same.

And if you have been asked about possession, whether the one who has asked you will attain it or not, look at the third sign from the ASC, which is the tenth house of slaves; if you have found the ruler of the third joined to the ruler of the ASC, he will get them. Similarly, if the ruler of the ASC and the Moon was in the third or the ruler of the third was in the ASC; or, if there was a planet carrying the light between them, he will obtain the aforesaid possession through the hands of go-betweens.

The Seventh House on Matters of Marriage.

When you have been asked about a marriage, whether it will be perfected or not, and, if it is perfected, how the connection will be between them; but if it was not perfected, by whom is the separation or disunion made. Put the ASC and its ruler and the Moon for the Querent and the seventh sign and its ruler for the woman, if a man asks, or for the man if a woman asks; if the ruler of the ASC or the Moon was joined to the ruler of the seventh or was in the seventh, he will get the woman.

Similarly, if the ruler of the seventh was joined to the ruler of the ASC, or if the ruler of the seventh was in the ASC, the thing is done with facility, and the woman's wish for it will be as great as the man's; and if the Moon is carrying the light between them, go-betweens will run back and forth between them, and the thing will be effected through their hands. After this, look at the receiver of the disposition, that is a heavier planet; if it was impeded by malefics by square aspect or by opposition, or if it was cadent, the thing will be destroyed after it was once arranged.

The Impediment to the Marriage.

And if you have been asked in what manner there will be an impediment, look at that malefic that impedites; if it was the ruler of the second from the ASC or the eighth, there will be a disruption on account of the description of the dowry; and if it was the seventh from the ASC, disruption from dissatisfaction with the woman's rank; and if it was the fourth, it will be because of the [Querent's] father; and if it was the third, because of his brothers. Understand the rest of the signs[1] thus in accordance with their significations.

---

[1] That is, the rest of the houses.

And if there was a planet cutting off the conjunction between them, there will be a disruption according to the signification of its house, i.e. if it was the ruler of the second house or the eighth, there will be a rupture because of the description of the dowry; and if it was the third, because of the [Querent's] brothers; and if it was the fourth, because of his parents; and if it was the fifth, the occasion will be that the woman had been married and has a child; and if it was a malefic that was carrying the light between them, because of the go-betweens, from their quality of mind.

Look at the conjunction that was between the ruler of the ASC and the ruler of the thing, if it aspected from the seventh sign, which is the opposition aspect, it signifies malice of mind and much contention; and if it was aspected by square, it signifies goodness of mind, but sometimes there will be contention there; if the aspect was a trine or fifth [sign], it signifies delight and a good quality of mind; and similarly if the Moon was received, and if the ruler of the ASC was in an angle, and if it was a weightier planet, i.e. the receiver, he will be a person of high degree, dominating and conquering the woman; and whichever one of them you have found to be cadent or giving testimony,[1] the ruler namely of the ASC, or the ruler of the thing, will be defeated and subjected.

But if they were conjoined in one sign, it signifies disputes; and if the Moon was aspecting the ASC and she was impeded, there will be loud wrangling in it; and if there was a malefic in the ASC, this will be instigated by the man; and so understand the rest according to the significations; and when you have seen the Sun impedited, the impediment will fall upon the man; and when you have seen Venus impedited, the woman will be impedited; but when the Moon was impedited, it will impedite both of them.

---

[1] Not 'striking', as the Latin has it.

Whether a Woman who has fled from her Husband will Return.

And if you have been asked about a woman who has left her own home because of anger at her own husband, whether she will return to her own home or not, look at Venus and the Sun, which are the significators of the man and the woman; if Venus was above the earth in the best house from the ASC, and the Sun was under the earth, declare the return of the woman to her own home with considerable delay and difficulty; and if the Moon in the hour in which she went out of her own home was already at the full, i.e. at the half-way point of the month, her return to her own home will be hastened; and if she was increased in light, i.e. at the beginning of the month, her return will be with slowness; and if Venus was retrograde from her own domicile and occidental, her return to her own home will be from a spontaneous decision and she will be penitent; and if Venus was oriental and emerging from being under the Sun beams and retrograde, she will return, and her husband will be penitent about her having left, but he will regret what he did just as he is penitent in the first chapter, and she will be penitent about her return.

Whether a Woman is a Virgin or not.

And if you have been asked about a woman, whether she is a virgin or corrupt, look at the ASC in the hour in which you were asked and its ruler and the Moon; if it is in fixed signs, she will be a virgin free from any fault and free from him by whom she was defamed; and if it was in mobile or common signs, she will be corrupt, for she has already been married; and if the woman thinks that she is a virgin, she is deceived, and her virginity has been taken.

And if the Moon is in a common or a mobile sign, and the ASC and its ruler in a fixed sign, she has already been attacked by someone, and her virginity was not really taken, and if the Moon is with Ma rs in a mobile or a common sign, her virginity has already been taken, in her friendship with men; and if Saturn was in the ASC with the Moon in a common or a fixed sign, the one who was joined with her used her in an unnatural manner, and her virginity was not taken; and if Mars was in an angle from Venus, i.e. in square or opposition aspect, and the Moon was impedited by Mars, and Venus was in Scorpio or its triplicity, she will not be a virgin.

And if you have found Mercury or Jupiter in the triplicity of Venus or in an angle to it, and if Mars fell away from it properly and did not aspect it and was in Aries or in Leo, or in Sagittarius, she will be a virgin.

Whether or not a woman will bear a Child.

And if you have been asked about a woman, whether she is carrying a child or not, look at Venus; if it was in Aquarius or Leo, and Mercury was with it, she will never give birth. But if Venus and Mercury were in Scorpio or in Taurus, she is carrying a child; and if Mars and the Moon or Venus were in any common sign besides Sagittarius, it signifies that she is carrying a child, for Sagittarius signifies that the woman is not carrying a child and will not ever give birth; and if she shall have given birth, it will die.

But if there were malefics in mobile signs, she will have a child from some improper act, i.e. from fornication and friendship, for she is not faithful to her husband; but if they were in common signs, [it will be] his child from proper action; and if both, namely benefics and malefics, were commingled in mobile signs, she will be saddened because of her own child.

Whether a Woman is Pregnant from Fornication.

And if you have been asked about a pregnant woman, whether her child is from propriety or impropriety, look at the sign of children, which is the fifth from the ASC, which if Mars or Saturn or Mercury aspected it, her child will be from fornication; and if benefics aspected it, her child will be from a just cause, i.e. it will be legitimate.

Whether a Woman has a Man she loves, or One who loves her.

And if you have been asked about a woman, whether she has a man who loves her or whom she loves or not, look at the ruler of the ASC and the Moon; if one of them was with Mars in one degree, she has a friend with her in her home; and if it was in one sign but not in one degree, he is a neighbor; and if one of them was separated from Mars, she has a friend whom she has loved, but she has already dismissed him; and if one of them was joined to Mars and was in either of his domiciles, she has loved a man who is [still] after her, and she wants him to have her. But if one of them was joined to Jupiter, she once loved a man who was higher and nobler than she, and she still loves him; and if it was joined to Mercury, she loves a young man who is better looking than her husband, but is younger, and he is a writer or a businessman; and if one of them was joined to Venus, she loves a woman and is involved with women. But if Jupiter aspected Venus, she will dismiss her because of religion, which happens to her. But if the Sun was in aspect, some great man has already admired her, but on account of this she has dismissed him; and if Venus was in aspect, the woman has already ordered this.

Similarly, all planets [act] according to their own kind. And know that Mercury and Saturn, if they were in one sign and aspecting the Moon and the ruler of the ASC, she has already perceived this. She was betrothed to a youth simultaneously to similar youths. And if the Moon is joined to them, she loves an effeminate man with such a figure, as I have said to you.[1]

Which of two will win a Competition.

And if you have been asked about a competition that was between two, [viz.] which of them will win and obtain victory, put the ASC and its ruler and the Moon for the Querent who is asking

---
[1] This last sentence seems to be defective. I have not found a parallel passage in Bonatti.

you, and the seventh and its ruler for his competitor, i.e. his adversary.

After that, look to see if both planets are mutually conjoined by sextile aspect or by trine, [if so] they will be reconciled before any competition; and if they are conjoined by square aspect or by opposition, they will not be reconciled except after war and competition; and if both of them come together in one sign, [there will be] peace between them without the intervention of another person, i.e., without anyone who comes between them for the sake of making peace; and if the ruler of the MC aspected them when it was in communication with one of them before one of them is conjoined to the other, they will not be reconciled until they come into the presence of the king; and if the Moon transfers the light between them, there will be the beginning of peace through the hands of go-betweens.

After that, look at the places of both planets, namely of the ruler of the ASC and the ruler of the thing, i.e. the ruler of the seventh, and their strength, because through this you will understand the [relative] strength of those who are in contention; for the stronger is that one of them whose significator was in an angle; of the two, he will have more helpers; and know the one from whom the beginning of peace will be from the planet giving testimony, i.e. from the one that goes to conjunction [and] that is lighter, and from the one falling away if it was lighter.

And know that if the ruler of the 7th is in the ASC, it signifies the strength of the Querent; and if the ruler of the ASC is in the 7th, it signifies the strength of the one who was asked about, who is like a person who is conquered and who is in the house of his adversary.

And if one of the significators was retrograde, it signifies something about low quality and flight and also business dealings and about the mendacity of the one whose significator it is, i.e. if the ruler of the ASC was retrograde, it will be the weakness of the

Querent. But if it was the ruler of the 7th, there will be weakness on the part of his adversary. But if the ruler of the MC aspects them and it was retrograde, it signifies the injustice of a judge, and that the contention will be prolonged.

Similarly, if one significator was received by the other, [and] by significators, I mean the ruler of the ASC and the ruler of the thing. And know that the Lights, i.e. the Sun and the Moon, if one of them was joined to one of the significators and was in its house, that one will be stronger and worthier; and if the ruler of the ASC was joined to the ruler of the MC, the Querent will seek aid from the king. But if the ruler of the MC was joined to the ruler of the ASC, the king will aid him without his having asked; and if the ruler of the 7th was joined to the ruler of the MC, his opponent will request aid from the king, but if the ruler of the MC was joined to the ruler of the 7th, the king will aid the opponent.

And when you have determined the strength of each one of them, and you have determined that they will not be reconciled, look at [the indications for] the king or judge who judges between them from the ruler of the MC; then look at the one of the significators that it aspects, i.e. whether the ruler of the MC, which is the significator of the king or the judge, aspects the ruler of the ASC or the aforesaid ruler of the 7th.

And know that the king or the judge will be with the one that it aspects; and if there was a peregrine [planet] in the MC that was not aspecting them, they will establish a judge between themselves who will justly decide between them; but if it was Saturn in the MC and it was also the ruler of the MC, that judge will not render a judgment, nor [if he does] a fair one. And if Mars impedites Saturn, the judge will be criticized because of this, and he will be denounced for it; and if Mars was in the MC, he will be a quick judge and very sharp of swiftness and rapid; but if it was Jupiter, he will be a just judge; and if it was Venus, he will be light-hearted of good spirit, and he is lightly admired; and if it was Mercury, he will be sharp in his orders; and if the MC sign was common, the first judge will not finish the judgment until it goes to another judge.

What will be the Action in Buying and Selling.

And if you have been asked about the buying or selling of anything, look at the ruler of the 7th for this and the ruler of the ASC; if they were joined together, there will be an agreement between them, and the lightness will be from the planet giving testimony which is lighter.

But if they were not joined and you have found a planet between them carrying the light of one of them to the other, there will be an agreement through the hands of another man who acts as a go-between; and if the ruler of the ASC was in the 7th, it will be the buyer pursuing the sale; but if the ruler of the 7th was in the ASC, it will be the seller pursuing the buyer; and if there was a benefic in the ASC, it will signify the ease of the sale and its integrity. but if a malefic was in it, it will signify its difficulty and delay and misrepresentation.

Moreover, if there was a benefic in the 7th, it will signify the ease of the buyer and his integrity and if there is a malefic, the opposite. And if the Moon was not separated from any planet, but it was joined to one, the seller will sell a possession or a thing that he has not bought but that he possessed from someone, or if he has bought it, he has not yet stated anything about the price of it. But if she was separated but not joined to any planet, there will be a delay in buying.

Moreover, if the planet from which the Moon was separated is going to combustion, the seller will die before his own substance, or the substance of anything lost, reverts to him.

Whether a Fugitive or Property or something else that is lost will be found or not.[1]

If you are asked about a fugitive, and about property, or about anything lost, put the ASC and its ruler and the Sun for the Querent, †the ruler namely of the fugitive, or the fugitive is a slave or something else†[2] But the 7th and its ruler and the Moon for the slave and the thing lost.

Then look to see if the ruler of the ASC is joined to the ruler of the 7th, [if so, then] the Querent will get the fugitive through inquiry and his own effort. Similarly, if the ruler of the ASC was in the 7th, and if the ruler of the 7th was joined to the ruler of the ASC or the ruler of the 7th was in the ASC, he will return of his own free will before he leaves the land.

But if you have found the Moon separated from the ruler of the ASC and joined to the ruler of the 7th, someone will come to the master of the one who is lost who will show him where his slave is. And if it was separated from the ruler of the 7th and joined to the ruler of the ASC, the slave will send a go-between to his master who will ask for security for him; and if after this, the ruler of the 7th was joined to the ruler of the ASC, the slave will return to his master of his own free will.

Moreover, if the ruler of the 7th was joined to an evil planet in an angle, the fugitive will be captured; but if the ruler of the ASC aspects a malefic or the ruler of the 7th, his own master will get him, but he will make a payment for him; and if any one of the Lights was joined to the ruler of the 7th, the place of the fugitive cannot be concealed. But if the ruler of the 7th is also under the Sun beams, it signifies the finding of the fugitive; and if the ruler of the ASC aspects it, he will be captured.

---

[1] MS **P** adds a heading in the margin *Si interrogatus fueris de fugitivo* 'If you have been asked about a fugitive'.
[2] Some words are lost in the passage between the two daggers.

Likewise, if the ruler of the 7th was joined to a malefic, the fugitive will be captured; and if it was joined to a benefic, he will not be captured, unless that benefic is going under the Sun beams or is retrograde or impeded, because if it is going into combustion, it will signify his death; and if it was joined to a malefic and that one was going into combustion, his body will be found; and if the Moon was joined to a malefic, [the Querent] will get the fugitive.

Moreover, if it was joined to a retrograde planet, he will come back by himself, but of his own free will; and if it was joined to a static planet, i.e. one that was in its own station in an angle or in a succedent to an angle, the fugitive is either wandering or will not move from his own place until he is captured; but if it was a planet in its own station about to go retrograde, the fugitive will likewise be captured and put in bonds and returned to his master. And if [the planet] was in its second station and about to go direct, he will be captured [while he is in flight],[1] and he will be put in bonds; after that, he will escape from that captivity, but he can be captured again. And if the planet to which the Moon was joined was direct, he will be returned without bonds. But if the Moon was under the Sun beams and was joined to Mars, the fugitive will be burnt up in a fire; and if it was joined to Saturn, he will die in water.

But if the Moon aspected the ruler of her own domicile, the substance of the fugitive will be captured; and know that when a malefic is in the ninth, the fugitive will be captured and brought back; and if a benefic was there, he could not be captured; and if the Moon was augmented in light and motion, his capture will be delayed, and in the diminution of the light of the Moon he will be captured more quickly.

The Place of the Fugitive or the Robber.

And if you were asked about the place of the fugitive and [who is] lost or about the place of the robber, look at the place of the Moon; if it was in the ASC, the fugitive is in the part of the east;

---

[1] Reading with Bonatti *in itinere fugiendo* rather than *in parte /////s* with **P**.

and if it was in the MC, the fugitive will be in the southern part; and if it was in the 7th, he will be in the western part; and if it was in the 4th, he will be in the northern part; and if it was in any angle, look at the direction of the planet from the sign in which it is [posited], and judge besides according to the direction of the place of the Moon and the sign in which it is [posited].

Whether it is Better to Flee or to Return.

But if a fugitive for whom you are looking [at the horary chart] has asked whether his return to the place whence he came would be better for him than to go where he wants to go, look at the Moon; if it was separated from the malefics, his return to the place from whence he fled will be bad for him; and if it was separated from benefics, his return will be better. Moreover, if it was joined to benefics, [the place] to which he is going will be better for him, and if it was joined to malefics, [the place] to which he is going will be evil for him.

Whether or not the Querent will get back what was Stolen.

If you have been asked about a robbery, whether or not the Querent will get back what [was stolen], put the ASC and its ruler and the Moon for the Querent, i.e. the one who has suffered the robbery, and the 7th and its ruler for the robber, and the MC for the things stolen; but the angle of the earth for the place of the robbery.

If the ruler of the ASC was joined to the ruler of the 7th or if the ruler of the ASC was in the 7th, the inquirer will get the thing sought, i.e. the robber by his own investigation.

And if the ruler of the 2nd, which is the House of Substance from the ASC, was with this conjunction, under the Sun beams, the Querent will get the robber, but he will not get what was stolen; and if it had gone out of combustion, he will find part of what was stolen; and if the ruler of the ASC was joined to a planet in an angle—and it would be better in the MC—the Querent will get the robber.

But if it was joined to a planet that was cadent and not aspecting the ASC, it signifies the going back of the fugitive; and if that planet was aspecting the ASC, it is can be hoped for, i.e. he will be able to have faith; and if the ruler of the 7th was under the Sun beams, it signifies the finding of the robber, and the more so if the ruler of the ASC aspects it, because it signifies that the master will have the robber; and if it was joined in the manner that I mentioned—the ruler of the 7th with the ruler of the MC—he will restore the property because of his fear of the king; and if the ruler of the ASC was joined to the ruler of the MC, the owner of the property will be threatened by the king or by someone to be feared.

And if they do not aspect each other—namely, the ruler of the ASC and the ruler of the 7th—the king or someone other than the Querent will take the property. And if the ruler of the 7th is joined with the ruler of the MC, it will help the robber. And if the ruler of the ASC is joined with the ruler of the MC, the king will help the ruler of the property.

And if the Moon transfers the light between both of the significators, i.e. between the ruler of the ASC and the ruler of the 7th, it signifies the finding of the robber; and if the ruler of the 7th from the ASC is joined to the ruler of the 3rd, the robber will go out of that region. But if the ruler was in an angle from the ASC, he will not depart from his own place; and, through the aspects of the malefics to the 7th, or to the ruler of the 7th, you can know what will happen to the robber.

And if the Moon was joined to the malefics, it signifies the taking away of the property; and if it was joined to a benefic and that benefic was under the Sun beams and impeded, it signifies the taking away of the property; and if it was joined to a planet in the ASC or in the 7th and that planet was free from the malefics, it signifies the finding of the property.

And if the Lights aspect each other by trine or sextile aspect, it signifies the finding of the robber and the thing lost; and if either of the Lights, i.e. the Sun or the Moon, was in the ASC or in the MC. But if they aspected each other by square aspect or by opposition, there will be recovery after desperation and complication; and if either one of the Lights aspected the Part of Fortune or was with it in one sign, what was stolen will be found, and that more quickly if the Sun aspected it. But if the Moon aspected the Part of Fortune or was joined to it in one sign, there will be some delay in finding what was stolen. But if neither of the Lights aspected the Part of Fortune or the ASC, and if the Lights did not aspect each other, that which was stolen will never be found.

A Question about something lost—will it be found or not.

And if you want to know whether or not that which has gone away may be found, look at the ruler of the ASC and the Moon; if either of them was joined to the ruler of the 2nd from the ASC and any planet transferred its light to it, i.e. that the light went from one to the other, i.e. between the ruler of the ASC and the ruler of the House of Property, it signifies the acquiring of the property; similarly, if any planet joined the light of them, i.e. if both of them were joined to any planet heavier than themselves.

But if the ruler of the 2nd, that is the significator of the property, was in the ASC, it signifies the acquisition of the property, although after a short time. Similarly, if the ruler of the 2nd from the ASC was joined to a planet that was in the 2nd sign from the ASC, and if the ruler of the 2nd from the ASC did not aspect it, the property will be lost.

Similarly, if the ruler of the 8th from the ASC was joined to the ruler of the 7th, which is the significator of the robber, and the ruler of the 7th was joined to the ruler of the 2nd, which is the significator of the loss of the property. But if the ruler of the 8th, which is the significator of the property of the robber, is joined to the ruler of the 2nd, which is the significator of the property of the Querent and also of those things which he has lost, he will find his property and he will receive a part of the property of the robber—and the more so, if the ruler of the ASC aspects them. For if the ruler of the MC aspected them, the king will receive what I mentioned; and if the ruler of the 8th was joined to the ruler of the MC, which is the significator of the king, the robber will placate the king with gifts.

But if the ruler of the 2nd from the ASC did not aspect the ASC and its ruler, the substance will in short be taken away, and there will be no mention of it. But if the ruler of the 2nd from the ASC was joined to the ruler of the 8th or the 9th or to any planet in them, and the ruler of the 2nd was in them, it signifies the exit from that region of the property that was stolen. And know that if the Lights are both under the earth, the thief will never be known. But if the Moon was in the ASC and its ruler and the Sun aspected them, judge that that which went away or perished or was furtively removed, will on that very day be found and returned, and the more easily if it was a trine aspect.

A Question about the Robber—is he a Foreigner?

And if you want to know whether the robber is a foreigner or not, look at the Lights. And if one of them is ascending, the robber will be from the house; and if one of them aspected the ASC, and the other did not aspect it, there will be some connection with those in the house, but he will not be of the house. Similarly, if you have found the ruler of the ASC in the ASC, or if ruler of the 7th was with the ruler of the ASC, the robber will be one of those dwelling in the house. And if the Lights were in their own domiciles or in the domiciles of the ruler of the ASC, aspecting the ASC or the ruler of the ASC, the robber will be one of those dwelling in the house; and if they were in their own triplicities, the robber will be a neighbor, but he does not stay with them in their house.

And if they were in their own terms or faces, he will be familiar to those dwelling in the house; and it may be thought that there is some closeness between them and that he visits them. And if there are two Lights in any of those things that I have said, he is familiar to the men of that house, and he visits them often. But if they aspect the ASC and do not aspect the 7th, he has not entered the house before the time when he robbed it, unless one of the Lights is in a common sign; then, he entered it again with the knowledge of the inhabitants, because a common sign signifies repetition. But if one of the Lights aspected the ruler of the ASC but not the ASC itself, he will be known to the inhabitants of the house, but he has not entered the house previously.

But if the ruler of the ASC has already fallen away from the degree of the ASC, and there was another planet with it in that sign in which the degree of the ASC is, it is more likely that the robber will be one of those dwelling in the house; and if the ruler of the 7th was in the 9th from its own domicile, the robber will not be from that region.

Moreover, if it was in the 6th or the 8th from its own domicile, the robber will be a male or female slave. But if it was in its own exaltation, the robber will be a noble; and if it was in its triplicity or in its terms or its own face, he will not be known in his own region, but nevertheless he will be known in that vicinity and in his own dwelling place.

And when you have determined that the robber is of the house, and the Sun is the significator of that house, i.e. of the House of Property, it will be his father. But if it was the Moon, it will be his mother. And if it was Venus, it will be his wife. And if it was Saturn, it will be a slave or a foreigner. But if it was Jupiter, it will be someone nobler than himself and all those [others] who are in the house. One who is also not known to be involved in robbery – that is one about whom there will be no suspicion. And if it was Mars, it will be his son or daughter or his brother. And if it was Mercury, it will be one of his close friends.

But if the significator of the robber was [indicative of] a foreigner, look at the Part of Fortune; if it was free from the malefics, the robber had not stolen anything before this incident. Similarly, if the ruler of the ASC was free from the malefics, and if it was separated from the 7th house, he was known by them before this; and if Saturn aspected the Moon or the ASC, that robber committed his theft with skill and intelligence.

Moreover, if Jupiter was the significator of the robber, i.e. if it was the ruler of the 7th, he did not enter the house to steal, but he entered because of some other business, but he saw an opportunity, and he stole. But if Mars was the significator, he did not begin the robbery until he had broken into the house and dug into a wall of the house in which the property was, or broke the locks, or found a key.

And if the significator was Venus, it signifies friendship and love and association and audacity while he entered into conversation with them, giving forth the image and likeness of a visiting friend, and so he stole from them. And if Mercury was the significator, he undertook the robbery with intelligence and skill or with some kind of trick.

For when the Sun and the Moon have aspected the ASC, the robber is one of the inhabitants of the house. Moreover, if the significator of the robber was a benefic, he will be a free man; and if it was a malefic, he will be a slave. And if Venus or Mercury was the significator, the robber was a young man or a girl, and Mercury is younger in age than Venus. And if Mars was the significator of the robber, he will be a mature young man, i.e. of perfected age and youth, i.e. more a youth. Jupiter, moreover, is older than Mars; and if it was Saturn, he will be a decrepit old man. But if the Sun was the significator and was [posited] between the ASC and the MC, the robber will be young in age, and so he will be increasingly older until it comes to the angle of earth, because that is the place of the end of life.

The Place of the Stolen Items.

And if you have been asked about the place of the stolen items,[1] look at [the sign of] the angle of earth; if it was Cancer or its triplicity, the things stolen will be buried close to water, and its place will be there. And if it was Aries or its triplicity, it will be in a place of wild animals and in a place of fire. But if [it was] Taurus or its triplicity, it will be in a place of oxen or cows. Taurus properly signifies a place of cows; and Virgo signifies a place of harvests and grain; and Capricorn a place of sheep. And if it was Gemini and its triplicity, it will be in a house, or in a box, or in a place high above the earth.

Moreover, if the theft was in the house and you want to know its place with relation to the house, look at the ruler of the 4th and the planet that was there. If it was Saturn, it will be in the latrine of the house and in a place that is longer and deeper and darker. And if it was Jupiter, it signifies a wooded place or a place of prayer; and Mars signifies the kitchen or a place of fire; and the Sun signifies an enclosed part of the house and the place where the master of the house sits; but Venus signifies the place where the women sit; and Mercury signifies the place of a decorated building and a place of books, or a place of grain and especially in Virgo; and if it was the Moon, it will be next to a well or cistern or a place for washing.

And know that when benefics are in the 4th from the ASC, the stolen goods will be in a clean and beautiful place, and they will already have been entrusted to someone noble. But if malefics were in it, they will be in a horrible and stinking place and already entrusted to some person of low degree.

Whether the Number of Stolen Items is One or More.

And if you were asked about the number of articles stolen, whether it was a piece of property or something else that was pos-

---

[1] Here, the word *latrocinium* seems to mean 'that which was stolen' rather than the act of stealing it.

sessed, look at the signs that are between the Moon and Mercury; if they were even [in number], then that about which the question was asked will be stuck together, or [it will be] more than one [article]; but if the signs between them were odd [in number], there will be only one item.

The Suspicion of the Robber.

Moreover, if you were asked about a man taken captive, whether or not he is a robber, look for this just as you look for rumors, whether or not they are true; and also make use of the testimony of the Moon, which if it is joined to a malefic, he will be a robber.

On the Same Subject.

And if you were asked about anyone, whether or not he has stolen something, look at the ruler of the ASC and the Moon, namely, the stronger one of those. If it has received anything from the malefics, i.e., if it was separated from them, he has certainly stolen, and all the more certainly if it was separated from the ruler of the House of Property, that is from the ruler of the 2nd from the ASC. And if it has not received anything from the malefics, he has not stolen anything.

What Sort of Thing Was Stolen.

And if you were asked what is that thing that was stolen, look at the place of the Moon in the signs and the terms.

If it was in the terms of Saturn, it will be one of those things that are necessary for the preparation of the earth,[1] if indeed Saturn was in the ASC or in the 10th or in Taurus or its triplicity. But if it was in the 4th from the ASC or in the 7th, it will be some other item, and if it was cadent from the ASC[2] and if neither of the Lights

---

[1] That is, something useful for agriculture.
[2] Cadent from *any* of the four angles, not just "cadent from the ASC," which would be the 12th house.

aspected it, or if it was in Aries, it signifies the badness and worthlessness of that thing and that it is horrid or stinking. But if Saturn was in Gemini or in its triplicity, there will be two items; and if Jupiter was in the MC aspecting Saturn, one of these items will be gold; and if it was in the 4th or the 7th from the ASC, it will be silver. But if it was cadent from the angles, it will be lead or something similar to that.

But if the Moon was in the terms of Jupiter, look at its essence and its place and which [planet] aspects it. If it was in Aries or in its triplicity, that thing will be gold or silver and everything that is made with fire. And if Venus aspects Jupiter or Jupiter was in her terms, it will be pearl; and if Jupiter was in Taurus or in its triplicity, it will be a thing useful to the rich, or clothing, i.e. something that was or will be an item of clothing or that will pertain to clothing. But if it was in Gemini or its triplicity, it will be some animated item[1] or something proceeding from animals. But if it was in Cancer and its triplicity, it will be [something] extracted from water, like a pearl, etc.

And if the Moon was in the terms of Mars, that thing has already passed through fire, i.e. it was worked by fire, or fire touched it in some way. But if the Moon aspected Venus, it was already worked with dye or dyed things; and if the Moon was in the terms of Venus and in Aries or its triplicity, it will be gold or silver; and if it was in Taurus or in Cancer or in their triplicities, it will be decorated clothing or something that is a kind of precious silk clothing woven with various colors and different kinds of pictures[2]; and you may know the goodness of the item and its beauty from the place of Venus [in the signs].

But if it was in Gemini and its triplicity, that thing will not be from animal substances; but still if Venus had emerged from under the Sun beams, it will be a new thing, but if it was retrograde or in

---

[1] Perhaps we should translate *substantia animata* as 'a living creature'.
[2] Embroidery.

the end of its course or diminished in its numbers,[1] it will be old and worn. And if it was in the terms of Mercury, it will be a book. And if it was in Aries or its triplicity, it will be coins; and if it was in Gemini and its triplicity, those coins will be taken from a purse or some jar that was covered with red leather.

After this, look at the place of the Moon. If it was in Aries, it will be a thing that is put upon the head or face. And if it was in Taurus, it will be an ornament, or a thing that is hung about the neck or [made of] some precious substance. And if it was in Gemini, it will be coins if Mercury aspects it, and if it does not aspect it, it will be [something made] of leather.

And if it was in Cancer, it will be a thing taken out of the water or something damp or moist. And if it was in Leo and the Sun aspected it, it will be gold or silver; and if it did not aspect it, it will be iron or brass. But if it was in Virgo and Mercury aspected it, it will be coins, and if it did not aspect it, it will be clothing.

And if it was in Libra and Venus aspected it, it will be a thing that is sold by weight and has a good odor, and it is also some of those things that adorn women; and if it does not aspect it, it will be an animal, and it will be sold so that there is blood in it. And if it was in Scorpio and Mars aspected it, it will be gold or silver, and if it did not aspect it, it will be bronze or something worked by fire, and it is shiny. And if it was in Sagittarius and Jupiter aspected it, it will not be a single substance, or it will be a tinted thing; and if it does not aspect it, it will be something common of less worth than what I have said to you, and it will not be valuable.

And if it was in Capricorn, it will be something old or dirty or common, and if Saturn aspected it, it will be of the substance of earth and seeds. If moreover it was in Aquarius, and if Jupiter aspected it, it will be gold or silver; but if the Sun and Mercury aspected the Moon, it will be coins, and they will be [contained] in leather. And if it was in Pisces and Jupiter aspected it, they will be

---

[1] That is, "slow in its motion."

pearls or amber or something brought forth from the water; and if it did not aspect it, it will be silk and of various colors.

{The Thing Stolen or Pilfered, What it is and the Type of Thing.}[1]

{And if you were asked about a thing that was stolen furtively, what it is and the type of the thing. But if you want to know the type of thing that was furtively stolen, then consider [the following]; for if the ruler of the terms of the degree of the Moon is going to Venus and the Sun aspects her, then it is coins or it is gold on which there is [something] sculpted, or an image or [something] purple, or what is similar to that from costly praiseworthy pieces of cloth well made.

And if it is Venus, and she aspects [the Moon], then it is a thing from his own person, in which there are shapes and things well made from pieces of cloth, such as scarlet pieces and those that are dyed with hemp and herbs and which are similar to them. And if Mercury aspects her, it something of things that are well made, such as pieces of cloth made of those things that are in animals, such as the cuckoo and silk and wool, and things of that sort; and things that were made carefully, neatly, and with correct measurement.

And if the one aspecting her is Mars, then it is a thing in which there are fabricated shapes, or which is [made] with fire and iron, and which are similar to those. And if the one aspecting her is Saturn, it is an old thing, in which there are shapes or dyes, or a stone nicely made, and it is one of those [things] that are [made] of clay or stones, and those things that are similar to them.

And if the one aspecting her is Jupiter, they are things in which shapes are made from the skins of an animal, and those things that

---

[1] This chapter is present in the printed edition **v**, but it is not found in MS **P** nor in **Bonatti**. Since it is not included in the latter two sources, and since its language is noticeably different, it may be that it is not part of Sahl's text. I have therefore enclosed it in braces. A similar text is in Aly Abenragel's *The Complete Book of the Judgments of the Stars*, ii. 37, but Aly does not attribute it to any source.

are similar to them. And if the ruler of the terms of the Moon [is] Mercury, then they are books, and if the Sun is aspecting him, they are [things] of the decorations of books and the throne of kings, and possibly there is something in them [made] of gold, or a diagram in something of gold. And if the Moon is aspecting that [planet], then they are things in which there are papers, either of mental skill, and of buying and selling, and of agriculture, and those things that are similar to them; and perhaps there is a text or inscriptions in silver.

And if the one aspecting it is Venus, then they are books and things in which there is sculpture and good shaping, and possibly there is silver and gold in them, or a similar drawing in silver and gold. But if the Sun and Jupiter aspect it, then it is some precious substance of those things that kings receive or make and adorn women with them, and possibly there is something aromatic of a sublime odor with them, which is pungent, such as musk and amber, and wood aloe, and such things.

And if the one aspecting that [planet] is Jupiter, it signifies the value of those things, and books in which are praise and preaching and parables on rights. And if the one aspecting that [planet] is Saturn, they are books in which there are poems and exorcisms, and things in which there are no truths; and possibly there are in them things made of iron or stones, on which there are diagrams.

And if Venus and Mars are aspecting it, they are instruments of delight, such as are the lute and the *tripana* and the *balmasis* and the *asclebm* and the harp and the flute and such like things, and instruments for drinking, such as flagons and cups, and big flagons and flagons suitable for wine or whatever is suitable for wine itself or something like that. And if it is Jupiter and Venus that are aspecting that [planet], then it is some adornment of women, which is for women to put on, and things made of the womanly instruments of women, and aromatic jars for characteristic things[1] and scents.

---

[1] The text has *moralia*, which is probably wrong.

But if Mars is in aspect with it, then they are bronze vases for the divine worship, having shapes of those things that kings make and that are made for kings from an instrument of glory, and those things that are similar to them. And if Jupiter and Mars are in aspect, they are of those things that majors and minors make for purification, and arms of iron and bronze, and those things that are made with fires from those things that are made for ships.

And similarly, combine the virtues of the aspecting [planets] for the joint composition—namely, according to their intentions in their simple [effects]. And if the ruler of the terms is Saturn, then it is an earthy thing of those things that are made from clay and stones and iron; and if the Moon aspects it, then it is just like something that is made from royal things. And if the one aspecting it is Jupiter, then it is just like something that is made from those things extending from men.

And if Mars aspects, it is that thing of the instruments of battle and from the restraint of slanderers and of the departure to justice and equality. And if the one aspecting is Venus, then that thing is from the instruments of man that women make for speech and action that is good and correct in faith, about which admiration is made. And if the one aspecting is Mercury, then it is like instruments from books and from those things for which books on law are made, and those things that are similar to them.

And if it is the terms of Mars, it is that thing that is from the instruments of iron and arms, or from those things that are made with fires. And if the one aspecting is the Moon, it is from the arms of the common people, and from an instrument of battle, and from those things that the messengers of kings receive. And if the one aspecting is Venus, it is that good thing in which there are shapes and a good image and sculpture. And if the one aspecting is Mercury, it is that thing from the instruments of girls and from the operations of castles, and those things that are similar.

And if the one aspecting is Saturn, it is something of a rod and a quiver and an arrow and a bow. And if the one aspecting is Jupiter, it is something from the arms of the common people covering the head, such as a breastplate of a shield, and [it is] yellow, and those things that are similar to them. And if each ruling star, namely of the terms of the Moon, is aspecting its own terms, that thing is of good substance; and if it is oriental, it is new; and if it is occidental, it is old; and if it is in its descent, which is before retrogradation or after retrogradation, it is intermediate between age and newness; and if it is direct, it is of course of equal figure; and if it is retrograde, it is of a crooked figure, or there is a crack in it, or a stain from the road of crookedness; and if it is not properly supported by adherence to its condition according to its diversity that is hammered out.

And if it is in an angle, it is made nicely and strong of its own substance; and if it is cadent, it is something weak of its own substance and not nicely made; and if it is in the succedent [of an] angle, it is between strength and debility and harmony and disharmony. And if it is fortified, it is sound in good nature; and if it is debilitated, it is foul, injurious, and there is a stain on it; and if it is in figure, it is harmonious in its goodness; and if it is in that which is outside the figure, it is disharmonious from its own goodness; and in these [states] there is something happening that prohibits it; and if that is because of its diversity, which arrives from the aspect of its ruler, then diversify your judgment through that which you have judged on the aspect of its ruler; and similarly the rightness of a good ruler is testified to, and its retrogradation, the likeness is testified to over that the ruler of the Moon, and all things that are testified to from the dispositions of the ruler of the Moon.}

{A Question about the Robber, Whether it is a Male or a Female or an *Imbrio*.}[1]

{And if you were asked about the robber, whether he is a male

---

[1] This chapter is possibly not a part of Sahl's Book 3, since it does not appear in MS **P**. I have therefore enclosed it in braces. I do not know what the word *imbrio* signifies unless it is "a youth."

or a female or an *imbrio*, then consider that which ascends of the forms of men in the face of the ASC in which the question is made, and declare according to the substance of those forms.¹ And you may know that in the first face of Aries, there ascends the form of a black man dressed in a white tunic; and there ascends in the second face, the form of a woman over whom there are red strips of cloth; and the third form [is that] of a man of a pale color with red hair.

And there ascends in the first face of Taurus, a man looking around and a naked man; and there ascends in the second face, a naked man in whose hand is a key; and in the third face, a man in whose hand is a snake and an arrow.

And there ascends in the first face of Gemini, a man in whose hand is a rod, and another who is a slave; and in the second, a man in whose hand [there is] a flute, and another [who is] bent over; and in the third, a man [who has] arms.

And there ascends in the first face of Cancer, a well dressed man and a young woman; and in the second, a young woman who is not a virgin, and another girl who is a virgin; and in the third, a man and woman [who are] angry.

And there ascends in the first face of Leo, the form of a lion, and a man above whom strips of cloth are elevated; and in the second, the image [of a man] having his arms raised, and a man on whose

---

¹The brief descriptions of the forms that arise with each face (decan) of the twelve signs are very similar to those given by **Bonatti** in Book 6, Chapter 18 of the 7th House Questions; he attributes the forms to Albumasar. They resemble those given by **Albumasar** (c.787-886) in *The Great Introduction*, Book 6, Chapter 1, and by Abraham Ibn Ezra (1089?-1167) in *The Beginning of Wisdom*, Chapter 2. In both books the majority of the forms given above are usually attributed to the wise men of India. **Ibn Ezra** is even more precise and in one place says "whose chief is Kanka." Al-Nadîm tells us in his *Fihrist* that the Hindu Kanakah came to Baghdad during the reign of the Caliph al-Ma'mûn (754-775) and wrote (or had written for him) several books in Arabic on astrology. The earlier Hindu astrologer **Varâhamihira** (6th century) also describes the decanates in his *Brihat Jataka*, Chapter 27, and attributes them to the Yavanas, i.e. the Greeks. Of all these, **Albumasar** and **Ibn Ezra** give the most details, but **Bonatti** is closest to the text given in the printed edition **v**.

head is a crown; and in the third, a youth in whose hand is a whip,[1] and a man of a very sad and dirty face.

And there ascends in the first face of Virgo, the form of a good girl; and in the second, a black man on whom there are leather clothes, and a man having a crown; and in the third, a white woman [who is] deaf.

And there ascends in the first face of Libra, the form of an angry man in whose hand there is a pipe[2]; and in the second, two men quarreling and angry; and in the third, a man in whose hand is a bow, and a naked man.

And there ascends in the first face of Scorpio, the form of a woman with a good face and body; and in the second, a naked man and a naked woman; and in the third, bent over onto his own knees.

And there ascends in the first face of Sagittarius, the form of a man of sordid appearance; and in the second, a woman above whom are strips of cloth[3]; and in the third, a man of a color similar to gold.

And there ascends in the first face of Capricorn, the form of a woman and a black man; and in the second, two women; and in the third, a black woman knowledgeable in her work.

And there ascends in the first face of Aquarius, the form of a man[4]; and in the second, the form of another man with a long beard; and in the third, an angry black man.

And there ascends in the first face of Pisces, a man on whom are his own good clothes; and in the second, a woman with a good face; and in the third, a naked man.}

---

[1] **Bonatti** says he carries a wand.
[2] **Bonatti** says he carries a flute, but the other writers say that he holds a balance in his hand.
[3] **Bonatti** says that she is well clothed.
[4] **Bonatti** says he is a youthful man.

A Question about Association and its Outcome.

And when you have been asked about partnership and association with someone, look at the ASC for the Querent and at the 7th for his associate, and at the MC for their essence, and at the angle of earth [IC] for the end of their [association]. if the ruler of the ASC and the Moon were in mobile signs, they will have a partnership, but it won't last long; and if it was in fixed signs, their partnership will be durable. But if it was in common signs, their partnership will be with profit, and their association will be with security and fidelity of each towards the other; and if there were malefics in the ASC, injury and lying and separation will come from the Querent.

Similarly, if there were malefics in the 7th, injury will come from his associate; and if the Moon was conjoined to the ruler of its own house, they will be separated with affection and profit; but if it does not aspect her, they will be separated through the bad opinion they have of each other. And if there were benefics in the MC, their profit will be multiplied, but if malefics were there, it will be diminished. And if the Moon was joined to the ruler of its own house in one sign, and both were joined to a malefic, they will not be separated except by death.

And when a man has wished to go to a great man and has asked whether he will find him or not, look at the ruler of the 7th; if it was in an angle, the man will be in the place where he is thought to be; and if it was in a succedent to an angle, he will be near his own place; but if it was cadent, he will not be in his own place.

A Question about a General going to War.

And if a general setting forth to war has asked a question, or if someone who is concerned about him has asked, because even if his kingdom was stable, it can nevertheless occur that the general himself will win the battle and be killed, and another will come.

Therefore, put the ASC, its ruler, and the planet from which the Moon is separated for the Querent and the one taking action; and the 7th and its ruler and the planet to which the Moon is joined for the enemy.

Moreover, if the Moon is neither separated nor conjoined,[1] and you should not change the matter in this work[2]; and know that the superior planets are stronger than the inferior planets in the matter of war; look, therefore, at both the significators, i.e. the ruler of the ASC and the ruler of the 7th; if they were joined by trine or sextile aspect and one of them receives the other, there will be peace, and it will be initiated by the one giving disposition, i.e. by the lighter planet; but if they were conjoined by square aspect or by opposition and one of them receives the other, there will be peace after a struggle.

But if one of them was retrograde or in an inconvenient place from the one that receives it, i.e. in the 6th or the 8th or the 12th, there is no dissension, [but] he will betray his associate, and he will act towards him in accordance with the quality of the substance of the house in which it was [posited]. And if it was in the 2nd from the ASC, it will give him security, after which he will take his property; and if it was in the 6th or the 12th, he will give him [a promise of] security, after which he will hold him, and he will suffer from him desertion, i.e. distraction; and if it was in the 8th, he will kill and destroy him; and if the ruler of the 7th was retrograde along with what I have said, it signifies his flight after security; and if one of the significators was separated from the other, the war between them will be prolonged; and if one of the significators was one of the superior planets and it was received in an angle, say that the person represented by that significator will win, unless it is entering into combustion.

But if the ruler of the ASC is one of the superior planets and it is cadent from the ASC, and the ruler of the 7th is in an angle and it is

---
[1] Something may be missing here.
[2] This presumably means that the question should not be changed.

one of the inferior planets, you shall not judge that the question is a winning one until you look at which planet the ruler of the 7th is joining, because if it was joined to a planet in an angle that is receiving it, the enemy will win, and he will capture the Querent, and he will have strength and victory over him according to the quantity of that planet to which the ruler of the 7th is joined.

Moreover, if the ruler of the 7th was strong and was joined to a cadent planet that impedites it, the person represented by the ruler of the 7th, i.e., the enemy, will not cease to have strength, so long as he stays in his own best place. And when it was threatened by that same place, it is weakened, and it will not cease to be weak, until it is impedited by the malefics, i.e., the ruler of the 7th, or is combust, and then the enemy will perish. But if it is joined to any planet in the sign where it is, it will change it to the 2nd sign.

After that, look at its conjunction with the planets, and thus you may judge through the strength of the inferior planets, unless through the goodness of that same place from the ASC and through its liberation from the impediting planets, and through the aid of the higher planets towards it. And if the ruler of the ASC was in the 7th, it signifies the strength of the enemy, because it is like someone conquered, and all the more so if the ruler of the ASC aspects it, because it signifies that the enemy will capture the Querent. And if the ruler of the 7th was in the ASC, the Querent will capture the enemy. And if the ruler of the ASC was in the 8th or joined to its ruler, it signifies death to the ruler of the question. Similarly, if the ruler of the 8th was in the 2nd from the ASC or was joined to the ruler of the 2nd, it signifies the death of the enemy, and more so if the ruler of that house was impedited by the malefics and does not receive the one giving testimony to it, sc. the one which is joined to it.

And if the ruler of the ASC was joined to the ruler of the MC, or if the ruler of the MC was joined to the ruler of the ASC, and the ruler of the ASC was in the MC, it signifies the good fortune of the Querent in his own kingdom, and that he will capture the one who contends with him, and the more so if the receiver was in an angle because it will be joined. For no one will be able [to contend successfully] with him, and he will not have confidence in his own kingdom, and he will capture the one who contends with him. Similarly, if the ruler of the 7th from the ASC was in the 4th and was joined to its ruler, or if the ruler of the 4th was joined to it, and the receiver was in an angle, the enemy will be unconquered by those who contend with him; and it must be feared for the kingdom of the Querent.

And if one of the significators was joined to any planet in an angle or to the ruler of an angle, and the more so if the significator itself was in an angle, because then it signifies the strength of that signification; and similarly if one of the significators was in an angle free from the malefics; and if it was in a mobile sign, it signifies death to him through being quickly seized. And when the ruler of the ASC was in the 12th from the ASC, it signifies the flight of the ruler of the question. Similarly, when the ruler of the 7th was in the 6th[1], it signifies the flight of the enemy; and if one significator was retrograde, it signifies a rupture and weakness of the house of that same signification; and if the ruler of the 10th was in the ASC, it signifies that the king will offer aid to the Querent. Similarly, if it was in the 7th from the ASC, it signifies that the king will aid the enemy. But if either of the Lights has from its own disposition givven disposition to one of the significators, i.e. if it was joined to it, it signifies the strength of that significator and that it will have aid from the king. And if the Moon was separated from the ruler of the ASC and joined to the ruler of the 7th, the enemy will be victorious.

And know that when Saturn was in an angle at the hour of the question and if it had no testimony, it signifies a lengthy continuation of the war until it recedes from that [position], and all the more so if it was retrograde, because the war will often be resumed. And if the Moon was with Mars and the benefics were cadent from her,

---

[1] Because the 6th is the 12th from the 7th.

then the Querent will be captured and slain. And if the Sun was in the [Dragon's] Head or Tail when the war was begun, there will be the greatest slaughter between both of the armies, and there will be no peace between them. But if the ruler of the ASC was with the [Dragon's] Tail, only a few [soldiers] will be left from either army.

For the severity of the war and the terror incurred by it, look also at Mars and at its place from the ASC, and look at the one that aspects it; and for the small size of the war and the number of men involved, look at the Moon and its condition and its place [from the ASC]; and look at the significators to see the condition of the military commanders and their state; and look at the planet from which Mars is separated, and put it for the significator of the enemy. After that, look at one of the significators, because the one that was in a mobile sign will be weaker, and its flight is feared; and that one that was in one of the common signs signifies that the ruler of its significator will persevere in the war; and a fixed sign signifies stability.

Then look at the strengths of those just as I shall say to you. If one of the significators was in its own exaltation, it will be stronger than if it was in its own domicile, and domicile is stronger than triplicity, and triplicity is stronger than the terms, and the terms are stronger than the face; and that one of the two planets is the stronger that aspects the ruler of its own domicile because it doubles its own strength; and then a planet will be more crafty when it was in its own fall or in the domicile of its own enmity[1] and it does not aspect the ruler of its own domicile; and if one of the significators was in its own exaltation, it will be the ruler and king of that significator; and if it was in its own domicile, it will be from neighbors or domestics of the king; and if it was in its triplicity, it will be from the children of nobles.

Moreover, if it was in its own terms, it will be [something] below that; and if it was in its own face, it will be thus to them; and if the

---

[1] That is, in its detriment (the sign opposite a sign that it rules).

ruler of the domicile of the significator was aspecting it, it signifies the boldness of the military commander and his armies, because he is faithful to the king. But if the ruler of its own domicile does not aspect it, he will not be of good faith; and whichever one of the significators was retrograde and impedited, that one provokes to flight; and whichever one was direct and fortunate, that one provokes civility and trust.

Look also at Mars to see if it was in its own exaltation or in the exaltation of the Sun, [for then] war will be manifest, and it will be called; but if it was in that [position] in the MC, it will strengthen the war until it is heard about in both the East and the West; and if it was in the ASC, it will be just as I have said to you; and if it was in the DSC, there will be craftiness and firmness, and the battle will be enlarged.

Moreover, if Mars is in a fixed sign and in an angle, there will be a war of that sort; and if it was in a common sign, there will be an often repeated war, and it will be stronger and larger; but if in a mobile sign, the war will be short; and if it was in its own domicile or its own triplicity, it will be of medium duration; and if it was in its own fall, the war will not be enlarged, but it will be broken off after a medium length of time.

Announce in accordance with what you have seen of the strength of Mars or its debility; and know that the Moon, when it was in the ASC and Mars in the 7th or the other way around, the one who goes to war and who starts it will be slain; and look at the number of soldiers and auxiliaries from the aspects of the planets to the significators and from their presence in their own domiciles; and put the sign of the 2nd and its ruler as significators of the soldiers of the Querent, and the 8th and its ruler as significators of the soldiers of the enemy, and the 11th sign and its ruler [as significators] of the agents of the king, the 5th and its ruler as significators of the city and those who live in it. But if there were benefics in the 2nd sign from the ASC or if they aspected it, and the ruler of the 2nd house was in a good place, it signifies the strength of the soldiers of the Querent and their fidelity and aid.

Similarly, the strength of the soldiers of the enemy are signified by the 8th from the ASC. And if there were benefics that were in a common sign in the 2nd from the ASC, or if they were in a sign of many children or in a mobile sign, announce that the Querent will have many soldiers; and if the significator [was after the Sun], i.e. oriental in its own domicile, or oriental in the 2nd house, the Querent's soldiers will seek truth, but if it is retrograde, they will be disobedient to him; but if a retrograde malefic is found in the 11th house, those serving the king and his auxiliaries will be traitors, especially if there was a malefic in the 8th house from the Sun, or if Mercury and the [Dragon's] Tail were with the Sun, because the king also with his associates is a malefactor to the soldiers of a noble.

But when you have recognized that military commanders will be reconciled, look at the planet that signifies this; if it was in its own domicile, the one who enters between them will be one of their own, and if it was not in its own domicile, a foreigner. But if it was Saturn, he will be an old man; and if it was Jupiter, he will be noble and great. But if it was Mars, he will be one of their own military commanders, and he wants to perpetrate an evil lie. And if it was the Sun, he will be a king and the head of the go-betweens. And if it was Venus, it will be a man who does not having any training nor any evil design. And if it was Mercury, he will be learned and wise or else a secretary. And if it was the Moon, he will be a man who goes between them with goodness and justice. But in the matter of treachery and craftiness, look to see if Mercury was impedited under the rays of one or the other planet, [for then] there will be treachery and craftiness in turn by each one of them, sc. towards his associate; and if Mars was with Mercury, that same craftiness and treachery will be apparent, for it will be divulged, and it cannot be restrained.

The witnesses are the planets by which it is aspected or which are in the same sign with it; and if the Moon and Saturn were the witnesses of the ASC, judge that the treachery has already taken place or that it will take place. Similarly, when Jupiter has offered its testimony both to the ASC and to the Moon, it signifies good. but if Venus has offered its testimony to the Moon and to the ASC, it does not signify treachery. And if Mercury has aspected the Moon or the ASC, it signifies craftiness or treachery.

For [the circumstances of] that peace-maker that was between them is declared by Mercury, which if it was under the Sun beams, and the Moon was with Mars or with the planet from which Mars was separated, the peace-maker himself will suffer; and if that one was an oriental Mercury, he will come with destruction, and he will be liberated by it; and if Mercury is in a common sign, the peace-maker that goes back and forth between them will not be just one person; and if there was an evil planet exalted over Mercury, he will encounter a heavy sentence and he will be thrown down; and if a benefic was exalted over him, he will evade it; and if it was impeded by Mars, it will be one of the warriors who impedes him; and if it was the Sun, it will be the king or the head of the armies.

The Cause of Wars.[1]

But when you want to know the knowledge of the cause by which a war was instigated, look at Mars, because the planet from which Mars is separated signifies those starting the war, and the one to which Mars is joined signifies their adversary; if it was separated from benefics, the beginner and Querent seeks the truth; and if it was separated from malefics, he does not seek the truth; and if it was joined to benefics, Mars or the enemy seeks the truth. But if it was joined to malefics, he does not speak the truth; and if it was joined to Mars in the ASC, there will be war because of fear; and if it was in the 2nd, it will be because of assets; and if it was in the 3rd, because of faith and religion; and if it was in the 4th, it will be because of land.

If it was in the 5th, it also signifies a war that is because of assets and because there is a relationship between the military com-

---

[1] I have added this chapter title.

manders, and perhaps they will be reconciled, or there will be war because of a woman or because of a city, and especially if you have found the Moon joined to Mercury,[1] it will be from love, then the war of the city toward which those who are wanting to accept her are going; and if it was in the 6th, the war will be because of some weak thing; and if it was in the 7th, it will be because of some old enmity, and they do not seek any gain; and if it was in the 8th, it will be because of some old thing with a seeking of blood, but if the Moon aspects the ruler of the MC, this will be because [of orders] of the king, and the killing will be multiplied in both planets.

And if it was in the 9th, it will be because of faith. And if the Moon was in the MC and was joined to Mars by a square aspect or by opposition, or if it was in one sign with it, there will be war for the honor of the king or for the magnification of the king and the seeking of the king; and if it was in the 12th, there will be a cause due to some old enmity, but there will be no war, because Mars in the 12th does not signify war, because it is cadent from an angle, for the one who goes forth to them will hear and obey if God is willing.

The Quality of the Army.

And if you have been asked about an army, whether it is big or of medium size, take the number from the Moon to Mercury, sc. how many signs are between them; if it was an equal number, the army will be big. But if it was an unequal number, the army will be small.

After that, look at this chapter for all matters pertaining to the war, that is so that you may know that the ASC is the significator for those beginning the war and for its cause, and who it was who instigated the war and truly whether he began it with truth or with falsehood; and the 2nd from the ASC signifies whether there will be a war or not and whether it will be for gain or destruction; and the 3rd from the ASC signifies the arms, by which kinds of arms

---
[1] Or perhaps we should read 'Venus', rather than Mercury.

there will be victory and attainment [of goals], and what kinds of arms are not necessary in that same war.

And the 4th from the ASC signifies where the war will take place, whether it will be flat ground or mountainous, and whether it will be on the shore of a great sea in fact or a little one or next to a river, and whether there are fruit-bearing trees in that same place or a wood; and the fifth [signifies] the honesty and ability of the soldiers and their [rate of] advance and their boldness or sluggishness; and the 6th signifies the many animals of the soldiers and what they are, i.e. whether they are horses or asses or mules or camels.

And the 7th signifies the enemy and a siege-work, i.e. an instrument by means of which stones are thrown,[1] and whether the war will be [conducted] with craftiness and skill or the contrary; and the 8th signifies wounds and captives and death and breaking to pieces and the flight of the victors; and the 9th signifies the activities of spies and the knowledge of the enemy's assets and his rumors and crafty actions.

And the 10th from the ASC signifies the action of the major military commander and the habits of those others who are under his command; and the 11th signifies their organization and their battle-order and the troops and how they will advance and what their formation will be around the enemy; and the 12th signifies a city and those who besiege and storm it.

Look, therefore, at these twelve houses and the houses of their rulers and the aspects of those [planets] that are cast to each one of those houses by the malefics, namely, and by the benefics that are also in them, either a benefic or a malefic, and which one of those benefics and malefics aspects the ruler of a house. After that, speak in accordance with what you have seen of the aspects of the benefics and the malefics and about their strength and debility, be-

---

[1] A *mangonel*, which is a catapult used to throw heavy stones in military operations.

cause when a benefic aspects the sign, it signifies good fortune and good to that same sign; and when a malefic aspects by a square aspect or by opposition or was in the same sign, it sends impediment and evil to it, sc. to that which pertains to that same sign in accordance with its own significations, about which I have set them forth to you in this chapter.

The Eighth House in Connection with an Absent Person.

When you have been asked about a man who is absent or about any other man, whether he is alive or he is dead, look at the ruler of the ASC and the Moon; if it was in the 4th from the ASC or in the house of death, which is the 8th from the ASC, or if it was combust or in its own fall or with the ruler of the House of Death, he will be dead. And if you have found any one of these, then look at the aspect of the malefics and the benefics to them; if the ruler of the ASC was in the 4th, retrograde, or retrograde in its fall, or retrograde in the house of death, or separated from the ruler of the House of Death by retrogradation, look to see if it turns back to the degree of combustion—[if so], he will be dead; and if the Moon is joined to a planet above the earth, he is alive; and if you have found the ruler of the ASC in the 12th with malefics or if malefics were aspecting it and either of the Lights was impeded, you will indicate death for him.

Also, if there were malefics in one sign with the Lights, which are the Sun and the Moon, without any aspect of the benefics, it signifies death; and similarly if the Moon was with Mars in the 4th and the benefics did not aspect her. Similarly when the Part of Fortune was with malefics in the 4th from the ASC or in the 6th or in the 12th, and the benefics did not aspect it.

And know that that which is above the earth signifies life, and that which is below the earth signifies death! When, therefore, you have found the ruler of the ASC combust under the Sun beams and no benefic has aspected it, and the Moon was under the earth, cadent from the ASC in the 3rd or the 6th, know that the one about whom you have asked is dead, and especially if the Moon was in Scorpio in the 3rd degree of it impedited by Saturn, which naturally signifies death; then you will verify the death of that one who is the subject of the question.

The Ninth House on the Matter of Travel.

When you have been asked about a journey, whether it may occur or not, and, if it can not be accomplished, what it will be that prohibits it, look at the ruler of the ASC and the Moon, which are the significators of the one who is traveling, and the sign of the 9th and its ruler, which are the significators of the journey itself. If the ruler of the ASC and the Moon, which are the significators, are in the 9th, or one of them was joined to the ruler in the 9th, the journey made by the Querent for himself will not be horrible; and if the ruler of the 9th was in the ASC and was joined to the ruler of the ASC, a journey will come to pass for him that cannot be frustrated in any way. Moreover, if the situation of the ruler of the ASC and the ruler of the 9th was what I have said to you, and any other planet has returned the light of one of them to the other, the translation of light signifies travel.

But if this was not the case, and you have found the ruler of the ASC and the ruler of the 9th joined to a planet weightier than themselves, and that planet has aspected the ruler of the 9th house of travel, it signifies travel; but if it does not aspect them, there will be no travel. Likewise, if the ruler of the ASC was in an angle and was joined to a planet that is to the left of the ASC, i.e. between the ASC and the 4th, and it was free from the malefics, it signifies travel. But if the ruler of the ASC and the Moon were joined to any Planet in an angle, there will be no travel; and if the significators are joined together—namely, the ruler of the ASC and the ruler of the 9th—and there was a peregrine malefic in the ASC impediting the ruler of the ASC or the ruler of the 9th, there will be [no] travel; and this will happen because of him, i.e. because of the Querent, [for] something will happen that will disturb [him] and prevent his travel.

And if that malefic was in the 7th, something will come to him about that land that he was wanting to go to, or something about the thing that he was seeking, that will frustrate his [desire for] travel and prohibit it. And if the malefic was in the MC, some burden will come to him from the king or from someone who is over him or who is in charge of him. And if the ruler of the ASC was joined to the ruler of the House of Travel, [and] afterward was joined to a malefic by opposition or by conjunction or by a square aspect or was with it in one sign, [then] announce a hindrance that will happen to him after his journey in accordance with the amount of enmity of that planet.

That is, if it was the ruler of the 6th from the ASC, it will be sickness; and if it was the ruler of the 4th, it will be imprisonment and other such sorrows; and if it was the ruler of the 8th, death; and if it was the ruler of the 7th or the 12th, the ruler signifies destruction by armed robbers and enemies; and if it is aspected by the ASC, his killing is to be feared. But if it is aspected by the 2nd from the ASC, it signifies loss of property. Similarly, the square aspect of the ASC signifies a bodily defect; and the other square aspect, the second one, i.e. from the 10th sign, a loss of property. and if you have found the ruler of the ASC in the 7th or the 8th, it signifies hardship in travel, and especially if it was a malefic.

But if the ruler of the ASC had already begun to emerge from under the Sun beams or was already freed from its own impediment in which it was [situated], i.e. under the Sun beams, it will be an easy journey; and if you have found that same ruler of the ASC in the ASC or in one of its own domiciles and it is not joined to the ruler of the 9th, he will not travel, especially if the sign was fixed, because a fixed sign destroys a journey. And when you have found the Moon to be received, it signifies ease. But if it was not received, it signifies delay and complication and that nothing is gained after that journey; and he will be odious and a burden upon the one to whom he comes.

The ruler of the ASC signifies similarly if it aspects it by opposition. And know that the ASC signifies the journey, and the MC his gains and what he wants to gain, and the 7th from the ASC signifies the land to which he is going. But the fourth from the ASC signifies the end of that thing.

Therefore, if there was a benefic in the ASC, the condition of his mind and body will be useful; and if there were benefics in the MC, his things will be useful and beneficial; but if there were benefics in the 7th, he will see in the land to which he has come what he wanted and desired. And if you have found any of the malefics in the ASC or in the MC or in the 6th, there will happen to him both labor in vain and sickness and diminution; but if you find benefics in the 4th from the ASC, the end of that thing will be in accord with what he wants and desires; but if you find malefics, the reverse.

And if you have seen that there will be a journey and you want to know to whom the traveler is going, look at the Moon. If it was joined to the Sun, he is going to nobles or to the king; and if it was joined to Saturn, say that he is going to low-born and common persons; and if it was joined to Jupiter, say that he is going to nobles; and if to Venus, to women; and if to Mercury, to writers and merchants and learned persons.

But if the Moon was void of course, he will go out seeking someone known to him who is absent; and then if it was separated from Saturn, he has gone out on account of a debt because he was being hounded by his creditors; and if it was separated from Mars, he will be a fugitive from the king or someone like a fugitive.

Then look at the planet to which the Moon is joined; if it was in its own domicile, the man to whom he is going will be a citizen of the region; and if it was in its own triplicity, he will not be one of those citizens, but he will come into the region and stay in it; and if the ruler of the house of the planet to which the Moon is joined aspects it, he will be known in the region; and if it does not aspect it, he will not be known in it; and if it was aspected from the 4th, he will be [somewhere] between praised and detested in that same region, i.e. he will not be universally praised nor universally detested; and if it was aspected by opposition, he will be odious and contentious. But if it was a sextile or trine aspect, he will be beloved; and if it was conjoined to it in one place, i.e. in one sign, he will be one of those who carry off the substance of men by force.

After that, look at that same malefic that is impeding the ruler of the ASC or the Moon; if it was in human signs, which are Gemini and its triplicity, it is a warning to him that he should beware of armed robbers and those who blockade roads; and if it was in watery signs, he should beware of shipwreck; and if in animal signs, he should beware of an accident involving animals or by being attacked by them; and if it was in signs of seed, he should beware of trees and thorns and of a high place and of food that has been poisoned.

But if the malefic was in Leo, there will properly be an impediment from wolves or from a scorpion or from reptiles; and in Pisces properly from those creatures which loiter in waters; and the greatest impediment of Mars is on the land, but Saturn impedes more on the sea.

The Entrance of a Traveler into a City.

For the entrance of a traveler into a city, look at the time when [as] a foreigner he enters the city and at what sign is ascending at the hour of his entrance. If it was the ruler of the 2nd house and it was retrograde, it signifies his quick return without the completion of his business and that he will not find anything good; and if it was in its own first station when it is about to turn retrograde, it will cause a delay, and he will return without the completion of his business. If it was in its own second station when it is about to turn direct, he will return between quickly and slowly, and he will accomplish his business after having lost hope of doing so; and if the ruler of the 2nd was in the ASC, in the MC, or in the 7th, it will be a satisfactory and profitable trip; and if it was in the 7th, some restriction and contention will occur during his trip.

But if it was in the 9th or the 3rd, he will not stay quietly in his own country, but he will set out for another one. And if it is in the 4th and a malefic aspects it or was with it, that will be his last trip, and it may be feared that he will die in that region, and he will not go on to another region.

Moreover, if the Moon was joined to the ruler of the 2nd from the ASC in one sign, or if it aspects her, or if she was joined to Mercury in one sign or if Mars aspects her, he will find injuries[1] and prostrations from illness and some horrible thing. But if the Moon was then in the angle of earth,[2] he will die from that. But if it was in any other angle than this, some vestige of that destruction and prostration will remain in him; and if the Moon aspects Mars, and no benefic aspects it, he will find plagues according to the substance of the sign in which it is posited; but if then the benefics aspect the Moon, he will have freedom and health from those restrictions that I have mentioned, and he will find a remedy for that infirmity and prostration and the injuries. But if the benefics do not aspect it, he will remain in that condition until he dies of those causes.

The Journeys of Princes and Kings.

And if you have been asked about the circumstances of the journey of princes or of kings and the circumstances of those who will succeed them, i.e. who will remain in their place in their own land, look at the 2nd from the ASC; if there was in it a malefic that does not have testimony to it, after his exit among those that will remain after him in neighboring [regions], sc. of his, and in his own kingdom [there will be] some detrimental occurrence. If it was Mars, [there will be] contention and war and destruction by fire; and if it was Saturn, armed robbers and infirmity or shipwreck.

---

[1] I have translated the Latin word *plagas* as 'injuries', but it has a variety of meanings, including 'blows', 'plagues', etc.
[2] The 4th house.

Moreover, if that malefic was received, it will not impede this, but it will ameliorate it. But if it was in its own fall, that will be perfected and magnified, and all the more if it was retrograde, because then it will signify dissolution and loss.

Say something similarly about the benefics when they were in the 2nd from the ASC or when the Moon was impedited, [for] they signify sorrow and hindrance on the road; but if the malefic was above the earth between the ASC and the 10th, this will happen to him on his return; and if it was between the 7th and the 10th, on his departure; and if it was below the earth between the ASC and the 4th, in those things that he acquired on his departure. But if it was between the 4th and the 7th, on his return.

What Land Would be Better for the Querent.

When someone has asked you, saying "Is the land I am in better for me, or the other one that I want to go to?" Look at the Moon; if it was separated from a malefic, his departure will be better for him. But if it was separated from the benefics, it is better for him to remain; and if the situation of the ruler of the ASC was good, it is better for him to remain. But if the situation of the ruler of the 7th was better, it will be better for him to go.

Whether it Would be Good for the Querent to Set Out on a Journey.

And if he has asked you, "See if it is good for me to go forth to this business or for me to do this or that." Look at the ruler of the ASC and the Moon; if they were separated from malefics and joined to benefics, admonish him to do whatever he wants to do. But if they were separated from benefics and joined to malefics, he should not [even] approach that work.

Release from Captivity.

If you have been asked about anyone who is a captive, look into this just as you look in the case of travel, because each of these questions looks into their departure from their [present] place. If the rulers of the angles, or some of them, are in the domiciles of those in the angles, it signifies their retention in that same year.

After this, look at the ruler of the ASC and its position, which, if it was in an angle, it signifies the prolongation of his imprisonment, and even more so if it was the angle of earth and the ruler of the 12th and any of the malefics aspected it, he will find some punishment along with imprisonment. But if the ruler of the ASC was cadent from the ASC but was joined to a planet in an angle, his imprisonment will be prolonged after he was hoping to escape. And if it was in an angle and joined to a cadent planet, it signifies his liberation after having lost hope. But if it was joined to an evil planet that is in the angle of earth, which is the 4th sign, or if the ruler of the 8th was in the ASC, which is a sign of death, he will not emerge from prison until he is dead.

And if the ruler of the ASC or the Moon was joined to any planet in the 3rd or the 9th, it signifies his liberation, and all the more so if it was not the ruler of any angle of the angles of the ASC. And if one of them, i.e. the ruler of the ASC or the Moon was joined to the ruler of the 3rd or the 9th, or to its receiver on the left of the ASC, it signifies his liberation, and this will be the result of some action on his own part, and no one will plead for him.

But if the ruler of the 3rd or the 9th was joined to the ruler of the ASC, someone will effect this for him, and he will be freed without any action of his own. But if the ruler of the ASC was joined to the ruler of the 12th and was to the left of the ASC, it signifies his escape from prison. Similarly, if the ruler of the 3rd or the 9th was joined to the ruler of the 12th. Moreover, if the ruler of the ASC was joined to the ruler of the 3rd or the 9th, but the receiver was in an angle, i.e. a weightier planet, he will [not] come out [of prison] until the receiver has gone out of its sign and receded from the angles. And if the ruler of the domicile of the Moon was joined to the ruler of the ASC, it signifies a delay in his release.

After this, [and] after you have ceased to look at the ruler of the ASC and its connection with the stars and at the connection of the stars with it, look at the place of the significator, i.e. the Moon; if it was in a mobile sign, it signifies the swiftness of his liberation, except for Cancer, which is slow; and Aries and Libra are swifter in liberation than Capricorn; and he will not linger in prison, and he will find many helpers there. But Capricorn signifies slowness and loneliness and sorrow, and that enemies work to keep him in bondage.

And if it was in a fixed sign, it signifies slowness in his release, and the slowest of all is Aquarius.[1] But if the Moon was in a common sign, and he was not set free before the Moon goes out of that sign, his imprisonment will be prolonged, and all the more so if it was a domicile of Jupiter and he did not aspect her. But if he is placed in that prison when the Moon is on one of the domiciles of Mercury, he will find good and joy.

Then look at her connection; if it was in an angle, and she was joined to a planet to the left of the ASC and the ruler of the ASC testified, it signifies his liberation similarly. And if the Moon was cadent and joined to any planet in an angle, it signifies the prolongation of his imprisonment, unless the planet was the ruler of the 3rd or the 9th, and then he will be liberated when that planet shall have been changed.[2] And if she was cadent and joined to a cadent planet that is the ruler of any angle, there will be hope of his release until that planet goes out of any of the angles of the ASC, and then he will lose hope.

But if there was a [planet] to which the ruler of the angle is joined, and it was in the 3rd sign or the in the 9th, it will be better and easier for his release. And if she was joined with the ruler of any one of the angles, and especially with the ruler of the ASC, it signifies slowness. And if the ruler of the ASC is going under the

---

[1] Because it is ruled by Saturn.
[2] Presumably, when it shall have moved into another sign.

Sun beams and there was a malefic in the 4th, he rarely is [still] alive. But if that malefic was Mars, he will be put to death. Afterward, he will go out of the prison.[1]

But if the ruler of the ASC has already passed through combustion, he will be made ill by a severe illness; and if any of the malefics was in any angle, the more distant you see that it is from the degree of the Sun, the lighter will be his infirmity, and the quicker he will be set free; and if it was joined to the ruler of the 8th from the ASC or to a malefic in the angle of earth, he will die in prison; and if it was with Saturn or if it aspected him strongly, it signifies a prolongation of his imprisonment and sorrow and some damage in his property and in his body.

But if it was with Mars, it signifies impediment and constraint; and if the Moon was then impeded, some punishment will find him, but he will not be whipped; and if the Moon aspects the ruler of her house, it will be lighter; but if she does not aspect it, it will be harsher.

After these things, look at the condition of the Querent from the ruler of the ASC and the condition of the one who is contending with him from the ruler of the 7th; if they aspect each other by trine or sextile aspect, the one that provokes the other will seek him out with pleasantness and peace and good wishes. But if they aspect each other by opposition or by square aspect, he will seek him out with seriousness and intemperance, and he will be very persistent in seeking justice for himself.

The Return of Someone Absent.

When you have been asked about the arrival of someone absent, look at the ruler of the ASC and its place; if it is in the ASC or in the 10th or it does not commit its own disposition to a planet that is in those [houses], it signifies his arrival; and if the ruler of the

---

[1] Either there is something missing, or else it must mean that his body will be released after he has died in prison.

ASC was in the 9th or in the MC, or if it commits its own disposition to a planet that is in those [houses], it signifies his arrival. But if the ruler of the ASC was in the 7th from the ASC or in the angle of earth, there will be difficulty and delay in his arrival, and it signifies that the absent person is in some land or other and he is not going out of it; and if the ruler of the ASC was in the 9th or the 3rd from the ASC, and it is joined to a Planet in the ASC, he will be on the road wanting to return. Similarly, if the ruler of the ASC was in the 8th from the ASC or in the 2nd and was joined to a planet in the 10th, that is in the MC.

Moreover, if the ruler of the ASC was cadent and was not joined to any planet in an angle and does not aspect the ASC, it will be bad because it signifies delay; and if the ruler of the ASC or the Moon was joined to a retrograde planet, or if the ruler of the ASC was retrograde and aspecting the ASC, it signifies his arrival; and if the ruler of the ASC was impeded, it signifies difficulty and prolongation [of the time] of his arrival.

But if the house of the ASC was not as I have said, look at the significator, which is the Moon, which if it commits its own disposition to the ruler of the ASC in or near to the ASC, namely within 11 degrees, it signifies the swiftness of his arrival; and if the ruler of the ASC was in the 7th or in [the house] succeeding it, this will be prolonged.

Moreover, if the Moon was separated from the ruler of the 4th or the 7th, or else of the 9th or the 3rd, and it was conjoined to the ruler of the ASC, it signifies his arrival. Also, if it was separated from a planet to the left of the ASC, that is under the earth, and it was joined to a planet to the right of the ASC, i.e. above the earth, it signifies his arrival. But if the Moon was cadent and was joined to a planet to the right of the ASC in the 10th, it signifies his arrival but with some delay because when the Moon was impeded to the right of the ASC, it signifies difficulty and the remoteness of his arrival.

[Here, edition **v** inserts a chapter entitled "A Question about a Vision or a Dream." This chapter does not appear in the Paris MS **P**, nor does **Bonatti** make any mention of it (from which we may infer that it was not present in his MS of Sahl's works), so it may not be a genuine part of Sahl's Book III. I have, therefore, chosen not to insert it here, but I will put it in an Appendix.]

The Tenth House, About a Kingdom.

When you have been asked about a kingdom in which someone has faith—that is, whether he will get it or not—look at the ruler of the ASC and the Moon. If the ruler of the ASC or the Moon was joined to the ruler of the 10th and the receiver aspected the MC, it signfies his acquisition with progress [of time] and effort and with the seeking of the Querent and his inquiry.

Similarly, if the ruler of the ASC or the Moon was in the 10th, it does not impede [his acquisition]. But if the ruler of the MC was in the ASC or was joined to the ruler of the ASC, he will get the kingdom without seeking [it] and without difficulty; it will be similarly if the ruler of the MC was joined to a benefic in the ASC.

But if there was nothing that I have mentioned, and you have seen a planet returning their light, i.e. transferring the light from one to the other, then the Querent is not seeking the thing himself, but he he is seeking someone who will work at this for him; and if the receiver of the disposition aspects the MC and was free from the malefics, he will get [the kingdom]. But if it was impedited and did not aspect the MC, that work will be destroyed after [he has made] an effort.

And know that when the malefics impedite [the receiver of the disposition] by square or by opposition, the ruler of the question will be turned back by the disgraceful turning back of his own companion, they destroy the question; but if by trine or sextile aspect it is turned back, they impedite less; and if they have conjoined the light of the ruler of the ASC and the light of the ruler of the MC to any planet, i.e. if they were both joined with it and that planet was in the ASC or in the MC, then look at the Moon, which, if it was joined with a good or beautiful turning back and to the ruler of the ASC or the ruler of the 10th, there will be the attainment; but if it was not joined to any of them and was free from the malefics, he will get and hold [it] with the aid of many men.[1]

Moreover, if the Moon was not [posited] just as I have said, and there was a planet that conjoined the light in the MC or aspected it, and it was not cadent, nor was it going out from that same sign until there was joined to it the ruler of the ASC and the ruler of the 10th, and it was free from the malefics, he will surely get it.

Question about Anything, Whether He will get it or not.

When you have seen the ruler of the ASC and the ruler of the 10th conjoined, look to see if the Moon has committed its disposition and its strength to one of them and was received and and free from the malefics, announce and expect the [desired] effect. But if none of them has committed its own disposition, but it was received, it will be slower.

If, moreover, it was not received and it was not impeded, look at the receiver of their disposition; if it was free from the malefics, aspecting its own domicile, he will get a part of those things that he sought; and if it was impeded, in accordance with what I have said about the impediment of the Moon, he will not get it; and if the ruler of the 10th house was conjoined to the ruler of the 4th, and the ruler of the 4th to the ruler of the ASC, he will get it. But if the ruler of the ASC is joined to the ruler of the 4th, and the ruler of the 4th is joined to the ruler of the MC, he will get it after having given up hope.

And when the ruler of the ASC has received the disposition of the Moon, there will be the seeking of a kingdom. And know that when the ruler of the ASC is in its own domicile, he will be estab-

---
[1] This paragraph seems to be *corrupt!*.

lished over the land in which he is; and if it is posited in its own exaltation, he will be established over many lands and [some] business of outstanding dignity; but if it is in its own triplicity, it signifies [some] great business, but it will not be in his own land in which he is. Moreover, if it does not have testimony in the house, he will be unknown in the land over which he will rule.

And know that perchance the ruler of the ASC and the tenth will be the same planet, as if the ASC was Virgo and the tenth Gemini. But if it was so and that planet was received and the Moon committed its own disposition to it, and it [has] strength from an angle, he will get it; but if the planet was received and the Moon was similarly received and in a good house, and it aspects the house of the thing or its own houses, he will get a part of those things that he is seeking; if, moreover, it was not received, and the Moon was also impeded, he will not get what he is seeking.

And perchance it will not happen that the ruler of the ASC aspects the ruler of the tenth, as if it was Leo ascending and the right angles. Then, look at the place of the Sun and Venus, and whichever Planet received them and aspected the MC, it signifies the perfection of those things. But if one of them was received and the other was not, look at the Moon [to see] if it commits its own disposition and strength to the one that is not received; he will get it. But if it was not received, and the Moon was impeded, and she was not received and did not aspect any of them, and the one that receives her disposition aspects the MC and was not impeded, he will get a part of those things that he is seeking.

And if a planet in an angle conjoins their light and it does not go out from its own place until it is joined to it, it signifies success and the getting of those things that he is seeking.

After that, look at the Moon [to see] if she is received and aspects the MC, [if so] his strength and good fortune is already complete. And if the Moon is joined to the light of the ruler of the MC, or if she has passed by it and is joined to its body and aspects the

MC, he will get it; and if the ruler of the domicile in which the Moon is receives her, and they both aspect the 10th, he will get it.

And if the Moon in the sign in which she is does not approach the light of any planet before she goes out of it,[1] the one seeking that thing will not get his own thing, unless the ruler of the ASC and the ruler of the thing have strength and testimony in their houses and both of them aspect the house of the thing.

And know that a defect of the Moon and of the ruler of the MC signifies a diminution of the thing in the work, and it will be all the worse if it was an impeded receiver of the Moon's disposition, because it signifies the detriment of the work; and if the Moon was joined to the ruler of the ASC or to the ruler of the MC, it will aid in the success.

But if the ruler of the MC gives[2] its strength and disposition to the planet that receives them and which has strength in its own house, and [in the house] of the thing, and it does not aspect the MC, the thing will not be perfected in the same manner in which it is sought. And when the significator is inimical to its own ruler, it signifies difficulty and complication in the seeking of the thing; and its enmity is as it is in its own twelfth house, or in the second, or in the sixth, or in the eighth.[3] And if it aspects it from the seventh, it signifies opposition.

And know that the ruler of the ASC is the significator of those things that happen to the ruler of the kingdom from [either] praise or censure, and other things that concern him. And the ruler of the 7th is the significator of the work of his citizens; and the MC and its rulers are the significators of those things that are done in his kingdom, of good or evil. And the eleventh and its ruler are the significators of those things that come after him in his own work,

---

[1] That is, if the Moon is void of course.
[2] The Latin text has *pulsat* 'strikes', but this is a mistranslation of the Arabic, which should have been rendered as *donat 'gives'. I have corrected it.
[3] These are all evil houses.

that is in the kingdom. And the ninth and its ruler are the significators of those things that were before him. And the fourth and its ruler are the significators of the end of his work.

Therefore, find the signification of his acquisition and his wealth from the second sign and its ruler and from the Part of Fortune and the goodness of its house, and writers from the second sign[1] and its ruler; and [also] from the 11th and its ruler, find his revenue and his friends[2]; and his brothers from the third sign; and his slaves from the 6th and its ruler; but his enemies from the 12th and its ruler. Look, therefore, at the aspect of the benefic and the malefic planets to these houses, where, when it was a benefic, there will be good joy and profit; and from wherever you have found a malefic, there will be hindrance and fear and the removal of hands from obedience, and war.

Royal Expenditures.

When you have been asked on what he expends the revenue that he collects, look at the ruler of the House of Assets. If it was Mars he will spend it and squander it on evil works, war such as war and luxury and drunkenness and other such things. And if it was Saturn, it will agitate his mind, and he will squander his wealth and that of others. But if it was Jupiter, he will expend it for the love of God and in charitable works, or in every kind of good work. And if it was the Sun, he will give[3] it because of his parents, and in the acquisition of nobility. And if it was Venus, it will make his own mind to enjoy every kind of delight. And if it was Mercury, in seeking profit in buying or selling. Moreover, if it was the Moon, it will act in accordance with the nature of the planet to which it is joined; and if she was void of course, he will spend it until it is all gone.

---

[1] 'Second sign' is equivalent to 'second house', since Sahl used the Sign-House system of house division.
[2] His revenue, because the 11th house is the 2nd house from the 10th House of Profession.
[3] The Latin text seems to have the word *donabit* 'he will give', but it is blurred in my copy.

And the ruler of the ASC also signifies the condition of his end, because it is the fourth from the 10th and its deposition.[1] If indeed you have found the ruler of the ASC either in the 12th or in the 6th or in the 8th, it signifies the disgraceful nature of his end, and all the more disgraceful if it was in the 6th or in the 12th; [for] then it signifies that he will be angered and mistrusted and cursed,[2] so that someone will rise up against him who will be put in place after him.

Moreover, if the ruler of the ASC is received, the evil will be taken away, i.e. he will not suffer any persecution, and he will not be defeated. But if it was not received, and it was impedited with that which I have said, there will be something that will happen to him after his deposition that is worse than his own deposition; and if the ruler of the 12th was joined to the ruler of the ASC, and it does not receive it, the one mentioned before as being put in charge will be defeated; and that is the more likely if it was in any angle.

But if it was in the 10th, he will be defeated in his own kingdom in the eyes of all [his subjects], and he will be put down in their presence; and if it was in the ASC, he will be below what I have said. But if it was in the 4th, this will be in secret, but nevertheless in his own honor. Moreover, if it was in the 7th, he will be brought together with the citizens of that honor, and he will have hindrance from it.

But if it was cadent from the angles, to the right of the ASC and was joined together with the 12th, he will not be defeated in his own honor until he is brought to the land in which he is going to be retained. But if it was to the left of the ASC, he will be defeated during his journey; and if it was joined to the ruler of the 8th after its separation from the ruler of the 12th, it signifies his death in his captivity; but if it was joined after the ruler of the 12th to the ruler of the MC, he will find a kingdom after a defeat. and know that

---

[1] That is, its "finish" or "end."
[2] Reading *exsecrabitur* 'he will be cursed' instead of *exrecitabitur* 'he will be coughed up'.

Mars also signifies some kind of defeat just as the ruler of the 7th does if it is inimical to the ruler of the ASC. That is, if it was the ruler of the 2nd or the 8th or the 6th or the 7th or the 4th or the ruler of the 8th is prompter, because it signifies death in captivity. And look at the malefic that impedites the ruler of the ASC; if it is Saturn, there will be that which I have said about hindrance; and he will be martyred from prison and be beaten with rods. And if Mars is impediting, the hindrance will be from chains and punishments by iron and from being beaten with whips.

A Question about Someone's Condition put by a Representative.

And if you have been asked to know the condition of someone by a person who represents him, for the Querent, look at the ASC and its ruler, and for the one who represents him, at the 7th and its ruler. If the ruler of the 7th receives the ruler of the ASC or gives its own strength to him by trine or sextile aspect; or by square, their matter will be very well resolved. Also if the Moon carries the light between them when the Moon commits her disposition to the receiver from the House of Love.[1] And the malefics are generally crafty from the square aspect or the opposition; and they operate fortunately from the square aspect and the opposition; but if the two significators are not mutually conjoined, and no star carries its light between them, things will not be between them as they would wish.

Where is the Ruler of the Kingdom?

Moreover, if you have wanted to know in what land the ruler of that kingdom is, look at the sign of the MC. If there is a Planet there and it was in its own domicile, it will be [a place] of men of that land and of middle class men; and if it is in its own exaltation, it will be [a place] of more noble men. But if it was in its triplicity, it will be less than that. And if it was not in its own domicile nor in its own exaltation nor in its own triplicity, it will be a foreign [place].

---

[1] The Latin has *ex loco dilectionis* 'from the House of Love', but perhaps we should read *ex loco delectionis* 'from the house of the choice?

And if it was an oriental planet, it will be one of the cities of the East; and if it was occidental, it will be one of the cities of the West; and if it was in the 4th from the Sun, one of the cities of the North; but if it was in the 10th from the Sun, it will be one of the cities of the South.

Moreover, if the planet is peregrine in the sign in which it is, and it does not aspect its own domicile or its own exaltation, it will not be a noble [place]; and if the planet is not in the sign of the MC, say about the ruler of the MC, just as I have already said to you.

A Question about his Taking his Seat.

And look at the hour of his taking the seat of his own kingdom—when he has sat upon the seat of his own empire and has begun to command and prohibit. If his entrance is by day, and the Sun is with Saturn, judge for him the swiftness of his being deposed from that work, namely from his kingdom. And if fortunes aspect the Sun, and if you find the ruler of the ASC and the Sun in the best house from the ASC, and it is in a fixed sign, his rulership will be prolonged, and he will see what he wants to see in it. But if the malefics aspect the Sun, and the malefic is Mars and it is exalted over it from the MC, and the Sun is in the ASC in a mobile sign, someone of the citizens of that kingdom will be opposed to him and will often frighten him; or, his end will be by death and murder.

Moreover, if you have found Jupiter in the MC and it is in a fortunate position, and the Sun is in the best and strongest house, his work will be exalted and augmented and memorable and productive of wealth. And if you see the Sun in the 8th or in the 6th, and the ruler of the ASC is in the ASC or in the MC, and it is a benefic, it will be the best thing for that prince; but it signifies the death of the one who appointed him.

And if his entrance into his kingdom was at night, look at the Moon just as I have said to you about the Sun; and look to see if the

Moon is free from the malefics; and if it was free from the malefics and in a good house, it signifies the health of his body. But if the Moon is with the malefics or joined to them, he will be quickly deposed from his own honor, and he will have great and strong complaints.

And if the Moon is with Caput or Cauda, and there are 4 degrees or less between them, he will not make progress in that same work; but if there are more than 4 degrees between them, the impediment will be less, until it passes 12 degrees from the hour of its freedom from their malice.

Look also at the Moon and the ASC and the rulers of their houses and the aspects of the benefics and the malefics to them. If benefics aspect them and their rulers, and their rulers are in good houses; and the malefics are cadent, and the benefics are in the MC, that prince will see what he delights in; and if the Moon and the ruler of her domicile are in evil houses, he will find evil in that region.

After that, look at the ASC of the hour of his entrance to see if it is in the terms of the malefics, and if the malefics aspect the terms of the ASC; [if so], he will be weak in that work, and a very bad crime will be attributed to him. But if the degree of the ASC is in the terms of the benefics and the benefics aspect them, that work will make progress, and he will go out honored; and every good thing will be said of him, together with the wealth that he will find from his own work.

And if a malefic is in the ASC, his work will be evil, for he will find hindrance in it; and he will perhaps die while engaged in his own work. Moreover, if there is a benefic in the ASC and a malefic in the 4th, the beginning of his work will be praiseworthy and good, but the end will be evil. And if there is a malefic in the ASC and a benefic in the 4th, the beginning of his work will be evil, and the end of it will be good.

And if you find Cauda in the ASC, and the ruler of the ASC is in an evil house, and there is a malefic in an one of the angles, and the moon is also impeded by the malefics, he had bad counselors from the lower classes who destroy his rule; and he will not cease to be sad and troubled and in fear as long as he continues in that work.

But if you find a benefic in the ASC of the hour of his entrance; or if you find the ruler of the ASC, and the ruler of the MC is in a strong house free from the malefics, it signifies the good condition of that same prince and the prolongation of his rule. But if there is a malefic in the ASC, and the ruler of the ASC is a malefic, and the ruler of the MC is in an evil house, indicate that he will soon be deposed.

And if you find the ruler of the ASC and the ruler of the MC in the 12th or in the 6th, indicate that his fall will be quicker, unless Jupiter is oriental in the ASC or in the MC, because that will delay his deposition somewhat.

After that, look at the sign of the MC and where its ruler is, and which Planet aspects it and the ruler of the MC; and if it is in an angle and the benefics aspect it, it signifies the goodness of his condition. And if there is a benefic in the MC, he will come to better things in that work of his and things more worthy of his own faith and will; and his dignity will be increased by that honor; and his rule will be strong; and his wealth will be multiplied.

But if malefics were there, he will find much hindrance in that same work; and whatever profit he gained will be taken away by martyrdom and conviction and deposition from the wrath that his own king will have towards him. And if a benefic aspects the MC, and no malefic is there, there will be the thing sought and good. But if a malefic aspects, it will destroy that work for him.

Moreover, if both a benefic and a malefic aspects, see which one of them has more degrees and that one will prevail over the other, but the other one will receive a part of it. And if Mercury is with Jupiter in the MC, his work will abound in wisdom and good counsel and reason and intelligence; and from this he will gain a name and fame; and it will increase his own work which he rules over and extend it in the regions; and especially if it aspects the Moon. But if the Sun is in the MC with them without an aspect from the malefics, it signifies the prolongation of the sound of his name and the attainment of his work in everything that he wishes for and his life will be long in that time.

It will be similar when Jupiter is with the Moon in the MC and Venus is in the best house. And whenever you find a benefic in the MC, it will lessen his hindrance, and he will find good. But if there is a malefic there, and the ruler of the MC and the ruler of the ASC were cadent, he will last a small time in his own work. And whenever you find a malefic[1] in the 7th from the ASC, and there is no benefic in the ASC, he will die during the course of that same work.

But if Saturn is there, and a benefic is in the ASC or in the 7th, he will not die nor will he be killed in that same work. But if there is a benefic in the 7th, he will be deposed decorously with honor and safety. And if the benefic is in the 4th, he will be sound in body, and his end will be according to his own wish. But if there is a malefic there, he will find evil and impediment after he has been deposed from his own work, along with imprisonment and martyrdom and hindrance and long imprisonment.

Moreover, if a benefic aspects the 4th, he will escape after the affliction and hindrance that he will find. But if a benefic does not aspect that malefic that was in the 4th, he will be defeated, and he will undergo punishments.; and he will die in that same prison. But if the ruler of the 4th is in the ASC or in the 10th or in the other best houses free from the malefics, and the ruler of the Moon's domicile is similar, it signifies a good end for that same work.

---

[1] Reading *malum* 'malefic' rather than *mortem* 'death'.

The Current Condition of a Kingdom.

And if you have been asked about the stability of a king or about his departure from his kingdom, look at the ruler of the ASC and the ruler of the 10th. If they were conjoined and the receiver of the disposition, i.e. the heavier of them was in an angle, that king will not move and he will not go out of his own kingdom; and if the receiver of the disposition is on the left of the ASC, i.e. under the earth, he will go out of it, but he will be returned.

But if the receiver of the disposition is [itself] received, it signifies the quickness of his return with honor. Moreover, if the ruler of the ASC and the ruler of the tenth pass their light across to each other in turn, i.e. if they were separated from each other in turn, it signifies the departure of the king. But if the Moon gives[1] her disposition to a planet slower in its course in an angle, he will remain in his own kingdom until that planet is combust or impedited in its own place, or until it retrogresses, then it will signify the taking away of his kingdom; and if the ruler of the ASC was joined to the ruler of its own fall, it will produce some action in which he will perish.

But if the ruler of his own fall is joined to the ruler of the ASC, lies will be said about him, and that which he has done previously will be remembered. And if the ruler of the MC was joined to the ruler of its own fall, he is put aside or a general will destroy his own territory; but if the ruler of the domicile of the fall of the ruler of the MC was joined to the ruler of the MC, his territory will be destroyed.

And if the ruler of the ASC has given[2] its own disposition to a planet in an angle, the ruler of that kingdom will remain in his own kingdom, and all the more so if the ruler of the disposition [is] in any one of the angles except the fourth, which is opposite the tenth and contrary to it.

---

[1] The Latin text has *pulsat* 'strikes', but this is a mistranslation from the Arabic. I have changed it to **donat* 'gives'.

[2] Again, reading **donat* instead of *pulsat*.

But if the ruler of the ASC was joined to any planet in the ninth from the ASC, or in the third, or was with their rulers, there will be no doubt about his exit from his own kingdom; but if afterwards it was joined to any planet in an angle, he will be returned to his own kingdom after his departure [from it].

And if the ruler of the MC was in its own place, that king will not depart from his own kingdom if the Moon was joined to it. If Jupiter was also in an angle, it will have some part in that, or if it receives the Moon or the ruler of the ASC, he will remain in his own kingdom, until Jupiter encounters a malefic, or becomes combust, or recedes from its own place.

And know that the ruler of the ASC and the ruler of the MC, when they are joined together, and the receiver of the disposition is in a good house not combust and not received, but it does not aspect the MC, that prince will be established over a kingdom that is not his own, but a foreign one; but if it does aspect the MC, it signifies his stability within his own kingdom; and if the ruler of the ASC and the Moon were in angles in mobile signs, and the Moon was not received, the king will depart.

After these things, look at the moon; if she has given[1] her own disposition to any planet in an angle, the ruler of the kingdom will not depart from his own kingdom if the ruler of the MC aspects its own place; but if the Moon was joined to the ruler of the ASC, and it was removed from the angles, and a malefic will come to the ruler of the ASC before the Moon is separated from it, he will be deposed from his own kingdom. Likewise, if the Moon was joined to a peregrine planet in the ninth or the third or if their ruler was in the house of travel, he will go out of his own kingdom; moreover, if it was in the fourth sign [and it was] mobile, that king will be removed, and that all the sooner if the Moon is joined to the ruler of the end of the thing, i.e. to the ruler of the fourth [house] from the ASC, unless its ruler is in its own domicile, because then that will

---

[1] Again, reading *donaverit* rather than *pulsaverit*.

be better for him, and the more so will the Moon be prompt if it was joined to a planet in its own fall or if it was in opposition to its own domicile; but if the Moon was strong in her own place, and she was void of course, it signifies the cutting off of that kingdom.

A Person or a King Absent from a Kingdom.

And if you have been asked about a man who departs from his own kingdom or about a king who is absent, whether he will return or not, look at this just as I have already told you in the first chapter on the conjunction of the ruler of the ASC and the ruler of the MC in turn, which, if they were joined together, and the receiver of their disposition aspects the MC, that king will be returned to his own kingdom; but if it does not aspect the MC, and the Moon was joined to a planet in the MC, he will be returned.; and if the ruler of the ASC is retrograde, he will be returned again to his own kingdom. And if the Moon was with that which we have said to you in a mobile sign, it will be swifter for them.

But if the ruler of the ASC is not retrograde, and the Moon was joined to a planet in the ASC or in the MC, he will be returned. Similarly, if the Moon was joined to the ruler of the ASC, and if the ruler of the ASC was joined to the ruler of the House of Travel, i.e. the ninth from the ASC, he is seeking a return by himself; and if the ruler of the MC was joined to the ruler of its own fall, it signifies the removal of the king; also, if it was in the angles; and if the ruler of the ASC was joined to the ruler of its own fall, it also signifies [his] removal; moreover, if the ruler of the MC was in its own house, having been removed, he will be returned to his own kingdom.

And if the ruler of the MC was separated from the light from the ruler of the House of the End of Things, i.e. from the fourth from the ASC, he will be returned; moreover, if it was joined to it, he will be removed; and if that same ruler of the fourth was joined to the ruler of the MC, he will remain in his own kingdom, and another kingdom will be given to him.

But if the ruler of the fourth was joined to the ruler of the ASC, he will not be removed, and a kingdom will come to him without his asking. And if the ruler of the ASC was separated from the ruler of the fourth, it signifies the firmness of the kingdom if the king was removed. Similarly, if the ruler of the fourth was joined to it; and if the ruler of the ASC and the ruler of the MC were joined, and the ruler of the MC did not aspect its own house, he will be established over another country, which he is in command of.

After these things, look at the significator, i.e. the Moon, which, if she were joined to the ruler of the MC, and the ruler of the MC aspected its own house, he will be returned, and all the more so if the Moon was in a mobile sign. And if she gave her own disposition to a peregrine planet in its own house to the left of the ASC, he will be removed. Moreover, if the significator was received, he will return to his own kingdom; and if it was not received, he will be removed.

And if the Moon was joined to a planet in the ninth from the ASC, pronounce the departure of that king; moreover, if that planet was a benefic and it was in a mobile or fixed sign, he will return to his own kingdom; but if it was in a common sign, he will go to his own kingdom beyond his first kingdom, and he will rule for three years, so long as the receiver of the Moon's disposition does not become cadent until it comes to the 12th house from the ASC; and there will be better action in the second year to the excessive satisfaction of his own will, unless a malefic first comes to the MC and retrogrades in it before the predicted hour.

But if a malefic comes to the same house, it will destroy his kingdom. And if the Moon is joined to benefics or is received, he will be praised in his kingdom. And if the Moon was joined to malefics, he will be cursed; and if she was joined to a planet in the 10th, he will not go back, and he will function for two years; and if she was joined to a planet in the 11th, he will rule for one year.

Nevertheless, if a malefic does not come into the MC and was not retrograde there; and if she was joined to a planet in the 5th from the ASC, he will rule for two years, and he will go back in the third year; but if she was joined to a planet in the fourth, he will rule for one year, and he will be removed in the second [year]. And if you have found the Moon and the ruler of the MC to be both of them impedited by a conjunction by body in an angle, he will not ever be returned to his own work; and he will be deposed, and he will remain deposed in accordance with the quality of the place of the work. But if you have found the Moon and the ruler of the MC debilitated, and if they were in common signs, his other work will be increased, and he will be stronger in his own work; and if he had gone out from his own work, he will be returned to it.

Will he Remain in his Kingdom or not.

And if someone has asked you whether he will remain in his kingdom or not, look at the ruler of the ASC and his significator, which is the Moon, if they were joined to the ruler of the MC or the Sun, or if they were in the MC, say Yes, but if not say No.

The Eleventh House, About Hopes.

When you have been asked about anything that is hoped for in which there is faith, as about stays by kings or about honor, look at the ruler of the 11th from the ASC; if it was joined to the ruler of the ASC or if the ruler of the ASC was joined to it, he will get that thing of his in which he has faith. Moreover, if there was a connection by trine or by sextile aspect, there will be what I have said, with ease. But if it was by square aspect or by opposition, it will be on account of difficulty.

And if the ruler of the 11th is in an angle, and the Moon is received, that faith will be perfected in accordance with what he wants; and if the receiver of the Moon's disposition is in a common sign, he will get a moderate amount of what he wants of it; and if it is in a mobile sign, there will be difficulty in that which I have said. But if it was in a fixed sign, he will get what he was hoping for perfectly. But if you have found the receiver of the Moon's disposition impedited, that thing will be destroyed after its attainment; and if the receiver of his disposition is received, he will get more of it than he was hoping for; and if the ruler of his ASC is received, he will have everything that he wished for.

The Relationship Between Two Persons.

And if [the Querent] has asked you about someone who he says is his friend, and he has said [for you] to see whether he will be joined to him or not, look at the ruler of the ASC and the Moon [to see] if they are joined to the ruler of the 11th from the ASC, and similarly [to see] if the ruler of the 11th is joined to the ruler of the ASC. Moreover, if that configuration is by trine aspect or by sextile, there will be joy, delight, and happiness in their relationship. But if it is by square aspect or by opposition, there will be contrariety and contention in their relationship, and one of them will be contrary to his companion; also, the contention will be stronger from an opposition.

The Realization of Something Hoped For.

If you have been asked about something that was not stated to you, and [the Querent] said to you "[it is] a thing that I hope for, and in which I have faith; see whether I will have it or not." Look at the ruler of the ASC and the Moon [to see] if they are joined to the benefics from the angles or from the succedents to the angles, [if so] he will get [his wish]. But if they were not [so] joined, say No. And if he has named the thing, look at it from its own house in the circle, in accordance with that which I have set down for you about the substances of the 12 significators.

The Twelfth House, On the Matter of Animals.

When you have been asked about animals, what sort of animal will win in the race, and the Querent had an animal in contest for a prize, or it is surmised that it was about another one of the animals, look at the ruler of that hour in which it was asked, which, if it was in the ASC, the animal about which it will be surmised will win over all the other animals.

And if it is in the MC, it will come in second, i.e. it will come in after the first [animal] and similarly in the 11th [house]; and if it was in the 7th from the ASC, it will be in the middle of them; and if it was in the 4th, it will be the very last, and no other animal will be after it.

And if the ruler of the hour was in its own fall, while running that same animal he will be frightened by that motion, and he will fall from it; and if, along with what I have said, malefics aspect it, that part of his body will be broken that that sign signified. But if a malefic aspects it by opposition or was with it in one sign, and the ruler of the ASC was in the 8th house of it, the one who is running will die from that accident and the more quickly if the ruler of that house or the Moon is impeded.

The Condition of the Animal.[1]

If anyone who does not have an animal among the other animals has asked you, namely saying, "Which of them will win?" Look at the ruler of the hour, which, if it was in the ASC, or if you find any planet in the ASC or in the MC or in the 11th, the owner that wins on that same day will have an animal according to the color of that planet that was in any one of those houses.

And if the significator of the victor was in its own domicile or its own exaltation or in its own triplicity or in its term or its own face, that same animal that wins will be noble and famous, and it will be [even] more worthy if it was [in its] domicile or exaltation. But if it was outside of this, it will be bad, but if it was not in any one of those that we have mentioned, it will be unknown.

And if it was with that which I have said to you in its own fall, it

---

[1] This chapter is about camels or horses entered in a race.

will have an ill-natured temperament and a very bad spirit. And in its own exaltation it will be noble, and in its triplicity it will not be known in its own country and it will not be noble; but in its terms or face, it will be known in the country, but it will not be noble, for it is not known from what country it comes.

A Question about the Age of the Animal.

And if you have been asked about its age, look at its significator. If it was oriental, it will be of two teeth,[1] and if it was occidental, it will be perfect. And if it was between both of those, it will be first, namely of four teeth. And if you find nothing about those that I have said to you, look at the ASC.

If it was [in] the domicile of the Sun, it will be a conquering one of the king's animals; and if it was [in] a domicile of Saturn, it will be an animal of great age, and perhaps it will not be a noble one, unless Saturn is in an angle or in the best house. And if it was [in] a domicile of Jupiter, it will be an animal winning well any prize that stands by the king. And if it was in a domicile of Mars, it will be the winning animal of some general, equipped for arms and warriors. And if it was [in a domicile] of Venus or of Mercury, it will be [the animal] of some noble or king or woman or writer. But if it is [in] the domicile of the Moon, it will be [the animal] of some businessman; and that same animal is shown as for sale.

Enemies.

And if you have been asked about enemies in general, [this is known] from the 12th house and its ruler, or, if one particular man was named to you, from the 7th and its ruler. Look at what will be between them from their connections, just as I have explained to you.[2]

---

[1] I suppose that by "teeth" he means "years." At any rate, he refers to some measure of an animal's age.
[2] At this point a new chapter should begin, because the subject has changed from 12th house questions to questions that are not assigned to one or more of the houses.

Therefore, I have explained to you the things in the questions of the 12 signs[1]; and now I shall explain to you those things that are not in the 12 signs, lest perchance you might err, because the wise men have erred in that which was not in the 12 signs. Take that from the substance of the planets, because there are more things than can be comprehended.

Letters.[2]

When you have been asked about a letter or something that has been read, look at the ASC for the one who wrote the letter and by whom [it was sent] from the one from which the Moon has separated; and from the 7th and its ruler for the one to whom it is written. But whatever was hoped or feared or whatever was in the mind of both men, and their conditio, from the ruler of the ASC and from the ruler of the 7th, and from their houses in accordance with the aspect of the benefics and the malefics to them.

Whichever one of them is in the angles, or in a house in which it receives and aspects its own house, it will be greater and more worthy than the other; and if the planet from which the Moon was separated is a benefic, or if it was in its own exaltation, the letter will be from the ruler of the kingdom. But if it was remote from the angles, he formerly had a kingdom, but now he is removed from it.

But if it was in its own domicile and it was in an angle, it will be from those known members of the household. It is also from the more important members of his own household and [those] having some dignity; and the [dignity of] triplicity is below [that of] domicile; similarly, the terms are below the triplicity; and the face is below the terms; moreover, if it is in a good house from the ASC, and it was not received, he will have [some] dignity, but it will not be

---

[1] Since Sahl used the Sign-House system of house division, by "12 signs" he means "12 houses."

[2] We must remember that Sahl lived in the early 9th century, when the *receipt* of a letter was a rare and often unexpected event, and one liable to make the recipient apprehensive. Further on, Sahl talks about *sending* a letter, which was also a rare action for most people.

praiseworthy—and he will be unwelcome among the members of his own house.

But if it was in its own fall and it was in an angle, he who wrote the letter will not be a noble, but he will be with the king, and one who is honored. And if it was in its own fall, and it was cadent, he will not be noble, nor will he be known among men.

If it does not aspect the ASC nor the ruler of the house or the ruler of the letter, he cannot [do] anything, i.e. he has nothing besides what he eats daily he eats daily; and if it does aspect it, then there will be good fortune from those things that are done by his own hand, and thus they will eat. But if the Moon was separated from the malefics, and it was [located] just as I have said to you, there will be with this that which is suffered from an evil condition hard in the heart; and if the Moon was separated from a square aspect or from an opposition or from conjunction, it signifies the strength of the ruler of the letter, and this will be stronger when the Moon was in an angle in her own sign, because that signifies that the one who wrote the letter is benevolent in his own matter, and that there is in the letter something that disturbs him.

After these things, look at the one to whom the letter came from the planet to which the Moon is joined, and announce that he is in accordance with that which I have said to you about the planet from which the Moon was separated. And know that when the Moon is separated from Saturn and Mercury is impedited, there will be a hardship in the letter and some strong thing. And if it was separated from Jupiter, the letter will be from a noble man. And if it was [separated] from Mars, it will be from a warlike man who uses blood and who uses iron. And if it was [separated] from the Sun, it will be from a king. And if it was [separated] from Venus, it will be from a woman. But if it was [separated] from Saturn, there will be some fault in it. And if it was [separated] from Mercury, the letter will be from a writer or from a businessman.

Another Chapter on Letters.

And if you have been asked about the condition of the man to whom the letter came, look for this at the Moon and her connection, which, if she is joined to Saturn, the letter will have been sent to an old man; but if it was Jupiter, to a noble; and if it was Venus, to a woman; similarly with the rest of the planets in accordance with their substance.

Whether the Letter is Good or Evil.

And if you have been asked about a letter in general whether there is good or evil in it, look at the separation of Mercury, because [the quality] of the letter will be in that, for all writing belongs to Mercury. Rumors also [belong] to the Moon. Also, the rulers of the 9th and the 3rd have a moderate participation in this.

If, therefore, Mercury was separated from the benefics, there will be good in the letter; and if it was separated from the malefics, there will be evil in it. After that, look at the planet from which Mercury is separated and Mercury itself, namely at the stronger of them, and take that one to be the significator, which, if it was in the ASC, there will be good will and advantage and recompense; and if it was in the second from the ASC, the letter will be for wealth in giving, namely, and in receiving, and similar things of good that pertain to wealth.

And if it was in the third, it will be from a brother or a friend. He related in the letter about a journey about which he was concerned, or it asked about its condition. And if it was in the fourth from the ASC, there will be in the letter something about some land; or it will perhaps be a letter from some neighbor of his, who is older than he is, or about some old thing. And if it was in the fifth, the letter will be about something that he hopes for, and it will be from a child or from a friend. But if it was in the sixth, the letter will be about a slave. If, moreover, a malefic aspected the same house, the letter will be about someone who is sick or about the case of someone who is sick.

And if it was in the 7th, the letter will be about a woman or about the condition of a woman. And if it was in the 8th, the letter will be about a dead person or about the estate of a dead person. And if it was in the 9th, there will be some admonition in the letter, or some proclamation or some commemoration of God, and some mention of travel, or of the removal of a king.

And if it was in the 10th, the letter will be from a king, and there is a mention in it of nobles and princes. And if it was in the 11th, it will be a letter from a friend, and there will be [something] in it that is pleasing to the recipient and that may make him return. And if it was in the 12th, the letter will involve contention, or [it will be] from an enemy.

What will be the Response to the Letter.

And if a letter has been written, and you want to know what its response will be, look at this from the second conjunction, because the first conjunction is the significator of that which went before concerning the letter, and the second conjunction is the significator of the response to that same letter.

Whether the Letter is Delivered or not.

And if you have been asked about a letter, whether it is delivered or not, look at the Moon. If it was joined to Mercury, it will be delivered; and if has already been conjoined to it and has gone past it by two or three degrees, say that it will be delivered, but otherwise not.

Whether the Letter is Signed or not.

And if you have been asked about a letter, whether it is signed or not, look at the Moon. If it is joined to Mercury, say that it will be signed; and if it was separated from it and has gone past it by a quantity of about two degrees, and it has not passed it [out of] the terms, say that it has already been signed. And if you have found Mercury with the Sun and both of them aspecting the ASC, say that it will be signed, but if not, No.

The Man Who is Sending the Letter.

And if you have been asked about a letter, whether it comes from a prince or a king, look at Mercury. If it is separated from the Sun or from the MC with a moderate [amount of] separation, say that it does, but if not, [then] no.

Whether a Letter has Reached the King or Not.

And if you have been asked about a letter, whether it has reached the king or not, look at Mercury. If it was joined to the ruler of the MC or to the Sun, say that it has reached [him], but if not [that it has] not.

Rumors.

When you have been asked about rumors, whether they are true or false, look at the ruler of the ASC or the Moon, namely the one of them that is in an angle, and begin with it. Which, if it was in an angle free from the malefics, and it was not joined to a cadent planet, the rumors are true; but if it was in an angle and was joined to a cadent planet that did not receive it, [then] it was their intention, but they will not continue with it, and it will not be perfected; and if the ruler of the ASC was in an angle and was joined to a Planet in an angle, the rumors are true, and they will become apparent if it was a benefic.

Moreover, if it was a malefic and it does not receive the ruler of the ASC, the rumors will be false. And if the ruler of the ASC was joined to a cadent planet, the rumors will be false unless that planet receives the ruler of the ASC. But if the ruler of the ASC was joined to a malefic that does not receive it, it signifies the destruction of the rumors, and that will be on the part of the ruler of the Querent. And if a malefic was joined to the ruler of the ASC, there will come about the destruction of the rumors by someone else, and he will destroy the rumors.

After that, look at the Moon and her testimony along with [that of] the ruler of the ASC; [and] if the ruler of the ASC has more testimony, use its testimony. But if the Moon was stronger, use its testimony along with [that of] the ruler of the ASC if the ruler of the ASC was in a mobile sign or if the ASC was mobile, and some of the malefics aspect it, the rumors will be lies.

Similarly, if the Moon was void of course. Similarly too, if the Moon was joined to a retrograde planet, even if it receives her. Similarly, if the Moon was joined to a cadent planet; and it will be more devious if it was a malefic, because it signifies a lie, even if it was received. But if she was impeded in an angle and that malefic does not receive her, the rumors will be false. And if she was joined to a planet in an angle that does receive her, it signifies the truth of the rumors; therefore, you should not look for any other testimony from it.

But if she was joined to a benefic in an angle, and the more so if it was in the MC or in the ASC, it signifies that the rumors are true. But if the receiving planet is then free from the malefics and from retrogradation, the rumors will be borne out and they will be better. But if it was impeded by a planet that does not receive it or by a retrograde planet, it signifies the destruction of the rumors after their correction.

Similarly, if the Moon was joined to a planet in an angle or outside it that does not receive her, and if the Moon was impeded or it was joined to a retrograde planet, it signifies destruction after correction; and if the Moon was impeded in an angle, it signifies the destruction of the rumors.

And if she was joined to a cadent planet, it signifies a lie if she was not received. And when she has passed[1] her own disposition to

---

[1] Reading *donaverit* 'passed' instead of *pulsaverit* 'struck' (a mistranslation from the Arabic).

a planet in an angle, the rumors will be true; moreover, if the planet was in the MC, there will be rumors [of things] that men have already known and [that] have already become apparent. And if it is in the ASC, it has already begun to appear; and if it was in the 7th, it already was, and it has appeared, and it is apparent; but if it is in the 4th, it will be secret.

A Question about Something that is Feared.

And if a man has asked about something that he fears, look at the ruler of the ASC; if it was in any angle, and it was free from the malefics, those same rumors will be false, and nothing that he feared will happen to him; and if the ruler of the ASC was in evil houses, i.e. in the 2nd or the 6th or the 8th or the 12th, he has already become fearful of that thing that he fears; but if the ruler of the ASC was in evil houses and the planets testifying to it are evil, he will fall into that which he fears; but if there were no planets testifying, the fear will be removed and not increased above that fear that is already in him; and if the malefics were in an angle and they aspected it, his condition will be worse.

But if that malefic was the ruler of the 8th from the ASC, it signifies his death and destruction; and if it was otherwise, punishments will find him; and if that malefic is the ruler of the 12th, they will fear penalties and fetters.[1] But if it was the ruler of the 2nd, it will be received for personal wealth; moreover, if the ruler of the ASC is in the 12th and the ruler of the 7th or the 12th does not aspect it, he will flee and he will be freed and he will not have power over it.

Similarly, if along with this, the Moon is joined to a malefic, it will show him to you unless that malefic is ruler of its house, it signifies nothing then, because labor and difficulty will occur for him in his flight. Moreover, if he it is not the ruler of its house, it will show him.

---

[1] The Latin has †*iunctione* 'union', but perhaps we should read *vinctiones* 'fetters'.

If a Slain Person will be Avenged or Not.

When you have been asked about someone who has been slain, whether he will be avenged, or, about someone who has suffered injuries, whether he will overcome the one who has injured him, or whether he will restore the injuries that he made to himself. Look at the ASC and at the angle of the end of the thing, which is the 4th [house] from the ASC.

If they were mobile signs and the Moon is in a mobile sign, nothing will be done; moreover, if the ruler of the ASC aspects the ASC, and the ruler of the Moon's domicile aspects the Moon, he will get his own thing rapidly; but if it is just as I have said, and the ruler of the 4th aspects the 7th, he will get his own thing, and he will pour out the blood of the killer, unless the Moon is joined to the benefics.

If after that, that benefic is not joined to a malefic, because then he will be killed, unless there is a connection by trine or by sextile aspect, [for] then it signifies that he will sustain punishments, and he will be fettered by iron.

But if the malefic is in a fixed sign, he will die in prison. But if it is in a mobile sign and the ruler of its sign is swifter in its course and it aspects him, he will abandon it quickly. And if it is the one to whom the Moon is joined in a mobile sign and it aspects the ruler of its own house with a friendly aspect, he will escape easily. And if it is aspected by opposition or by square aspect, he will escape in a battle or in something like a battle.

But if there is a conjunction in one sign, he will be let go quickly, or he will flee, and he will go away; and if you find a benefic in the ASC, that anger on the part of the loved ones will be extinguished. And if with this the Moon is joined to a malefic strong in its own house, that same revenge will not be from loved ones; the king will be revenged on him. And if there was a malefic in the ASC, and the Moon was fortified, the loved ones, namely of the killer, will bind him, and the king will help him, and he will support getting him out. Because if the ruler of the ASC aspects the ASC, his loved ones will get him after exertion during the king's anger. But if the ruler of the ASC does not aspect the ASC, and the ruler of the domicile of the Moon aspects the Moon, the king brings him out without the will of his loved ones.

And know that every punishment that Mars has signified will be with iron and a whip; and Saturn's signification will be punishment by wood and by prolongation of prison and close confinement.

Whether Anything is True or False.

If you have been asked about anything, whether it is true or false, look at the ruler of the ASC and the Moon, which, if they are free from the malefics, the thing will be true in its effect and advantageous. But if they were impeded, the thing will be false. And if it is gold, have the Sun as witness, and for silver, the Moon.

Many Things.

And if you have been asked about two or three things, which of them is more worthy, and which of them is true or false; or for two rumors, which of them is true or false; or, about one thing, or about two things, which one of them he will get; or about two or three animals, which one of them will win; or, about two men, which one of them will get his own thing.

Look at the ruler of the ASC [to see] if it is in the angles, free from the malefics, and received, the thing that is named last is more worthy, and he will acquire it. And if it is impeded in the angles, that which is named first will be, [and the things] after that will be destroyed. And if the ruler of the ASC aspects the ASC, and it was in [the houses] succedent to the angles, free from the malefics, [and] received, he will acquire the second one of the things named, and it will be the worthier one; but if it is impeded, it will be had, but afterwards destroyed.

And if the ruler of the ASC is cadent, free from the malefics, and received, the third one of the things named will be the more worthy, and it will be acquired. If it was impedited, there will be none of those things that I have said, and the question will be destroyed. And judge similarly about the Moon.

More things.

And if you have been asked about many [different] things, you will take the Moon to be the significator of the Querent; and the stars, i.e. the planets, will be his things. Therefore, consider the connection of the Moon according to the numbers of those things, because the first connection will be the significator of the first question, and the second connection will be the significator of the second question; similarly, of the [other] things according to the number which I have mentioned to you.

Look, therefore, at the strength of each planet—in the angles or in the succedents of the angles—and in their safety from retrogradation, and from the malefics; then, mix together those planets in strength, and pronounce [your judgment] in accordance with that quantity.

Hunting on the Land.

If you have been asked about an inquiry about hunting and what will be its result, look at the ASC and the ruler of the hour because it is strong in hunting; and know the substance of the ASC, whether it is [one] of the quadrupedal signs; and after that, look also at the substance of the 7th sign and that of the ASC when you go hunting. Or, you should look at which one of the signs it is, and where is the house of its ruler with respect to the ruler of the ASC in their configuration; and then, if they are favorably [configured], it signifies [that he will get] the result that he wants from hunting with ease; and if they are conjoined in a square aspect or by opposition, he will get hunting with labor and fatigue.

But if they were not conjoined [at all], he will have nothing, and he will not get what he wants. And if the 7th sign is [one] of quadrupeds, and its ruler or the ruler of the hour is fortified in it or in any other angle, he will get the hunting; and [if it is] the hour of Jupiter, or it is in any of the angles, he will have roebucks.

Moreover, if the ruler of the 7th is a malefic, and the benefics fall away from it, he will painfully injure himself in the quest, and he will hunt only a little, and some failing must be feared for him or some impediment in his body if Saturn is the ruler of the 7th.

But if Mars was [the ruler] of the hour, and it had some strength, he will have his hunting, and some of those things that [necessitate] labor will cause a loss for him, and [yet] he will be freed [from them] because Mars has the substance of hunting.

Moreover, if Jupiter aspects Mars and it is the ruler of the hour or the ruler of the ASC, he will be safe from everything that he fears, and he will hunt with ease, and he will have his own [desired] thing without labor and fatigue; and if the 7th sign is [one] of the airy signs or the earth signs, and there is a benefic in it, and its ruler is a malefic or the ruler of the hour is a malefic, he will be safe in his own hunting, and he will not get everything that he wants, and the game will be frightened and will flee from him; and his search will be strong, and he will injure himself in it, unless Jupiter or Mercury is with the malefic that is ruler of the hour; for that breaks down the evil of the malefic, and it does not prevent the hunting because Mercury has the greatest participation in hunting along with Mars.

The Quantity of Hunting.

In addition, if you were asked about scarcity in the hunt or about its abundance, look at the MC when you go on the hunt; if Mars is the ruler of the MC, or if you find him there, and he is in aspect with Mercury or Jupiter, or he is in aspect with one of them and one of them is the ruler of the hour or the ruler of the ASC, he will have much hunting, and it will happen for him, and he will be able to hunt with his own hands, and he will not have any hardship unless Saturn is aspecting Mars from an angle or unless Saturn is in the MC or is its ruler, for it sends to the master of the hunt an intense sadness about that which he will hope for.

Moreover, if Jupiter has fallen away from it, and Saturn was just as I have said, and Mars was in an angle, the master of the hunt will find an impediment in his own body and delay in his journey, and with this [configuration] he will not acquire [any] hunting, because Saturn destroys hunting and causes delay for its master, especially if he was hunting on the land.

Moreover, in the case of hunting on the sea, look at the ruler of the ASC and the Moon and the ruler of the seventh sign. But if the ASC sign was a water sign, or if the Moon was joined to Mars, or the ruler of the hour was joined to Mars, and Venus has fallen away from any aspect to the Moon, dismiss [the idea] of this hunting as a possibility for you, because an impediment of the Moon from Mars in hunting on water is a worse thing and one of little success, because he will have no strength or advantage except with [some] impediment.

But if the Moon was joined to Saturn, and Venus aspects the Moon, the hunting will be abundant, and Saturn does not impedite the Moon in hunting on water, unless Mars is aspecting the Moon, and Venus must also be thanked for this, because Mars is an enemy of Venus. Instead, when Saturn aspects her, then a shipwreck must be feared for the master of the ship, and a soaking, and other things similar to these, namely from the dampness of water.

A Banquet to Which You have been Invited.

When you have been invited to a banquet or to any kind of dinner; or, when you have been asked about the foods, how many of them they[1] will eat, look at the ASC. If it is a mobile sign they will

---

[1] The invited guests.

eat many foods; and if it is a fixed sign, they will eat one kind of food; but if it is a common sign, they will eat two [kinds]. And if the Moon is in the ASC, their food will be salty.

And if Mars is in the ASC, there will be some saltiness in it; and Jupiter signifies sweetness. But the Sun [indicates] sharpness, and Venus gassy foods, that is a taste of celery or colewort or mustard and other things of that sort, and of rich foods, i.e., of *sepus* or thick meat and beef.[1] And Mercury signifies a pungent flavor and everything mixed. But Saturn signifies a wild and insipid flavor.

After this, look at the Moon's separation and her conjunction; if she was separated from a malefic and was joined to a benefic by square aspect or by opposition, the master of that food will not be able to give it for a banquet, such as for a marriage or a circumcision, or in other such [occasions] that engage men and occur for them. And if it was by trine aspect or by sextile, the cause will be conversation or recompense, etc.

But if the Planet to which the Moon is joined in an angle, there will be a banquet involving them on one day; and if [the sign it is in] is a common [sign], it will be on more than one day. And if the ruler of the Moon's domicile aspects her, their banquet will be disturbed, for there will be in the banquet someone who will disturb them; then they will be pacified, and afterwards they will return to the banquet.

And if the Moon was joined to Jupiter, it signifies the nobility of the banquet and a multitude of condiments. And if she was joined to the Sun, it signifies elegance or the beauty of the condiments or the multitude of sharp-tasting things. And if she was joined to Venus, it signifies the beauty of the foods and the multitude of their sweetness, along with games and things to listen to and laughter and a pleasant odor. And if she was joined to Mercury, it signifies the pressure of [many] men in the same place, and

---

[1] The Latin has *saporem sepi vel carnis crasse & bus*. I cannot identify *sepi*, and *bus* I have rendered as 'beef', but that is a guess.

that there is someone who speaks wisdom and relates it, and condiments will be numerous there, and relations of stories or fables; and they will employ the flesh of birds for food.

And if there is a conjunction with Saturn, it will signify the uncleanness of their foods, and that there will be many condiments [made] of fish and whatever comes out of the water. But if the conjunction was with Mars, it will signify that quarrels will occur among them, and that they will eat everything hot. And if it is in the MC, it will signify that quarrels will occur among them; and a planet that is in the MC will [also] signify that there will be quarrels among them.

When, therefore, you have been invited to the banquet, and the Moon was with Mars in one sign, or she was joined to him from any angle, you should not go to that banquet, because you will be sorry [that you went] at the end of it. Similarly, when she is with Saturn, because it signifies the uncleanness of the foods and their poor quality; and if you have gone, you will not find foods among them that were sweet.

But if she was with Venus or with Mercury, [then] go, because you will see something that will please you; and if it was Jupiter, [then] similarly, and in that banquet there will be much *alozor*,[1] that is some kind of grain, from which the best condiment and grains are made.

After that, look at the ruler of the hour. If it is in the ASC or in the MC, the food will be brought in in the first of their sittings; and if it was remote from those two houses, they will eat before it is brought in; and it will not be brought in until that star is removed from the ASC or from the MC. And if it is in the 7th or in the 4th, the food is not brought in until the house is filled. And whenever the Moon was joined to Mars, their food will be hot.

And if you have asked or have been invited, and the Moon is in

---
[1] An Arabic word that I have not been able to identify.

a water sign aspecting Saturn by trine or sextile aspect, they will eat trout.¹ But if the Moon is in Libra, they will eat grains or beans. And if she was in Gemini or in Aquarius, they will eat the flesh of birds. And if Saturn aspects the Moon by square aspect or by opposition, they will eat cold meat, and if the Sun was joined to Mars, all of it will be burnt.

And if the Moon was in Libra or in square aspect, you should not eat vegetables, either cooked or raw. And [when she is] in Virgo or in Libra, you should not approach grains. And if she is in Scorpio with Cauda, beware of fat. And if she was in Leo, beware of eating meat. And if she was in Sagittarius, you should not approach the flesh of wild animals, that is of hares or of bears. [When she is] in Pisces, you should not eat salted trout, nor fresh ones [either].

Beware, therefore, of what I have said to you about the places of the Moon with the malefics in those signs that I have named to you, because they impedite the body with a great impediment.

The Cause of the Banquet.

And know that the ASC signifies the cause of the banquet. If it is [in] a domicile of Venus, the cause will be a marriage. And if it is in a domicile of Mercury, it will be on account of a child or because of children. But if it is in a domicile of Jupiter, a friend prepares that dinner for him.

And the second [sign] from the ASC signifies a vessel in which are carried the household goods² of the house. But if the second sign is common, it will be a colored vessel of those things; and if Mars was in that same sign, there will be bronze in that same vessel; and if it was Venus, there will be silver in it; and Jupiter, silver and gold; the Moon, glass; but Saturn, wood and tile. And if there

---

¹Reading *tructas* 'trout' rather than the simplified spelling *trutas*.
²The late Latin word *suppelictilia* means "household articles," "furniture," or "goods."

were benefics in the second sign, it signifies the beauty of the ornaments of the house; moreover, if it was a peregrine benefic, they will be foreign; and if there was testimony in that for it, they will be [things] of the house.

And the third [house] signifies those things that are important for a banquet. But the fourth from the ASC signifies the place where the banquet is held. But if it is a common sign, there will be a banquet of them in the portico; and if the Sun is in it or Jupiter, their banquet will be in the *claustrum*¹ of the house or in the middle of it.

And the fifth from the ASC signifies their drink; if it is a common sign, their drink will be diverse; and if Jupiter was in it or Mercury, their drink will be various kinds of wine; and if it was Saturn, it will be a sugared drink; and if it was Mars in it, their drink will be very sharp from *daptili*.² Moreover, if Mars is impedited by Saturn, their drink was already made sharp; and if it was the Sun, there will be in it sharpness and bitterness; and if it was Venus, they will drink unfermented wine of the *daptilorum*. But if it was the Moon, their drink will be water.

And the sixth from the ASC signifies servants. And the seventh from the ASC will be butlers. But the eighth [signifies] bakers and cooks. And the ninth signifies the one who serves its courses. The tenth also signifies the goodness of the foods, and whether he will rejoice with the invited guests or not, because when the benefics are in the MC, he will rejoice with them; and if there was a malefic in it, they will be odious to him and to his friends. And the eleventh signifies brothers and friends. But the twelfth signifies the master of the house, and whether he will desire this or not.

Look, therefore, at the places of the benefics in these 12 houses. In whatever sign³ there was a benefic, and its ruler was fortified,

---

¹A closed-off part of the house.
²I am unsure what the late Latin word *daptilis* means here; it usually refers to something in the household. As a guess, it might refer to homemade wine.
³Understand that by "sign" Sahl means "house."

judge for him who belongs to that house goodness and joy; and in whatever [house] there was a malefic or its ruler there is a hindrance—everything that pertains to that same house and to all the things in it will be destroyed.

The Significations of the Planetary Hours in Questions.

And there are three divisions of the Hours. First, it is divided into three parts. The one who comes in the first part of the Hour of the Sun asks for a king or a lord or a man, or a great evil about which he is fearful; in the middle, either about fear or about someone who is ill; in the end, about his own livelihood or about trading or seizing.

In the first part of the Hour of Venus, he asks you about the capture of a woman or about cures for women; in the middle [part], about women's clothes or their ornaments; at the end, about a situation that arises or about a friendship that cannot be made.

In the first part of the Hour of Mercury, about things that have happened or about his grandfather or about something engraved; in the middle, about suitable clothing or about the mind of the Querent; at the end, about a loss.

In the first part of the Hour of the Moon, about a move from place to place or about a sick person, or about something that has some stain in it; in the middle part, about something that has gone out of hand and is not returned, or about a man who comes off the road, or about an animal; in the end, for what is going to be completed, or something that arises from the earth.

In the first part of the Hour of Saturn, about a runaway slave, if you worry about whether he will return; in the middle, about a strong man, or an association that he wants to make, or that he wants to go from place to place, or about some request; in the end, about some bad situation from which he has already escaped.

In the first part of the Hour of Jupiter, he comes to you to ask in his own name or about something outside; in the middle, about a choice of clothing or about a sick person to be cured; in the end, about a man who was getting ahead and then lost from his own desire.

In the first part of the Hour of Mars, first about the theft of something red or gold or bronze or clothing; in the middle, either about a sick person badly afflicted or about heat; in the end, about deception or something that is worked in fire.

The End of Zahel's Book on Questions.

Book IV

The Book of Elections

All the wise men are in agreement that elections are weak unless they are made for kings, for, even though their elections are weak, those persons have radixes, i.e. their nativities, that strengthen every planet that is weak in the way; but for those of low or moderate degree[1] and for those that follow, you shall not elect anything unless [it is based] upon their nativities and upon the revolutions of their years and upon the nativities of their children.

But if these are unknown, horary charts may be taken for them. And the effects of an action of theirs may be known from these [charts]; afterwards it may be elected for them according to this, because when someone has asked about something personal, it has already arrived at good or evil in accordance with his nativity, wherefore he has asked you; and indicate to him according to his own question.

Beware, therefore, in elections of this sort how you elect for him, whose radix is distracted, especially when this is a first beginning and an old radix in which there is faith.

Beware, therefore, to elect for him, for whom the radix of his nativity or the horary question signifies anything horrible, because when it has happened that you have put all the benefics in angles, and you have made all the malefics to be cadent, [still] nothing will profit him, and every planet that does not agree with the ruler of the ASC will not profit that man anything, and especially those

---

[1] The printed text has *mulieribus uero et mercatoribus* 'but for women and merchants', but this must be a misreading of *uilibus uero et mediocribus* 'but for those of low or moderate degree', a phrase that occurs below. **Bonatti** has *vilibus et mediocribus*, although he cites the phrase from **Abû 'Alî al-Khayyât**.

[men] who are of low or moderate degree because you do not know whether you should elect his ASC or a star that is inimical to him in the radix or a malefic is in the same rising sign that you have elected for him.

For we may be surprised at nothing in [the case of] those who ride upon the sea or those who travel in the same hour, whose intention is upon a trip. But some of them will experience shipwreck, while others will evade it, and some will find their wealth, but others will find nothing, for the essence of some of them is not compared to the essence of others; and I have already proved this many times in the comparison of some of those who went out from the same place at the same hour and arrived at the same region at the same hour.

But some of them returned more swiftly with the best wealth, and some went slow at the same place, and some of them in fact perished before they could return to their own homes, for this occurred because of their nativities and from their differences in those same years.

We also see some persons rejoicing and drinking on an evil day and on a day to be feared, namely one of many impediments, and some assembling and quarrels coming upon them on a good and praiseworthy day; and you will see strongly a significator joined badly by square aspect or opposition, or it will be with it in the same sign, and yet it will find good fortune in it.

Wherefore, this does not occur unless perchance the malefics are more conjoined to it because they were rulers of the first ASC or rulers of its division [triplicity] or rulers of the ASC of the revolution of the year.

And when you have elected on the ASC of a horary question or a nativity that you know or on the ruler of the sign of the profection of the year, your election will be more worthy because you will know what is agreeable to it from the stars and what its disposition is. Beware, therefore, in this chapter, and let your task be similar to your own election.

And know that the Omnipotent and Most High One created every creation, the world namely and whatever there is in it of the four natures, i.e. of the four elements, and he placed the land and everything that is rational or non-rational upon it, and everything that is mobile or immobile in the circle, and he also put among them a subtle circle, which the wise men know about, so that that subtle occasion which he put between the magnetic stone and the iron, and that which is between father and son, and between the one that eats and his food. Know this and understand it!

Therefore, from that agreement which is between both substances, namely the superior and the inferior, things are tempered and destroyed by adversity, and benefics are equal, i.e. of temperate nature, but the malefics are of a harmful nature, and that is why they want to impedite, and if they receive, their wealth will not at all be lacking and the skill of their diversity, and they are like thieves and citizens of the evils of men, and from them comes diversity and discord, also change and the confusion of things. Understand all of this!

The ASC and What is in it of Elections in the Knowledge of the Natures of the Signs, the First of which are the Mobile Signs.[1]

Know that the mobile signs signify the hasty mobility of things, and nothing is durable in them, and their time is not prolonged; but in them it is good to sow, to buy, to sell, to confirm [the honesty of] a woman; all of these profit under them, and a sick person will quickly be freed of his illness; also, contention is not prolonged in them, and a fugitive is quickly brought back; travel is also useful in them; and if anyone promises anything in them, he will not keep his promise; speeches, dreams, and rumors are false in them; no

---

[1] Beginning here **Bonatti**, Treatise 7, Section 1, Chapter 18 ff. sometimes quotes **Sahl** verbatim but more often paraphrases and comments on **Sahl's** text.

physician will effect a cure[1] under them; and no plantation will be planted under them; and no foundation will be established in them, because it is evil, and everything that you begin in them whose stability you desire, will be unstable.

Therefore, begin under them every unstable work and all the hurried things that you want to do. And the swifter among the mobile [signs] are Aries and Cancer, for they are more crooked [in their ascensions] and more mobile. But Libra and Capricorn are stronger and more temperate.

The Fixed Signs.

Next, the fixed signs are suitable for every work whose stability and prolongation of time is desired and which its author desires to be durable and good. And in them it is useful to build, and to celebrate marriages after there has been a betrothal under the mobile [signs]. And if in them a woman is dismissed by her husband, she will not be returned to him.

But there will be no faith in beginnings and inceptions [undertaken] in them unless the testimonies of the benefics are multiplied in them; and whoever has been incarcerated in them, his imprisonment will be prolonged; and whoever becomes angry in them, will not be quickly pacified. But terms and payments in them are useful; and it will be good to build and to make a foundation.

And Scorpio is lighter than all the other fixed [signs], Leo is more fixed; Aquarius is slower and inferior, but Taurus is more level.

The Common Signs.

The common signs are useful for participation and fraternity. And whatever is done in them will often be repeated. But to buy and to celebrate marriages in them will not be useful or advanta-

---

[1] The text has *curret* 'will run', probably a blunder for *curat* 'cures'.

geous; and there will be ingenuity and deception in them; and that one who has anything thrown up against him in them will evade it, and he will be relieved from that which is thrown up against himself.

And whoever is incarcerated in these [signs] is not fixed [there], unless it is by his own fear because of the smallness of his own appearance and his exit[1]. And whoever goes out of prison will return to his own place; and if a fugitive is captured in them, he will return to his flight a second time;. And whoever goes to a judge in them, [will find that] the opinion will not be firm for him, nor will the judgment be firm. And one does not go in a ship in them, for whoever goes, is changed from that one to another. If anything is promised to someone in them, it is dissolved and nothing of it will be completed for him; and a sick person is cured in them, but then there will be a recurrence [of his illness].

All of good and evil, therefore, that happens to a man in them is doubled for him. And if anyone dies in them, then another in that place will die soon after him. And [any kind of] change, and washing the head and beard, and purifying gold and silver are appropriate [undertakings] in them, and also to send boys to school.

And if you want to begin any of those things I have mentioned to you, then put the Moon in the ASC of those houses appropriate to that which you want and conjoin the Moon with the benefics receiving in that sign, and the signs of that day in the comparison of the day that are stronger,[2] and make the ASC diurnal.

Air signs are appropriate for hunting on land or on sea, and royal signs are appropriate for kings, and the voiced signs are appropriate for those who sing and for those wishing to use musical instruments[3]; and the fire signs are appropriate for everything that

---

[1] The meaning is not clear.
[2] The meaning of this phrase is unclear.
[3] The printed text has *qui canunt fistula cum crudo & uoci alhool & cantilenae*, but I have translated **Bonatti's** *cantoribus & volentibus uti musicis instrumentis*.

is done with fire; and the signs of equality,[1] in which night and day are equal, are appropriate for truth and for speaking the truth and for those things that are done with scales.

And the mutable signs (and they are those in which night and day begin to be changed) are appropriate for change and for him who wants by means of change [to go] from one thing to another. And consider for every work that you want to begin what is the nature of that sign of the spheres, and join the Moon and the ruler of the ASC with that matter, and the root of its nature, and the virtue in that hour, namely the hour of the beginning.

But if you want that which belongs to lords and princes and magnates and those who are in charge of cities and of high officers of state,[2] then [that] is [shown] to you by the Sun; and that which belongs to elevated things, then [that] is [shown] to you by Jupiter; and [matters] of farms and the lowest things, then [that] is [shown] to you by Saturn; and battles of dukes and lords of battles, then [that] is [shown] to you by Mars; and that which belongs to women, then [that] is [shown] to you by Venus. Moreover, purchases and sales, and terms, and things that are written, and negotiations are [shown] by Mercury; and [matters concerning] queens and other important women and the investigation of those that are among them, by the Moon.

An Election for the Beginning of any Work, and the Ten Impediments of the Moon.[3]

When, therefore, you want to begin any work, fortify[4] the ASC and its ruler and the Moon and the ruler of the thing, and beware of an impediment to the Moon, just as Dorotheus said, and the other wise men in the beginning of their works, and there are ten modes.

---

[1] That is, the equinoctial signs.
[2] The Latin adds *pugne & langorum*. I don't understand that.
[3] Cf. Dorotheus, *Pentateuch*, v. 5 (ed. Pingree).
[4] Lit. 'adapt' in the sense of choosing a position that is suitable for the election. The usual term, however, is 'fortify'.

The **first** mode, that it may be combust beneath the Sun by 12 degrees and after it similarly, but it is less severe afterward. The **second**, that it is in the degree of its fall. The third, that it is in opposition to the Sun. The **fourth**, that it is joined to the malefics or within the orb of their square or opposition aspect. The **fifth**, that it is in the Head or the Tail [of the Dragon] from the [exact] degree up to 12 degrees, which is the limit of an eclipse. The **sixth**, that it is in the last degrees of a sign, which are the terms of the malefics. The **seventh**, that it is cadent from the angles or in the Combust Way, which is the end of Libra and the beginning of Scorpio, and this is worse because it is from the sixth impediment of the Moon, and especially if it is the inception of marriage, or of anything else of those things concerning women, or of buying, or selling, or travel. The **eighth**, that it is in the twelfth[1] sign from its own domicile, i.e. in Gemini, with a malefic, or when it is in opposition to its own domicile or not aspecting it. The **ninth**, that the Moon is slower in its course, and this is what the wise men call "similar to the course of Saturn," when its course in a day is less than 12 degrees, and if it is one minute less, that is, when its course in one day is less than its mean course in one day, which is written in the table, i.e. in the book of courses. The **tenth**, which Mashâ'âllâh and the wise men of our own time mentioned, is when the Moon is void of course.

And fortify the Moon for its own power, and you should not put it in anyone's ASC because this is to be feared on account of what happens to its ruler in connection with bodily infirmities, unless the ruler of the ASC or a benefic is aspecting the degree of the ASC, because a planet that does not aspect its own house is like a man who is absent from his own home and cannot repel anything from it nor keep them out; but when a planet does aspect its own house, it is like the master of a house who guards it, for whoever is in the house must fear him, and whoever is outside [the house] fears to enter it.

---

[1] The text has 'seventh', but if it is correct as naming the sign Gemini, then the ordinal number should be 'twelfth'.

And if the ruler of the ASC is a malefic, make it aspect by trine or by sextile aspect, and beware lest you put the Moon in the angles, when it is impeded,[1] but you should put the benefics in the angles of the ASC—or put the Moon there when the two benefics are aspecting it from an angle and you have put it in the angles of the ASC.

And you should not make the Part of Fortune in all inititiatives or questions to fall away from an aspect to the Moon or from conjunction with it, and you should not aspect the ruler of the Part of Fortune; and you should not care whether the Part is cadent from the ASC, and whether it is the same Part, and whether the same Part aspects the ASC and the Moon; and take care to put the ruler of the ASC with the Part because this is more useful and of greater gain.

And you should never put the Moon in the second or the sixth or the eighth or the twelfth [house] from the Part because that is horrible; and always establish the ASC and the Moon in all initiatives in the signs of direct ascension[2] because that signifies lightness and progress; and you should not put them in the signs of crooked ascension because that signifies complication and delay. The ASC also and the fourth [house] from it signifies what will happen from that election. Therefore, look at the benefics and the malefics in the houses, and the strong and the weak, and speak about the beginning of the same thing and its end from [the standpoint of] strength and debility.

And Dorotheus said, When you see the Moon impeded, and a thing is at hand that should not be done, but it cannot be deferred, you should not put the Moon in the ascending part, but make it to fall from the ASC, and put a benefic in the ASC, and strengthen the ASC and its ruler.

---

[1] That is 'put in a bad position' or 'afflicted in some way'. The word 'impeded' is obsolescent in modern English, but it is a useful term in astrology.

[2] The signs Cancer through Sagittarius are called "straight" because the ascend in more than two hours, while the signs from Capricorn through Gemini are called "crooked" because the ascend in less than two hours. Modern astrologers sometimes call the former group "signs of slow ascension" and the latter "signs of fast ascension." Cf. **Dorotheus**, *Pentateuch*, v. 1.6-9, and v. 2 (Pingree's translation).

The Second Sign or the Second House with its Elections, and First about Receiving and Allocating Money.

When you want to elect an hour for receiving or allocating money, let the Moon be in Leo or in Pisces or in Scorpio or in Sagittarius or in Aquarius, and let it also be waning in light, and let both benefics be declining and aspecting the Moon or the ASC; and let Mercury be free from Mars, and let the Moon be with Jupiter or Mercury, and beware lest the Moon be impeded by one of the malefics, and let Mercury not be joined to them or in square aspect with them, and let the benefics not be cadent, because if the Moon is with Mars, it will fall into toil and anxiety and denial[1] and difficulty. And if it is impeded by Saturn, it will fall into prolongation and delay, and it will come out after an extension [of time] and weariness.

And if you want to conceal an allocation, so that no one can learn about it, let the Moon, when you receive it or ask for it, be under the Sun beams, going to the conjunction of the benefics after its separation from the Sun, for this is indeed lighter of it, and you will not make it public[2]; for if the Moon in its exit from combustion is going to the conjunction of Mars, this will be made public, and you will fall into the mouths of men and into the mouths of those whom you do not wish to know about this.

And beware lest the Moon be in the circle of signs without any latitude, i.e. in the Head or the Tail [of the Dragon], or in the Combust Way, because this is horrible; and Dorotheus said, "Do not receive an allocation and do not allocate anything to anyone when the Moon is in the first degree of Leo or Gemini or Sagittarius, or when these signs are ascending because this is hateful to one's own allocation. Know this!

---

[1] Reading *negatione* 'denial' (with **Bonatti**) rather than *negotiatione* 'business'.
[2] This seems to be corrupt. **Bonatti** has 'lighter for the one that is elected...and in no way will that thing be made public'.

An Election for Sharing Money or Some Kind of Work with Someone.

And if you want to share money or work with someone, it is better for this that the Moon be free from [any aspect with] the malefics and joined to the benefics, and let it be in common signs, so that their profit will be multiplied, or let the Moon be in Leo or in Taurus; and it is to be dreaded for them if the Moon is in inferior signs,[1] and the worst of them is Libra because it is in the Combust Way, and Aquarius is similarly horrendous.

And let the Moon be received by trine or sextile aspect, so that their separation may be good, because if it is received by square aspect or by opposition there will be words between them, that is a quarrel when they separate. The aspect of selection also signifies the goodness or the honesty of their separation and their fidelity and good will.

And beware of the presence of the malefics in the angles, because it is the ASC of the one of them initiating the partnership or of the one who was of greater age. But the seventh is the partner of the other; and the tenth signifies what will be between them and the multitude or scarcity of gain; but from the fourth is known the outcome of their association.

And beware lest the ruler of the ASC does not aspect the ASC, or that the ruler of the domicile of the Moon does not aspect the Moon, because, when the situation is thus, each one of them will deceive his associate, and their action will be made worse after they separate.

An Election for Investing Money in Order to Profit from it.

And if you want to invest money, seeking some gain from it, fortify the Moon and Mercury and the ruler of the House of Money

---

[1] Presumably, those signs in which it is peregrine.

and also the ruler of the degree[1] of the House of Trust,[2] and let the Moon be joined to Mercury, and make Mars to fall away[3] from both of them as much as you are able; also, fortify Mercury and keep it away from unfavorable positions.

But if Mercury is retrograde, fortify the Moon and the degree [of the House of Trust], the ruler of the House of Trust, and their rulers, and make Mercury to fall away from the light[4] of Mars, but you should not make it to fall away from an aspect to Venus or from the ruler of the eleventh.

And in connection with money and seeking gain, always let your trust be based upon Mercury and the Moon and the degree of the House of Trust and their rulers, and make Mars and its light to fall away from them.

An Election for Buying or Selling.

And if you want to choose an hour for buying, fortify the Part of Fortune, and let it be in a domicile of Jupiter, joined to the benefics, because this will be better for buying than for selling.

And when the Moon is in the signs of straight ascension, increased in light and in motion, and joined to the benefics, whatever he will buy in that hour, its previous owner will lose in [the transaction]; and [so] this is better for buying than for selling.

Let Mars also be falling away from the Moon and Mercury, because Mars impedites [the deal] in selling and buying, and it is the [planet] that signifies toil and contention.

Similarly too, the Tail [of the Dragon]; make it to fall away from the Moon properly; and it is below Mars. But if you want to

---

[1] Presumably, the degree of the cusp of the house (when the houses are divided unequally).
[2] I.e., the eleventh house.
[3] That is, to be out of orbs of conjunction or aspect.
[4] That is, out of orbs of either the conjunction or an aspect.

sell, put the Moon in its own exaltation or triplicity, separated from the benefics, and aspecting the malefics, but let it not be joined to them.

An Election for Alchemical Operations.

And if you want to undertake an alchemical operation, or some work that you want to repeat, let the following be done: let the Moon be in common signs, free from the malefics, and let the ASC be similar; therefore, fortify them. And if your work is in gold, strengthen the Sun, and fortify it in its beginning.

The Third Sign or the Third House and its Elections.

And whatever kind of election falls in the third house, a part of it is in the ninth house, and the other part is in the house of friends; then we may say this, if God is willing.[1]

The Fourth Sign or the Fourth House and Whatever Kind of Elections are in it, and First for Building a House.

When you want to elect [a time] to build a house, fortify the Moon and its ruler and the degree of the ASC and its ruler, also the Part of Fortune and Mercury; and make Mars to fall away from these significators that I have named to you; and you should never give them any part in anything to do with the building of houses; and if it cannot be done that they have no part, put Venus strong in its own domicile, and you shall not put for it [any] strength over Mars; and join [Mars] to it by trine or sextile aspect because Mars does not impede the matters of Venus because of the multitude of Venus's friendship for Mars.

And make Saturn to fall away from Venus as much as you are able because of its enmity with Mars and with the Moon when they

---

[1] After this we would expect some discussion of third house elections. Apparently the text is defective. **Bonatti** has three chapters here: (1) On short journeys; (2) On the reconciliation of brothers, etc.; and (3) On religious matters and religious persons.

aspect themselves in a friendly [aspect]; and let the Moon be increased in light and in motion and joined to Jupiter by a square aspect because that is better than by an opposition; and this signifies the beauty of the building and its completion.

And beware lest the Moon be with Saturn or with Cauda, or lest Saturn be in the ASC or in the fourth, because this signifies slowness and harshness in the work, and because it will not be erected; or, if it is erected and it is inhabited, its inhabitants will not cease to suffer fears in it and hardships and troubles from death, and the house will be torn down, and perhaps it will fall down.

And if Mars aspects it, and it is ascending towards the perigee in its orbit, then it may be feared that shortly a fire or a collapse may come upon it; and let the Moon then be increased in its light, because then it will be useful for its own ruler. And let the ruler of the Moon's domicile be aspecting it. Similarly, let the ruler of the ASC be aspecting the ASC, and let these be free from the malefics because if they are not in aspect, the lord [of the house] will not die in it.

An Election for Tearing Down a House.

And when you want to tear down a house, let this be when the Moon is descending in its circle, and when it is separated from the malefics and joined to the benefics, and let the benefic itself be oriental or ascending directly, or let the Moon be joined to the ruler of its own domicile by a friendly [aspect], i.e. by trine or by sextile aspect, so that its destruction is lighter; but in square aspect or in opposition its destruction will be heavier.

An Election for Buying Land or for Leasing it, so that You may Receive a Return from it.

And if you want to buy land and to join with someone in doing this, or if you want to have a piece of land, so that you may receive its return from someone, let Saturn be in its own exaltation or in its triplicity or in its own terms, and let Jupiter be in aspect with it from an angle or by a trine aspect; and make Mars to fall away from them; and let the Moon be in the beginning of a month, aspecting Saturn by a friendly [aspect], increased in motion, and in aspect with Jupiter, for these things signify the population of that piece of land and its return.

But if you cannot have an aspect of Jupiter with Saturn, [then] put Venus in place of Jupiter, and you will fortify the water signs because when you fortify them with the benefics, they will be better than the air signs; and let the Moon be in its own exaltation or in the MC, and the ruler of the ASC aspecting it; and let the Moon also and the ASC be free from the malefics and from debilities.

An Election for Diverting a River or for Digging a Well.

When you want to divert [water from] a river or dig a well or canals, let it be done when Saturn is oriental and the Moon is under the earth in the third or the fifth, free from the malefics, fortified and received; and beware lest there be one of the malefics in the MC, because then it must be feared that the well or the canal may be destroyed or that the river may dry up; and let Saturn be in the eleventh [house] from the ASC, and let the Moon be joined to a benefic in a fixed sign; the ASC in the circle is better than the benefics and Jupiter.

But if you cannot do this, [then] put the benefics in the MC, because with [them in] this [position] the river will be more lasting and the canal or the well more dependable.

An Election for Planting Trees.

And if you want to plant palms and fig-trees and other trees, let this be done with the Moon in a fixed sign and the ruler of its domicile aspecting it from water signs, and let the ASC be a fixed or a common sign, and the ruler of the ASC ascending and oriental, because if it is ascending but not oriental, they will grow more quickly. But they will cause delay in bearing fruit.

And if it is oriental and descending, they grow slowly, but they will bear fruit quickly; and if it is occidental and descending, it will delay both risings, viz. of the trees themselves and their fruit; and let the ruler of the ASC and the ruler of the Moon's domicile be aspecting them, and let them be free from the malefics and from combustion.

An Election for Sowing Seed.

And when you want to sow seed that you also want to cultivate, let the ASC be a common sign, and let its ruler be in a mobile sign aspecting the ruler of its domicile, and let it be free from the malefics, because if a malefic aspects it, the seed will be found to be damaged.

Therefore, let the Moon be increased in light and in motion, because if the Moon is under the Sun beams and is declining in light and in motion, the seed will not sprout, and nothing will come of it[1]; and if it is just as I have said to you, with the Moon increased in motion, that seed will rarely sprout in accordance with the amount that is sown.

The Fifth Sign or the Fifth House with its Elections, and First about Begetting a Male or Female Child.

When you want to elect an hour for intercourse, i.e. when you want to have intercourse with your wife, so that you can beget a male child, let the ASC and its ruler and the Moon and the ruler of the House of Children be in masculine signs or in a masculine quadrant of the circle in the hour of intercourse, and in that hour you should not put any planet but a masculine one in the ASC and in the sign [House] of Children.

And if you want it to be a female, let these significators be in feminine signs and in a feminine quadrant of the circle.

But if you cannot do this, and these significators are different, i.e. if some of them are in masculine signs and some in feminine

---
[1] Reading *nascetur* instead of *uascetur*.

signs, let the ruler of the hour be taken into account and those that are received by the Moon, [and let there be] more testimony in masculine signs and in a masculine quadrant if that is what you want, and the child will be in accordance with it.

An Election for Removing a Dead Fetus from the Womb.

And if the child is dead in the womb and you want to bring it out, let this be done when the Moon is declining in light and in motion and descending from the circle of signs toward the seventh sign, i.e., from the MC to the seventh, aspecting the benefics by trine or square aspect along with an aspect to Mars; and this will be more and better and more suitable if the Moon's sign and the ASC are feminine signs that are of direct ascension, and if they are not in the crooked signs.

An Election if you Want to Enroll a Son in a Course of Instruction or Send him to a Place in which he may be Taught some Trade.

And if you want to enroll a son in a course of instruction, or if you want to send him to a place in which he may be taught some trade or service, let your election be done like this. Let the Moon be aspecting Mercury and let them be free from the malefics, and let the ASC be Gemini or Virgo, and let Mercury be oriental ascending and not descending or retrograde, nor in its first station,[1] nor in its fall, nor impedited, and let the ruler of Mercury's domicile be [situated] similarly, and you should not put the Moon descending and declining in light, because it makes the training to be slow; and let the rulers of their domiciles be aspecting them.

The Sixth Sign or the Sixth House with its Elections, and First about Expelling Devils and Ghosts from any Place.

When there is a devil in any place or in any house or a disturbance caused by evil dwellers, or when some terrible thing has

---

[1] Static retrograde.

taken place that causes fear, or when some ghost is appearing, and you want to remove it from that place or from any man by means of a song or by means of any kind of investigation or scheme, beware lest the Moon or the ASC be in any of these signs—that is, in Leo or Cancer or Scorpio or Aquarius—but let the Moon be in other signs besides these, separated from the malefics, and joined to the benefics.

An Election for Taking Medicine or Applying a Plaster or Any Other Kind of Medication to Any Part of the Body.

When Remedies for the Belly Should be Administered.[1]

And when you want to elect [a time] for taking medicine for those who are seriously ill, i.e. those who are having convulsions, or for taking medicine for stomach pain, or for applying a plaster, let this be done when the ASC is Libra, or when the Moon is in it joined to the benefics; and you will not put any of the malefics in the angles of the Moon.

But if this cannot be done, let it be by trine or sextile aspect, without any opposition, and without the projection of two rays from a square, or from an entering under the Sun beams, because if it is thus, it will make pain and hindrance.

The Head.[2]

But if you want a cure for the head and whatever comes down from it, such as humors in the throat[3] or vomit, let the ASC be Aries, or let the Moon be in Aries or Taurus, and let the Moon be declining in light and joined to the benefics; and beware lest [the Moon] aspect the Sun by square or opposition, especially in Aries, on account of the heat of the Sun. And for medicines that are inserted into the nostrils, such as inhalants and things that are

---

[1] Here and below, I have inserted titles.
[2] A marginal heading in the printed text.
[3] Lit. 'a gargle', but probably referring to mucus descending from the nasal passages into the throat necessitating a 'clearing of the throat'.

sniffed,[1] etc., let this be done when the Moon is in Leo or Virgo, joined to the benefics, and let it not be joined to the malefics or to a retrograde planet or to one that is impeded.

[The Body.]

And if you want a cure for the body, namely for the hands or the feet, let the ASC be Capricorn or Pisces or Aquarius or let the Moon be in them joined to the benefics.

[Cures for Diseases.]

And if you want a cure for any long-standing diseases, let your election to do this be made when the Moon is in Taurus or its triplicity, and the best of these is Taurus because it is of sicknesses of the earth; and let the Moon be free from the malefics, and let the benefics be in the angles of the Moon from Taurus,[2] and it will be stronger and better to make a long-standing[3] sickness go away, and it will not come back to him who is suffering from it; and beware lest the Moon be joined to Saturn in particular, because it signifies a prolongation of the infirmity.

And Mâshâʾallâh said, Look in every cure that you want [to make] at the place of the infirmity in the body, which, if it were in the head or the throat or the chest, cure it when the Moon is in Aries or Taurus or Gemini, which is the upper part [of the body]; and if it is in the part of the belly or inside the chest,[4] cure it when the Moon is in Cancer, Leo, or Virgo.

But if the sickness is in the lower part, sc. in the anus or in the lower part of the body, cure it when the Moon is in Libra, Scorpio, or Sagittarius, and let the Moon be joined to the benefics, in-

---

[1] Lat. *sternutamenta*, lit. 'sneezes', but probably medicines to be sniffed up the nose.
[2] The "angles" of the Moon in Taurus would be the signs Taurus, Leo, Scorpio, and Aquarius.
[3] Reading *antiqua* in place of *intiqua*.
[4] Reading *pectore* 'chest' rather than *pectine* 'comb'.

creased in light and in motion. And if the sickness is from the knee and below, down to the foot, cure it when the Moon is in Capricorn or Aquarius or Pisces.

And it was also said that every pain that is from the head down to the foot[1] ought to be cured when the Moon is between the angle of the earth[2] and the MC, namely rising from the angle of the earth up to the MC through that part of the circle.

And if it is from the chest[3] into the lower part of the feet, you will cure it when the Moon is between the tenth and the angle of the earth, sc. when it is descending from the tenth to the angle of the earth, which is the lower part of the circle; and let the ASC be fortified, because if it is thus, it signifies that [the patient] will be healed and will make progress.

The Eyes.[4]

And if there is any vesicle[5] or any other thing in the eye, and it is necessary that it be touched by an iron [instrument] or scratched open, if there is also a covering over it; or if there is another place in the body where it is necessary that it be touched by an iron [instrument], such as cutting off a vein, etc., let this be done when the Moon is increased in light and in motion, except in blood-letting of those swollen with wind, because then you will put the Moon to be declining in light and motion, joined to the benefics; and let Jupiter be above the earth, in the ASC above the earth, or in the 11th or the 10th or the 9th; and beware of its conjunction with Mars when the Moon is increased in light and motion.

But if you cannot put Jupiter in those places, let it be aspecting the ASC; and beware lest the Moon and the ASC be in fixed signs

---

[1] Reading *pedem* rather than *pecten*.
[2] The IC.
[3] Again reading *pectore* rather than *pective*.
[4] Again I have added a title.
[5] Perhaps a *sty*, which is a swelling of a sebaceous gland on the eyelid.

or in Gemini configured with Mars, i.e., having any connection with Mars; and beware then of the rising of the Moon, that is when the Moon goes past the Sun by 12 degrees, [and] similarly in its being before the Sun, and don't let Mars be in the ASC when this happens, or Saturn either, unless it is the beginning of a month; and let the Moon be increased in light and motion, because if you cut off anything from the body or you perforate it, it may putrefy, and the removal or perforation will not help the patient's infirmity.

And you should not cut off a vein or pull out a tooth with the Moon in a mobile or common sign, unless the Moon is free from the malefics or unless there is a strong benefic with the Moon, or the Moon is joined to it by trine or sextile aspect.

Moreover, [for] those pains that are in the eyes and that happen to them, such as burning and whiteness and other infirmities that are cured with an iron [instrument], let this be done in the waxing of the Moon and the increasing of its motion, as I have said to you above this topic; and in particular, let the Moon be free from Mars in treating the eyes, but if it is in aspect, hold off from this.

But if Saturn is in aspect, and if the Moon is increased in its light and motion in the beginning of the month, it does not impede [the treatment]; but when it is remote from full Moon, make the Moon aspect Mars by trine aspect, and let it be joined to a benefic; and you should not fortify Mars in any treatment of the eyes, because the wise men have agreed that Mars is an impediment in [cases involving] the head, and they have also said that [for] everything that is treated with an iron [instrument], look at its power from the body, and you should not put the Moon or the ASC in this sign, and you should not touch anything with an iron [instrument] when the Moon is in a common sign or in a mobile sign.

An Election for Shaving the Head with Medicine.

When you want to shave the head with a depilatory,[1] i.e. with a certain kind of medicine to remove hair, etc., let this be done when the Moon is in feminine signs declining in light. But if you cannot do this, you should not put it in hairy signs, such as Aries and Leo and the rest of the bestial signs[2]; and let the ruler of the ASC be descending from the MC to the angle of earth.

An Election for Buying Slaves.

And when you want to make a purchase of slaves, beware lest the Moon be joined to the malefics or lest it be in a mobile sign, because that signifies that that slave will be unfaithful to his master, and he will not be steadfast in one situation, or he will be a runaway; [but] if the Moon is separated from the malefics and is joined to the benefics and it is in Libra, it will be useful, [even] besides [being in] Libra, which is more useful for this.[3]

Moreover, in fixed signs he will be patient and supporting and honored by his own master, except in Scorpio, because then he will be whispering and an accuser and weak in speech. In Leo he will be greedy, and he will incur pain in the belly on account of gluttony, and he will be a bandit. And let the Moon be in common signs because this will be praiseworthy, except in Pisces,[4] because [if it is there] he will think to himself about betrayal and infidelity to his masters, and he will disparage them where they are not [present]. And fear the conjunction of the Moon with the malefics, because when it is joined to the malefics, it signifies that the slave may be sold.

---

[1]Lat. *annora* from the Arabic *al-nûra* 'lime' or 'depilatory'. **Bonatti** explains it correctly as *psilatum* 'depilatory'.
[2]**Bonatti** lists them specifically: Taurus, the last part of Sagittarius, and Capricorn.
[3]This sentence is unclear, but perhaps I have caught the meaning.
[4]Pisces, being the 12th sign, is evidently likened to the 12th house, which is the house of secret enemies, etc.

An Election for Giving Freedom.

And when you want [to set] a slave free, beware of the presence of the Moon in the 12th sign, just as it is [stated] in the fifth book of Dorotheus.[1] And when you want to set a slave free, let this be done when the Moon is free from debilities, increased in light and motion, and joined to the benefics; and let the fortune be increased oriental because if it is increased occidental, he will gain an advantage, but [if the Moon is declining in light][2] he will begin to have pains, and he will not cease to decline in health, until finally he may die.

But in the increase of the Moon's light[3] and its motion, it will signify [his] finding wealth; and let the Sun and the sign of the MC be free from the malefics because if they[4] are impedited, the master will encounter some impediment according to the nature of the sign; and let the hour of the setting free be when the lights[5] are aspecting each other by trine or sextile aspect, so that there may be friendship and delight between the slave and his master, and he will gain an advantage from this.

For the square aspect is middling and the opposition aspect signifies that the slave is contending with his master; and whoever sets a slave free when the Moon is impedited, [the slave's] servitude will be better for him than his freedom; therefore, put the Moon in the fixed signs.

The Seventh Sign or the Seventh House with its Elections, and First for Marriage.

When you want [to make] an election for a marriage, beware lest the Moon be in the 12th, and beware lest it be in signs that are

---

[1]**Bonatti** also says this rule comes from **Dorotheus**, but it does not appear in **Dorotheus**, *Pentateuch*, v. 13 (ed. Pingree).
[2]This addition is from **Bonatti** and seems to be necessary.
[3]Here, the printed text adds *erit Saturnus in corpore* 'Saturn will be in the body', which I have omitted, since it appears to be an interpolation.
[4]Namely, the Sun and the MC.
[5]The Sun and the Moon.

not useful for this, which are Aries, Cancer, Libra, Capricorn, and Aquarius; and beware of those signs in which the malefics and Cauda [are placed].

When you want to strengthen the woman, let this be done when the Moon is joined to the benefics, and let it be in a mobile sign, and the best of all of them is the sign Libra; and beware in strengthening lest the Moon be in a fixed sign, and particularly in their union, i.e. when anyone goes in to his wife to have union with her, beware lest it be in a mobile sign or in a common sign, but let it be [done] when the Moon and the ASC are in a fixed sign, and Leo and Taurus are better than the others, but Scorpio and Aquarius are more useful for the woman; and the first half of Taurus is better than the end, but the first half of Gemini is worse, and the end of it is good. Aries also and Cancer are evil; but Leo is praiseworthy, except that one of them will not cease to destroy the wealth of his partner; and Virgo is useful for the woman who has already been married and is not a virgin; Libra is also evil; the beginning of Scorpio is useful, and the end is evil because it signifies that their association will not be prolonged; Sagittarius also is evil, and similarly the beginning half of Capricorn, and the end is good; Aquarius also is evil and similarly Pisces.

And there is no utility in the marriage when Venus is aspecting the malefics; and let this marriage be when Venus is in the domiciles of the benefics and in their terms joined to the ruler of Venus's domicile; but if the ruler of Venus's domicile is a malefic, let Venus be separated from it; and let Jupiter be elevated over Venus or let Venus be joined to it by a trine aspect; and let the Moon and Jupiter and Venus be aspecting each other in turn by trine or sextile aspect, and the better of these is the trine aspect, and especially in the water triplicity; and let the Moon be increased in light and motion, free from the malefics; and let Venus always be in its own exaltation or triplicity, or in its joy, or in conjunction with Jupiter or Mercury; and let Mercury be fortified and strong.

Similarly, fortify the Sun, just as we have said to you, because from the Sun and the ASC is known the character of the husband, and from Venus and the Moon and a feminine sign is known the character of the wife; therefore, beware of an aspect of the malefics to them by conjunction or square aspect or by opposition.

And if the woman has been married, let the Moon be in common signs, and let the election be made in accordance with what I have already said to you; and let the ASC in the hour of the marriage be one of the signs that I have already said to you or let the Moon be in them; and you should not put any of the malefics in the ASC nor let them make a bad aspect to it; and let one of the benefics be in the MC, and Dorotheus said that then a child will be bestowed on them in the same year in which they are married; but if the benefic is in the degree of the MC, the woman will become pregnant in their first union.

An Election for Going to War.

The knowledge of hours for going to war. You ought to put the ASC in one of the domiciles of the higher planets, of which the strongest is a domicile of Mars, when it is [also] in sextile or trine aspect to the ASC; and let the ruler of the ASC be in the ASC or in the eleventh, and beware lest it be in the fourth, sixth, seventh, and eighth or ninth, and lest it be combust or cadent, or joined to a cadent planet that does not receive it; and make the ruler of the ASC to be joined to the ruler of the seventh, or put it in the ASC or in the second with Mars. And if you want to conjoin them, make them to be conjoined in angles, so that they oppose each other and war will come about between them; and put against Mars a benefic having its degree in the ASC, so that it can prohibit Mars from the ASC.

And you should not go to war unless Mars is in a friendly aspect with the ruler of the ASC, or unless Mars itself is the ruler of the ASC and is strong in a good house and is not impeded nor combust and is in signs of direct ascension. And beware lest you put it [anywhere] except in *hays*[1] of the ASC, so that its assistance may be directed towards the one whom you are sending to war.

Also, fortify the Moon while you are sending soldiers to war because they will be freed by the order of God; also, fortify the second [house] and its ruler for the soldiers of the one who begins the war, and the eight and its ruler for the soldiers of the enemy; and you should not put the ruler of the eighth in the seventh, nor in the eighth, but put the ruler of the eighth in the second or in the eleventh; and put the Part of Fortune and its ruler in the ASC or in the eleventh; and do not put them in the eighth and the seventh.

And you should not put the ASC and its ruler [so that they are] impeded when you are beginning this thing; [and deal] similarly with the dignity of the twelfth [house] from the Moon because it is necessary in matters of war to fortify the stars of war, i.e. Mars and Mercury, also the Moon and the ruler of its domicile. Look, therefore, to fortifying these, and do not be neglectful in [any of] this, lest you forget [some of] them.

And know [this], because when you have wisely brought forth both armies to war, just as I have already said, that one [of their leaders] will achieve victory who was born at night and in whose nativity Mars has the part[2] because Mars is the lord of wars, and wars are entrusted to him; and perhaps they will be pacified or they will abandon war, i.e. when the house [that rules] their going forth to war is a good one.

---

[1] This term is from the Arabic *hayyiz* 'domain'. It is a refinement of what the Greek astrologers called *hairesis* 'sect'. A planet is in *hays* when it is in a sign of its own sex and is also 'in sect', i.e. above the ground by day and beneath it by night if it is a diurnal planet or above ground by night and below it by day if it is a nocturnal planet. Mars, being both male and nocturnal, is in *hays* if it is in a male sign and above ground by night and below ground by day. This is a position of power. Cf. **al-Bîrûnî**, *The Book of Instruction in the Elements of the Art of Astrology*, trans by R. Ramsay Wright (London: Luzac & Co., 1934), Sect. 496 (p. 308).

[2] Something seems to be missing here. Perhaps we should read 'the Part of Fortune' or 'the rulership of the Part of Fortune' or something else instead of simply 'the part'. **Bonatti** cites the Latin text exactly (while attributing it to **Haly**), so his exemplar had the same reading as the 1533 printed edition.

An Election for Buying or Mutually Accepting or Returning Instruments of War, or for Destroying any Place or any Instrument.

And when you want to buy arms and instruments of war, let this be [done] when Mars is in its own domicile or in its own exaltation or triplicity at the end of a month, because the wise men warn us that the Moon should not be with Mars at the beginning of a month, but [this position] is more useful at the end.

And if you want to destroy your own forts,[1] let the beginning [of the work] be [done] when Mars is in debility, not having any strength. And when you want to destroy any instrument of war, begin [work on] this when Mercury is impeded and without any strength. And when you want to destroy a land, begin when the Moon is in debility, not having any strength. And when you want to destroy the opposition of a war, let this be [done] when Mars is impeded and without strength. And when you want to destroy a place of idols and a place in which prayer is said [for them], let this be [done] when Venus is impeded and without strength.

The Eighth Sign or the Eighth House with its Elections.

When any man wants to arrange anything or to recommend it [to someone], let this not be begun when the ASC and the Moon's sign are mobile signs, because this signifies that the recommendation will be annulled; moreover, it will be recommended when the Moon is slow and increased in light, and when the Moon is not joined to a planet under the Sun beams, because this signifies the swiftness of death; and there is more craftiness in it when the Moon is with Mars or in its square or opposition, or when Mars is in the ASC, or when she aspects him by an inimical aspect, because this signifies that the recommendation will not be annulled, and he will die sick from the same sickness, and the recommendation will not be accomplished after his death.

---

[1] Presumably, to prevent their falling into the hands of the enemy.

And similarly, when Saturn is with the Moon in the ASC, the life of that man will be prolonged, and that recommendation will be accomplished after him, and it will not be annulled during his life nor after his death. And if Jupiter and Venus in similar fashion were rulers of that recommendation from [their relation with] the Moon and the ASC, it will bring his life to an end, and the recommendation will follow.

The Ninth Sign or the Ninth House with its Elections, and First for Travels.

Do not dismiss [the idea] of directing travels by using the nativity, sc. on the ascensions of every nativity, and its angles, and let the Moon be in its ASC, or in its MC. And fortify the ruler of the thing you are looking for, and fortify the ruler of the year, viz. of the sign of the profection, and the ruler of the ASC of the radix and of the year of the revolution.

But if you ignore what I have said, look for yourself for the one that will come to you from the ruler of the thing that is sought, where its house is [as reckoned] from the ruler of the ASC; after this, point out to him the hour [of the election] from his nativity or similarly from the horary chart, i.e. you should not put the ASC of the horary chart and its ruler cadent from the ASC of his departure.

And let the ASC of the departure also be the 10th from the ASC of the horary chart or the nativity if you are going to seek a kingdom. And if you are going to undertake a negotiation, [then let it be] in the 11th from the ASC of the horary chart.

Similarly, in every thing that you are going to look into, put the ASC sign for him, and let the Moon be in the angles or in the succedents of the angles. And if it is free from the malefics, let it be aspecting the ASC. But if it is impeded, make it cadent from the ASC, and let the ruler of the ASC and the ruler of the domicile of the Moon be in angles, and let the Moon aspect the ruler of her own domicile.

And take care not to put the Moon with the malefics or in aspect to the malefics by square aspect or by opposition, because the aspect of the malefics to the ASC is lighter than their aspect to the Moon in travel principally because the conjunctions with Mars in the beginning of the month signifies robbery or fire. And take care lest you put the Moon in the fourth,[1] but always put it in the fifth, because if it is fortified in that house, there will be less toil involved in his travel and it will be greatly advantageous for his affairs, and there will be more to his profit, and less too to the disturbance of his body, and lighter to his journey, and more to his preservation [and] that which is with him, and his profit.

Also, the presence of the Moon in the ASC is horrible, both in the beginning and in the end, because then the sickness of the traveler during his trip must be feared or else some serious pain in his body. But if [he is going] to a king, put the Moon joined to the Sun or the ruler of the MC by trine or sextile aspect; and let the Sun be in a good house, in the ASC, or in the 11th or in the 10th, because if it is [placed] so, he will find good from it.

And if it is in the 9th or in the 3rd or in the 5th, it signifies difficulty and little profit. similarly, the angle of the west[2] and the fourth signify little good and that with difficulty and delay. And if you are seeking [a meeting with] nobles or judges or officials of religious sects, i.e. bishops and other such persons, let there be a conjunction of the Moon with Jupiter in the angles or in a good house from the ASC.

But if it is [a case of] your going out to the leaders of military conflicts, let there be a connection of the Moon with Mars by trine or sextile aspect, and take care lest it be by conjunction or in the angles; and [rather] let it be in *hays* in the succedents of the angles.

---

[1] Reading ...*in quarto, sed semper pone*... rather than ...*in quarto semper, sed pone*... Cf. **Bonatti** ...*in quarto sed <si potueris eam sub terra> pone eam in quinto*...
[2] The seventh house.

And if it is your going out to those who are elderly or to commoners, let the connection be a friendly one with Saturn, and let Saturn be in the succedents of the angles.

But if your going out is to [meet or visit with] women, connect the Moon with Venus, and let it be in a masculine sign; and if you are able, let it be in the houses that I have already mentioned to you for partnership, etc.

And if your going out is to writers and merchants and learned men, let the [Moon's] connection be with Mercury, and take care lest Mercury at that time be under the Sun beams or retrograde, or lest malefics be aspecting it, because often when the star with which the Moon is connected, or a planet that that is in opposition to the ASC, or the ruler of the 7th, is slow or retrograde, or impeded, it signifies involvement or difficulty in these modes.

And if there is travel by water, let the Moon be in water signs, free from the malefics, and [likewise] the ASC, and let it not be [connected] with Saturn. And in the case of travel by water, beware of the connection of the Moon with Saturn from an angle, and beware of Saturn lest it be in a water sign, and beware lest there be a fixed [star] in the ASC of the departure, or with the Moon; but if this cannot be done, let the Moon is joined to a benefic or in aspect with it by trine or sextile aspect, or from an angle, so that it may remove the malignity of Saturn from [the possibility of] shipwreck or [some kind of] hindrance or from some severe storm.

Also, in traveling on the sea, you should not put the Lights in an impeded position, because if they are fortified and safe from the malefics and if they are fortified by the benefics, they signify safety and prosperity. But if they are impeded, that man will be dead or lost in his journey.

And you should not embark upon the sea when the Moon is at new Moon with Saturn[1] because that is horrible. But if you embark

---

[1] The printed text has ...*interlunio Saturn*i... but **Bonatti** omits *Saturni*.

upon the sea for some business purpose, fortify Mercury and particularly the Moon, and let it be aspecting Jupiter from Cancer or Pisces. For Scorpio is horrible for sea travel because it is a domicile of Mars and because of its enmity to those traveling by sea.

And beware of the terms of the malefics in sea travel, but in travel on the shore it is less of an impediment than it is in sea travel.[1] And if it is [a question about] traveling on land, let the Moon not be in water signs, and free from the malefics. And beware of an aspect from Mars in traveling on shore, just as I have warned you to beware of Saturn in sea travel. And beware lest traveling be done, in whatever manner, when the Moon is in Scorpio.

And know that the earth signs are safer for him who wishes to travel on land, and the water signs for him who wishes to travel on the sea. And Saturn is more of an impediment in [sea] travel, and even more so if it does not aspect Jupiter. And beware of traveling on land or sea when the Moon is in the last part of the sign Libra.[2] Know all this!

An Election for the Entrance of a Traveler into a Region or a City.

The fortification of the region for the entrance of a traveler. And know that that when you want to fortify the region into which you will enter, you should fortify the second [house] from the ASC when you are going to enter whatever region or city you want to enter. And when you have done this, you have already fortified the region. And you ought to fortify the ASC and its ruler, and the Moon, and the ruler of the second if you can.

Therefore, make it a benefic, and let it be above the earth in the ninth or in the tenth or the eleventh; and you should never put it under the earth, viz. in the fourth or the fifth or the sixth, because this

---

[1] But cf. **Bonatti**, who has ...*the terms of the malefics always in travel both on the sea and on the land.*
[2] Because this is the first part of the *Combust Way*.

is horrible in traveling and in everything that you want to do in that region. And if it is above the earth, whether it is a benefic or a malefic, try to put the ruler of the Moon with the ruler of the second above the earth; and you should not put them under the earth, because that is not praiseworthy, unless in case you are seeking in that region something that you want to hide so that it will not be seen until it is completed.

And let the Moon then be 12 or 15 degrees below the Sun; and beware of this—so that the Moon, until it has emerged from being under the Sun beams up to three degrees may be fortified, for this is better and more praiseworthy for everything that you want to keep in hiding.

And if you are going to seek a kingdom in that region, fortify the MC and its ruler, along with the [ruler of the][1] second [house] from the ASC and the Moon.

After this, in the case of travels, look at the location of the Moon in the signs in the manner that Dorotheus mentioned with regard to travel by water. because if it is in the first face of Aries, whether there are planets in aspect or not, it signifies the abundance of the thing. and if it is in Taurus, the impediment of Mars will be less for him. But if Saturn aspects it, he will impede him and will involve him in a shipwreck.

And in the second face of Gemini, it signifies delay [but] after that, safety. And in Cancer [it signifies] safety from all impediment. But in Leo, say that there will be impediment, and all the more if a malefic is in aspect. And in Virgo, say that there will be prosperity and delay and [some kind of] reversion.

And in Libra, when it has passed 10 degrees, you will not travel on land or on the sea. And in Scorpio, say that there will be sadness. And in Sagittarius, say that before the journey is completed, he will turn back. And in the beginning of Capricorn, [say that

---

[1] The phrase in brackets is added by **Bonatti**.

there will be] some little bit of good. And in Aquarius, say that there will be delay and safety. And in Pisces, say that there will be impediment and destruction; and if a malefic is in aspect, the harm will increase; but if a benefic is in aspect, the impediment will be ameliorated and the good will be strengthened. Know this!

The Tenth Sign or the Tenth House with its Elections, and First about Going with the King to a Region that he Rules.

When you want to set out with the king or a prince to a region that he already rules, let this [be done] when Jupiter is in the ASC or in the 9th, because this signifies that he who goes will find good and joy in that journey, and he will see that which is pleasing to him.

And beware lest you put Jupiter in the fourth, because that is horrible; and let the Moon testify to him from some angle and [also] Venus; and beware lest Saturn and Mars be in the ASC or in any of the angles, or Venus.[1] You should not put the Moon under the Sun beams, and beware lest this be done with the Moon or with the malefics, because there is no good in this; for if he travels, he will not return; and if he is sick, he will die; and if he goes out to war, he will be killed or defeated.

An Election for Elevation to a Kingdom.

And when you want to be elevated and moved into a kingdom, let this [be done] with Leo ascending; and let the Sun be in Taurus in the MC; and let the Moon be in the ASC joined to the benefics or to the ruler of the MC.

An Election for Putting the King on the Seat of Empire.

And when you want to place the king on the seat of his own empire, let the ASC be a fixed sign and similarly the fourth, and the ruler of the MC free from the malefics, and let the ruler of the ASC

---

[1] Either something is missing here or else 'or Venus' has been mistakenly repeated from the previous line of the text.

be received in a good house; and let the ruler of the 10th not make a bad aspect to the 11th; and let the Moon be making a friendly aspect to the ruler of her own domicile; and also let the ruler of the fourth sign be in aspect to the benefics.

But if you are unable to do what I have just said, let the Moon be received; and let the ruler of the fourth be in a strong house aspecting the benefics, but if you can't do that, [then] make it be falling away from the ASC and its aspect,[1] and put the benefics [where they are] aspecting the fourth sign and the MC.

An Election for Putting Someone in Charge of a Restoration.

And when you want to elect an hour for someone to be [put] in charge of a restoration, let the Moon be joined by a friendly aspect to Saturn at the beginning of a month; and let it be in a domicile of Saturn; and let benefics be aspecting him, because this signifies stability and that the action will be lasting; and let the MC be a fixed sign, so that this may be done [only] once.

An Election for Strengthening a Rulership.

And when you want to strengthen a rulership or a position of command, let the Moon be fortified in one of the domiciles of Mars, and let it be in friendly aspect to Mars, with the benefics joined to them at the end of a month.

And the strengthening of a position of command, which is beneath that of a kingdom, is worthier when the Moon is free from [any aspect of] the malefics and is not in their domiciles, nor in Cancer, unless the Moon be free in this [and joined to?] the ruler of war; and let this be in the domiciles of Mars; and Scorpio is better and more useful because of the strength of Mars and its stability in it.

---

[1] This apparently means simply 'let it be in one of the cadent houses with respect to the ASC', i.e. in the 3rd, 6th, 9th, or 12th.

An Election for being Inimical to a King.

And if you want to be inimical to a king, and if you yourself are the one who is inimical, let this be done when the Moon is increased in light; and let the Moon and the ASC be free from the malefics; and let the ruler of the ASC be in the best house from the ASC, direct, in some of its own dignities, and safe from the malefics, whether it is a benefic or a malefic; and let the ruler of the seventh be in a bad house from the ASC, not aspecting a benefic nor the lights.

An Election for Mollifying a King who is Angry with You.

If in fact he is angry with you or inimical to you, you should not appear before him except when the Moon is decreasing in light and the ASC and its ruler and the Moon are impeded; and let the ruler of the seventh be fortified in a good house from the ASC, so that it may be stronger and [more favorable] to your case.

The Eleventh Sign or the Eleventh house with its Elections, and First for Making Friendship.

When you want to make friendship with someone, let the Moon be free from the angles of the malefics,[1] and let the ruler of the 11th [house] be making a friendly aspect to the ASC; and you should make the Moon to be joined with a planet related to that which you are seeking, such as Venus for women, and Mercury for writers and universal circles,[2] according to what will come from it.

An Election for Seeking Something from Someone.

And when you want to seek something from another person, let the ruler of the ASC be making a friendly aspect to the ASC; and let the ASC be a fixed or a common sign; and let the ruler of the ASC be in it or in its triplicity or in square aspect, but beware of the

---

[1] That is, let the Moon not be in a sign that contains a malefic or that is the 4th, 7th, or 10th sign from it.

[2] What 'universal circles' means here is unclear.

opposition; and beware lest the Moon be joined to the malefics or lest she not be in aspect to the ruler of her domicile. For if the Moon does not aspect the ruler of her own domicile, the matter will not be completed; therefore, always seek after a thing when the Moon is increased in light and swift, and the ruler of the ASC is direct, and the Moon is joined to the benefics. But if the benefic is direct and fortified and the Moon is joined to benefics, it will be increased because she herself is increased.[1]

And beware lest Mercury be in a bad condition, because if it is impedited and it is received, it signifies insolence or sorrow and harshness and a second reversion of the request. Therefore, dismiss the badness, and put the Moon in connection with the planet which pertains to your case, such as the Sun for a king, and Mars for military commanders and warriors, [and] similarly with the rest of the rulers of the circles.

The Twelfth Sign or the Twelfth House with its Elections, and First for Buying Animals.

When you want to buy an animal, let this be done when the Moon is joined to the benefics, and when she is direct, oriental, and ascending; and beware of a connection with the malefics, because then the animal must be feared; but if it has been broken and already ridden, [then] buy it when the ASC is a common sign and the Moon is in a fixed sign, with the exception of Aquarius and Scorpio.

And let the [planet] to which it is joined be direct and ascending, so that the animal may increase in price and in size, because if it is retrograde and ascending, there will be a decrease in the size of the animal, but its price will be increased. And if it is direct and descending, its size will be increased, and the price will not be proper for it.

---

[1] Reading (114,1) ...*fuerit directa fortuna, [& Luna iuncta fortunis] augmentabitur...*

But if the animal is not broken, let the ASC be a common sign, and when the Moon is in a mobile sign, joined to a benefic. After this, do just as I already told you in the first chapter.

An Election for Going out to Hunt.

And if you want to go hunting, go out under a common sign, and let the ruler of the 7th [house] be declining and descending; and let it be in the succedents of the angles, because if it is cadent, it signifies that the game will escape after it has been captured; and let the Moon, in the general departure on the hunt, be separated from Mars, fortified, in the best house from the ASC.

And you should not go hunting when the Moon is at the end of a sign, nor when she is void of course, nor when she is in a mobile sign; and beware lest the ruler of her own domicile not aspect her, because if the ruler does aspect her, it will signify [attainment of] the [hunter's] wish and ease in doing it.

And put Mercury free from the malefics for hunting on the sea. But if you want [a time for] hunting in the mountains, let the Moon be in Aries or its triplicity. But if it is hunting for birds, let the Moon be in Gemini or its triplicity, and joined to Mercury; or let her be separated from that same Mercury, and let it be descending, because that is better.

And if you want to hunt on the sea, let this be done when the ASC is a common sign and when its ruler is in a water sign, and beware lest the ASC be a fire sign; and let the Moon be aspecting the ruler of her own domicile.

And know that the impediment of the Moon with Mars will be worse for hunting on the sea and less productive. Therefore, beware of the impediment [resulting] from Mars in hunting on the sea; and beware of the impediment of Saturn in hunting on the shores.

And know that when Venus and the Moon are in good positions

and Mars does not impede them in hunting on the sea, the catch will be doubled for the hunter, and it will be multiplied, and it will bestow the greatest profit on him, and the hunting will make him prosperous. Therefore, let the Moon be joined to Venus, and let Mercury be with them too; but if Mercury is impeded by Saturn, it will not produce this. And beware lest Mars be in a water sign, and lest the Moon be joined to it, or lest Venus be separated from Mars.

An Election for Taking Flight, or for Whatever you Wish to do Secretly.

And if you want to take flight or to perform some secret work, and [indeed for] everyone who wishes to flee or to be hidden, let this be done when the Moon is joined to the benefics and separated from the malefics; and let the Moon be joined to Saturn under the Sun beams; and let her be joined to the benefics at the time of her emergence from under the Sun beams. And the Lights, when they have risen above anything, will disclose it, and they will make it appear. Therefore, beware of their aspects [when they are] in a similar condition.

An Election for Finding a Fugitive.

And when you are looking for a fugitive, let this be done when the Moon is joined to the malefics or when she is emerging from under the Sun beams; and let that egress occur with a malefic in square aspect or in opposition or in conjunction; and you should not put the Moon and the planet receiving her disposition in square.

An Election for Writing a Letter.

When you want to write a letter, let this be done when the Moon is joined to Mercury, free from the malefics; and let Mercury be strong and fortified, not retrograde, nor impeded; and let it and the Moon be free from the malefics.

The End of Zahel's Treatise on Elections.

Book V

The Book of Times.

Know that the earth excites motion; therefore, the beginning of the motion that is made in the circle up to the end of the time in which the hour is chosen for a particular motion that is beginning until it is finished with a completion that is suitable or unsuitable to itself. Because if that sign is good or evil; and the universal motions are according to what I shall relate to you, if God is willing. Know that the change of figures and the destruction or conversion of motions in the universal circle, signifies what is stable in the time of good or evil. And the conversion or change of figures is the change of the planets from the east to the west and from the west to the east, also from the north to the south and vice versa and from that in latitude and longitude.

Moreover, the motion of the circle that moves from the east to the west is every day and night, i.e. of one revolution. But the explanation of these motions in longitude is that for every Planet that is separated from the Sun and distant from it by 180 degrees, that is when they pass over the body of the Sun, then they are oriental from that time until the completion of 360 degrees, after which they are occidental; and this motion that I have said to be occurring from the east to the west is not substantial.

And the rising of the Planets is also partly the motion of the circle that signifies swiftness. That is, as it is making its path from the ASC to the 10th, and the 7th and the 4th; and the occident of these; namely as is made a Planet between the 4th and the ASC, and what that opposes—that is, the path between the 10th and the 7th; and that place in the circle signifies slowness and putting off according to the sayings of the ancients.[1]

---

[1] This is the definition of orientality given by Ptolemy in *Tetrabiblos*, iii. 3.

But Mâshâ'allâh[1] is different from them, i.e., he disagrees with them about this. He makes the higher place of the circle, whichever begins, namely to be elevated of the circle, and it hastens to rise and to appear; and from the 4th back to the 10th, and this is called the higher part, from the beginning of the motion of the circle in rising. After this, which is between the 4th to the 10th; and back to the slow part, and the one descending to the beginning is called the part near to the beginning of the descension of the circle, and its inclination is one of the slowness of its appearance. And this is a truer opinion than the others according to testing.

Furthermore, the rising point is the degree of the ASC; the setting point is the degree of the 7th [cusp]; and the 10th point is the MC; but in fact the 4th point is the angle of earth.[2] The motion of latitude is the part rising to the north and descending to the north, or ascending to the south and descending to the south. Also, a change of the figures of the Planets is a conjunction of the Planet with the Sun up to the hour of its own rising, and from this to its own first station is a time; and from its own first station to the end of its retrogradation and the beginning of its second station.

And the beginning of its direct motion is a change of time up to its conjunction with the Sun is a time. And from the motion of the superior part of the circle back to the Sun in its arrival at the degree of the Planets and of the signs is a time. And from the motion of the superior circle, which is from the east to the west, and their change to the places of the Planets by body or by light is a time.

And from the direction of the degree of the ASC or of any of the Planets to any particular degree [is] a year, a month, and a day, or an hour; or back to any one of the Planets to its rays and them, and to the degrees of the signs and to the Parts is a time; and

---

[1] Mâshâ'allâh (d.c. 815), the famous Arabian astrologer, gives a different definition of orientality.
[2] The IMC.

Mâshâ'âllah has already said this, and Abuabalgharat,[1] i.e. The Tailor, have [both] said not to direct the degree in longitude and latitude forward or backward. Therefore, it is from the motions of the universal circle that the times that are made from these motions are known.

The Principal Knowledge of the Times.

Know that the signs of the light planets and the signs of the weightier ones will be in the times of the light ones for days and months; and the signs of the weightier planets will be the years; and generally, if the significator is in the fixed signs, it will signify years; in the common signs it will signify months; and in the mobile signs, it will signify days. Also, a swift place from the ASC signifies the swiftness of the time, i.e. in a superior part; and a slow place of the circle, which is in the descending part, signifies slowness of the time. Also, the ASC and the 10th signify swiftness of the time; and the 7th signifies months, and it is slow; but the angle of earth is slow, and it signifies years. And when the Planet that is the significator of the time is in common signs, it doubles the time.

Finding the Significator of the Time.

Know that you do not ever take the time from just one planet even though it is strong, unless it is the significator of the same thing, or unless it has some part in the signification of the thing on account of the lights, which have a natural signification of the times which the others do not have. You will accept no time from the ruler of the ASC, or from the ruler of the thing, or from the receiver of their disposition, or from a Planet to which any one of them is joined, if they do not aspect themselves, either by their lights or by the receiver of the disposition of the Moon by the one that was the stronger and more dignified in the question; and the

---

[1] The badly garbled name, Abû ʿAlî al-Khayyât, more usually called in Latin Albohali, a 9th century Arabian astrologer (*al-khayyât* means 'the tailor' in Arabic). See his book, *The Judgments of Nativities*, translated into English by James H. Holden (Tempe, Az.: A.F.A., Inc., 1988).

one that wins out the most in that, establish it as the significator of the time, which if the likeness should deceive you, that is if you should not be able to elect a significator because there are many that you could place in signification, put one of the Lights for comparison with the significator—namely, the significator that aspects the ASC—and that one is found to be the significator of the time—the one that is more dignified than the Lights. But if you do take one of the Lights, take the one that aspects the ASC.

And know that the universal times in questions are made in five ways; of which, **The first** is that you should look at the degrees that are between the dispositor and the receiver by light or by body; and you shall put a year or a month or a day or an hour for each degree according to the quantity of the swiftness or the slowness of its partner.

The 2nd way is that you should look at when the informer will come to the one to whom the informing will come by body or by degree and minute; namely, when a light Planet will come to a heavy Planet by body.

The 3rd way is that you should look at how many degrees of longitude are between the one that joins and the one to which it is joined, and put them as days.

The 4th way is that you should count from the ASC to the place of the receiver of the disposition, or from the place of the receiver of the disposition to the ASC, at a sign for each month.

The 5th way is that you should look at how many are the minor years of the significator of time, and the time will be according to the quantity of months or years. These are the five ways.

And the time from the Moon is one month or two months in number and thing. And when it rules the disposition, 25 months. And the time of Venus and Mercury in thing and in number: the thing in Venus is 10 months and 8; and Mercury 5 months or 3 also months. Moreover, when she rules the disposition in Mercury, if she is above him, the cutting-off will signify 20 months; and in Venus, 8 years; and in the Sun, 1 year and 19 months; and in Mars, 10 [years] and 8 months, or 15 years; and Jupiter, 12 months or 12 years; and Saturn, 30 months or 30 years.

The knowledge of the recognition of the cause of time of the 5 modes in swiftness and slowness, i.e. which one of these is slower or swifter, and their slowness and swiftness, is according to what I am saying.

Know that a Planet that is giving disposition or is a receiver, when each is in the oriental part from the ASC, they ought to be like planets that are inherently oriental and swifter in course; therefore, put every degree that was between them as an hour of the day. And if there are two planets between the MC and the 7th, they signify months, according to the quantity of degrees that was between them; and [also] if both planets were between the 7th and the 4th. And the ASC signifies years and months when two planets agree between themselves in similar agreement [of distance] from the ASC. But if it was different, and there was a planet inherently oriental and swift, and occidental from the ASC and slow, it signifies moderation.

Therefore, establish the time thus. If it was the time from the degrees that were between them, put one month for each degree that I have said. Therefore, combine the times according to what I have explained to you about the part of the ASC and about the substance of the planet according to the sign in which it is, and the figure of the Planet. After that, appraise the measure of slowness and swiftness, and you will not err, if God is willing.

And know that here these are radices; and perhaps there will be a single time without these radices, because the Moon when she is in the place of the thing quesited, or when she aspects the place of the thing; and when the Moon is joined to the ruler of the ASC or when she aspects the ruler of the thing, because the place of the thing signifies the essence of the thing, i.e. on the same day. Because if it is a question, it is swift and it signifies days; and the days of slowness with the degrees belonging to the Planets, then you should not put the time in months until it crosses the orb of the Moon, which will perhaps be separated from one of the two Planets. It will enter in some way the ruler of the ASC and the ruler of the thing, or it will enter the ASC or the place of the thing; and the attainment of the thing will be at the same hour and on the same day.

And perhaps the hour from the degree of the significator to the degree of the ASC is also by one degree; or perhaps the time will be from the entrance of the Sun into the degree of the ASC or the place of the thing, or the place of the ruler of the thing; and the thing will be moved, and it will come with its own perfection through its work in those three, it will enter 4; and thereore they have made it similar to the spirit.

After that, look at the times of universal things, i.e. the 12 signs, according to that which I shall tell you, if God is willing.

The Life of a Man in the Ascendant.

When you have been asked about the life of a man, from the sayings of the ancients, look at the ASC in the hour of the question and its ruler, and the ruler of the New Moon or of the Full Moon that was before the question, and take the stronger of these significators of the things, which is more in testimony, because the time will be [from] the *alimbutar*,[1] which is the significator of the hour; moreover, direct this just as you direct the hyleg to the conjunction of the malefics and their aspects, giving to each degree through its ascensions one year.

But if the benefics do not project their own rays to that terminus, the Querent will die in that same year. But the stronger of the

---

[1] A corruption of the Arabic *al-jânbaḫtâr* from a Persian word meaning 'the giver or distributor of life'. It is something like the *alcochoden*, but it is sometimes restricted to ruling only a portion of life.

rays and the more killing is the one that is in square or opposition aspect, because it may perhaps kill when the benefics also project their own rays on that terminus. And if that *alimbutar* is received, or if it rules the hyleg, then if the one that rules is oriental in an angle, it will give its own major years; and if it is in the signs succeeding the angles, it will give its median years. But if it is cadent from the angles, it will signify its own minor years.

And Mâshâ'allâh said look at the ruler of the ASC and the Moon, if it is joined to malefics or to one of them, or if it is combust, take all the degrees that are between it and the malefics or the combustion and use them. Because if the ruler of the ASC is in a fixed sign, take a year for each degree; and if it is in a common sign, a month for each degree. But if it is in a mobile sign, you will take a day for each degree; and that which will be from the ruler of the ASC will be the number of life; that that which goes out from between the Moon and the malefics or the combustion will be the number of his suffering.

The House of Substance.

But the time of the question about substance, namely when he will find or he will get it. When you want to know, look at the number of degrees that are between both significators. And know that the time of it will be according to the number of those degrees in days or months or years in accordance with the amount of its swiftness or slowness. Look also when the ruler of the House of Substance enters its own house or the ASC, or when it will be joined to benefics, and then it will be.

The Times of the 3rd and 4th Houses are in the other Chapters below.

The House of Children.

When you have been asked about a pregnant woman, when will she give birth? Look at how many degrees there are between the ruler of the House of Children and an angle in signs and degrees, and put a month for each sign and a day for each degree; and in that same hour she will give birth, if God is willing.

The House of Illness.

Moreover, in the time of the health of an ill person, you should make the Moon to fall in her own course until she aspects her own place. Because if she is impeded when going to a degree of the malefics or to the degree of the House of Death, direct her to a degree of the malefics; then if the Moon is joined to the malefics before she comes to the degree of the House of Death, death will be feared for him before the Moon comes to the House of Death. Which if it is the malefic Saturn, according to the degrees that are between them, there will be months; and between it and Mars, a day or a month according to the amount of strength and the swiftness and slowness of the place; and you should not neglect the degree of the combustion.

The 7th Sign for the Times or Hours of War from the Sayings of Theophilus.

When you want to know the time or the hour in which a war ought to be waged, look at the hour that joins the Moon to the Sun; if it is opposed, the war will hasten. But if there were 20 degrees between the Moon and the conjunction, it will delay the war. And if the Moon was with some one of the planets in her own domicile, the war will be quicker, and especially if the Sun is in aspect. And if there is a dignity in the 12th of the Moon, in the ASC, or in the 10th, or with the Sun at the same time with the ruler of its own house, or with a Planet that is already rising, this signifies the swiftness of the war.

And he also said that when you want to know the hour of the battle and when it will be ended, look at the Lights; if they aspect each other by trine aspect, and they aspect the ASC, it will make the war soon. But if they aspect each other by square aspect, it will not occur quickly, and the battle will last; and it will be changed from its own place into the proper place of the recipient; and if they aspect each other by opposition, the battle will not be completed quickly.

And when the Part of Fortune is in the MC, the war will be made in those quadrants. And if the Sun in the hour of the question is in square aspect to the ASC, or if it aspects it by opposition, that which I have said to you will be the effect of the war in those oppositions, and from triplicities, and in triplicities. And this occurs when Jupiter and the Moon are aspecting the ASC in the manner in which the Sun was aspecting in the hour of the question.

And look also at the Part of Faith and the Planet that is with Mars or in its own square aspect; if it is fortified, it will be done quickly. If they are malefics, the war will not be halted, and it will be made more serious, and it will be prolonged. Moreover, if the benefics are configured with the ruler of the Part, it will not make delays, but one of the armies is conquered according to what you will see from the place of fortune partly.

And Hermes said, Look at the end of the breaking off of the war and of all the things to the Lights and to the ASC, and the last of their degrees to the benefics and the malefics; then you will know the times of the things and the breaking off of them in years and months or days. And he also said to look at the slowness of victory and its swiftness at the place of Saturn and Jupiter. If it is swifter in course, there will be a quick victory for the one in whose clime of those Mars is either oriental or occidental. But if it is slow in course, the victory will be slow, and the things of it will be prolonged; and it will not be easily broken off.

And if the significator of them is direct after Mars from Saturn and Jupiter, there will be a striking of it on the land that will be between both of them. But if it is in a common sign, there will be war in the whole land, and it will be many times; and if it is in a fixed sign, the war will be moderate and light; but in inferior signs, it will be heavy, and things of the world will be destroyed; and things will be built up just as they were before. And this opinion is from the sayings of the secrets of victories by Hermes.

Remarks on the 8th House were already given in the House of Life.

The 9th Sign on Travels from the Sayings of the Ancients.

When you want to know the hour of the return of a traveler to the near vicinity and to his own home, look at the ruler of the ASC and the Moon at the beginning of his travel. If you see malefics in square aspect or in opposition to them, that travel will be prolonged, and his return will be delayed; and if they are joined to benefics, it signifies the quickness of his return. If they were joined to benefics after the malefics, he will find evil in his travel. After that one has gone out and returned to his own vicinity, he therefore will experience with the benefics and the malefics a recurrence and a delay through him.

And if at the beginning of the journey you find the Moon in the ASC, his delay in that same journey will be prolonged, and especially if the Moon is in a domicile of Saturn or in its terms. And when you find the Sun at the beginning of a journey not impeded, then when it comes to its own square aspect or its own opposition or when it returns to its own place in which it was, it signifies a return for him who is traveling; and if it is not impeded in the same sign, that is when you direct the Sun into its own place in the radix and into the trine aspect of its place or into the square.

And if the Sun is impeded in the radix, his delay will be according to the exit from that malefic and the arrival of some one of the benefics to the place of that same malefic. Similarly, know the strength of those surpasses the enemy Planets; and say according to it in its circle of years and months, that Saturn when it is the ruler of the ASC, or when that same Saturn is in the House of Travel, the journey will be prolonged according to the quantity of the orb of Saturn. Similarly, if you find Saturn and Jupiter in an angle, and they are retrograde, the delay will be prolonged. But the rest of the Planets are lighter in their own motion than those Planets.

The Return of a Traveler.

Mâshâ'allâh said, In the hour that the travel begins, look at the Moon and the ruler of the hour, which of them is stronger; and if the stronger one is between the 10th and the 4th, take what is between it and the ASC. Moreover, if the ruler of the hour is a malefic that is going out in the degrees, they will be hours. And if the Moon is stronger, take the thirteenth that is going out from it, and what results will be the hours.

And if you do not take the signification from that; and the ruler of the ASC is in opposition of what I have said, and the Moon is the ruler of the hour, take what is between it and the ASC, and what will result will be days, and then he will come. Also, if the ruler of the ASC is in the MC or returning to the ASC, and if the Moon has more testimony and is strong, and if the ruler[1] of the ASC does not aspect the ASC nor the ruler of its own house, his return will be according to that. and if the ruler of the house of the Moon is in an evil house, and the Moon is in a good house from the ASC, and she does not aspect the ruler of her own house, [the time will be] according to what is between her and her own house in degrees; it will be the time of his return, if God is willing.

A Letter and Rumors.

When you have been asked about a letter or about rumors, when it will come, look at Mercury; if it was in the ASC or in the 12th wanting to enter into the ASC, or if the Moon was joined to the ruler of the ASC, or the ruler of the ASC was joined to the ruler of the domicile of the Moon, or the ruler of the domicile of the Moon was joined to it, or Mercury's ruler was ascending, the letter will come; and if it was not in the ASC, at the hour of its entrance into the ASC, it will come.

---

[1] Reading *dominus* 'ruler' rather than *domus* 'house'.

And if the Moon is joined to Mercury, in the hour of their conjunction, or the hour of the entrance of the Moon into the ASC, the letter will come. And if the Moon is separating from Mercury [and moving] into the degree of the ASC and the ruler of the ASC, it will be the time when the deliverer will arrive at the place of the recipient.

And if you are asked about a letter, when was it written, look at the degrees that are between the Moon and the Planet from which she is separated, and say that that same letter was written according to the number of those degrees. Similarly, look at how many degrees you find between the Moon and the Planet to which she is joined; and according to [the number of] those will be the time of arrival of the letter.

The 10th Sign in Connection with a King from the Sayings of Mâshâ'allâh.

Look at the hour of the departure of that king, of whom you have known the entrance or the time in which he received the kingdom, the testament, or its question; and from these, you will know the quantity of his stay in the work and what will be brought forth to him in it. And from the hour of the confirmation of his election is known his honor and victory. Moreover, whenever the Planet that signified the kingdom is combust in any one of the angles of the ASC, that king will be removed.

And if the Planet is not in the ASC, look at the Royal House; if you find there a Planet having testimony in itself, then when a malefic is retrograde there or the ruler of the descendant of the Royal House, and it then aspects the Planet from which you had the signification, the king will be removed. But if you do find a Planet in any one of those places, look at the one to which the Sun is joined.

If it is joined to Saturn and Mars, then when it comes to the degree of the one to which it is joined in an angle, the king will be removed. And if it is joined to Jupiter, his return will be when Saturn comes to the place of the Sun, or to its opposition, or to its square aspect, or when it retrogrades into the same place. Similarly, if it is joined to Venus, and if the Sun is remote, just as I have said, and it is [in] 1, 2, or 9 having testimony; then if Saturn or Mars is retrograde in that same place or in its opposition, the king will be removed.

And do by night in the case of the Moon just as you have done by day in the case of the Sun; but you will not look at the time from the times of the Planets, but look to see whether the Moon is joined to the Sun, or if she was joined to it or separated from it, as if she were joined to a malefic; then there will be the time of that thing from the Sun, just as I said to you previously about its time. And if the Moon was not separated from the Sun, and was not joined to him, look in this case at that which I have said to you, because he will not complete a year in his kingdom.

And know that when the ruler of the ASC and the ruler of the 10th are combust in angles, it signifies that the removal will already have taken place, and if the ruler of the exaltation of the Sun is impedited, his year will not be completed. Therefore, look in its hour before the year at the combustion of the ruler of the ASC and the ruler of the 10th and the arrival of the malefics in their own places; and if the Moon is not the ruler of the exaltation, look at her conjunction with the Planets, because if she is conjoined to Mercury and is in a fixed or common sign, it will signify 20 months; and if she is in a mobile sign, 10 months.

Therefore, look at the planet to which she is joined, but if it is impedited by the malefics or by combustion, look at the quantity of degrees that is between it and the strength of the malefic or combust [Planet]; and however much there is, that will be the time. But if indeed the Moon is received, and the ruler of his exaltation is received, his year will be completed. Look then at the second year, and revolve the years for him; and know that the ruler of his place, if it is free from malefics, the one who enters will remain in his own kingdom more than a year.

But if the Moon is received, look at the application of a malefic to the degree of the Planet that receives the Moon, or the minor years of the ruler of the ASC, and also mix with them the revolution of the year and its application. And if it is the ASC of the entering, or its beginning from the domiciles of the higher Planets; but if there is a retrograde malefic in the MC, or in that same MC the ruler is either combust [or] the ruler of the ASC is in angles, it signifies the destruction of the kingdom; and if there is a retrograde malefic in the ASC, or if the ruler of the ASC is combust in the 10th, he will perish in his own kingdom; and if it is retrograde in the 2nd, it signifies the destruction of his wealth; and in the 10th, it signifies the destruction of his work; and in the 11th, the restoration of the destruction; and in the 10th, the destruction of his soldiers.

Look at the Planets that are ruling. If they are in the angles and have strength, they give months according to the number of their own minor years, or years when it is Saturn in the ASC or the 10th; and if it will have testimony in those things; and if it was received by the testimony of the Planets, it will signify 30 years. When they are completed, revolve the year. Moreover, if the ruler of the ASC is combust, or the significator is in the angles, the thing will be destroyed. But if Saturn is strengthened much and is aided by the ruler of the year, he will not cease to be fixed [in place] until his return is destroyed, and if his testimony and his strength is removed. But if such testimony is not that of Saturn, revolve for him in 30 months, because the time is weak.

After that, look at the destruction of the year from impediment and combustion; but if the one that rules the disposition is retrograde at the end of any angle, that thing will be destroyed repeatedly and unexpectedly. And if it is Jupiter in the ASC or in the 10th, and it has testimony, it will signify 12 years. If it is Mars in the ASC, and the Moon in the 4th, or in opposition, or conversely, unless benefics are in aspect, it signifies a mortal impediment. And if it is Venus in the ASC or in the 10th, and it has testimony, you will note 10 months for it; and when it is combust in an angle, his kingdom will recede; but if Venus is received and free from the malefics, it signifies 8 years; and revolve the years.

But if a malefic opposes in the revolution of the 8th year, and the malefic is retrograde in its place, it will signify the destruction of the kingdom and its weakness and the entrance of some impediment for him.

And if Mercury is in the ASC or in the 10th, and if it has testimony there and is strong and received, it signifies 20 months; and you should revolve the year; but if it is weak and does not have testimony, reckon 5 months for it; also, if it is combust in an angle, and if a malefic or the light of a malefic should come up to the ruler of the 10th in an angle, he will depart.

And if Mars is in the ASC or in the 10th, look to see whether a combustion will occur for it in less than 20 months; because if it is combust in an angle, the king himself will depart; and revolve that year.

And if the Moon is his ruler and she is received and is free from the malefics and she has testimony, it signifies 25 years; and if she does not have testimony, 25 months. Or, look at the Planet to which she commits her disposition; if is combust and in an angle, he will depart; but if it is not combust in an angle and it is received, that same Planet will signify years and months.

And look about this topic just as I have indicated to you in the case of the Sun when its degree comes to the malefics. But if the Sun is the ruler, and it receives the testimony of a star, it signifies a year; if the Sun is strong and of great testimony, it signifies 19 years if the malefic that impedes the ruler of the disposition or the ruler of the ASC or the 10th does not impede its disposition in the first year; but if it is impeded, it will give 29 months.

And know that when a Planet signifies the number of any disposition, [and] afterwards it is impeded before that in an angle; revolve that year for it; if it is safe from combustion and from impediment, the thing will be saved until the number is completed, but there will enter upon it damage and diminution.

After that, make the projection of the rays in the revolution of the years of the king just as you do in nativities, namely for each year, a sign; and you will also look at the ruler of that sign and what is the nature of its house, and what is its own essence; and what is in the signs of the benefics or malefics, and where is the place in the signs of the ruler of the sign; and what is its own essence and place, and if it is received or not, and if it is impedited or not; also, what is its own situation with respect to the ruler of the 10th and with respect to the ASC of the year.

And let the revolution of your years [be made] by equal hours, so that the ASC of the revolution is not destroyed. After that, look at the ruler of the ASC and the ruler of the 10th; if they are conjoined, it signifies the stability of the kingdom; and if the Moon is free from the malefics and gives[1] her disposition to a Planet in an angle, it signifies his stability. Similarly, in the case of the Sun and the ruler of the ASC; and if the ruler of the 10th is combust in the revolution, or is retrograde, or if there is a malefic in the 10th, it signifies the departure of the king.

Similarly, the ruler of the ASC; and when it is the ruler of the 10th of the revolution [and is] oriental, it will signify the renovation of the kingdom and its stability; but if it is occidental, it will signify its destruction and its end. And when the ruler of the 10th of the revolution is joined to the ruler of the 4th, it will signify the departure of the king; but if the ruler of the 4th is joined to it, it will signify the stability of the king.

And the departure of the king will be more [certain] when the Sun has departed from the angles and the Moon is in the 6th or the 12th from the ASC of the year; and it is helped in this matter by the application of the year to the sign in which a benefic or a malefic

---
[1]The Latin text has *pulsaverit* 'strikes', but this is a mistranslation from the Arabic; it should have been *donaverit* 'gives'.

was; and mix with the Light of the Time of the revolution and the Planet that was in the 10th, and the ruler of the ASC and the ruler of the 10th in turn; and investigate their testimony according to what I have explained to you; and then you will find the time, and you will not make a mistake in the deposition of the king, if God wills.

The Treatise of Zahel on the Signification of the Times for Judgments is completed.

Appendix I.

[A Ninth House Question]

A Question about a vision or a Dream.

The knowledge of this is that you should consider the ninth house; then, if you a find a star in it, put that one for the significator of the goodness or the malice of the vision; however, if you don't find a star in it, then consider the tenth [house]; and if you find a star in it, then that one is the significator of the goodness of the vision. But if you do not find a star in it, then consider the ASC; and if you do not find a star in it, then consider the 7th; and if there is not a star in it, then consider the 4th; but if you do not find a star in it, then consider the 3rd; but if you have not found any star in that house, then the vision is not sane, and it is worthlessness of a vain form; and he does not see it or he has forgotten it; and if you find any one of the stars in the aforesaid houses, then you may know it [to be the significator].

But if it is Saturn or Cauda, then he will see a terrible thing of those things that bring in fear; thereafter, look at which house the star is ruler of, then that which makes him to be afraid and terrifies him is of the nature of the same house of that planet; for if it is the ruler of the 12th house, then that which terrifies him is enemies or things of their sort; and say similarly in [the case of] the rest of the houses.

And if Jupiter is the significator of the vision, then he sees kings and persons in charge or higher-ups and greater [persons] of all those that are similar to the nature of Jupiter.

Moreover, if it is Mars, then he sees hunting or a duel or a legal confrontation or a dispute or a fight or flesh or blood or arms or a weapon or those things that are similar to the nature of Mars.

And if it is Venus, then he sees clothing and pieces of cloth and a good beloved thing or something aromatic and delightful or pearls or women or girls or sodomitic boys and other things that agree with the nature of Venus.

And if it is Mercury, then he sees something aromatic and mixtures or some persons speaking or *denarii*[1] or images or voices or buying some things and selling and exchanging, and those things that are similar to the nature of Mercury.

And if it is the Sun, then he sees that he was flying between heaven and earth or he sees a light or fire or a king and those things that are similar to the nature of the Sun. And if it is the Moon, then he sees a woman or the sea or *verulas* or a river.

And if it is Cauda, then he sees darkness and dust and whispering and murmuring. And if it is Caput, then he sees greenness and something giving off an odor and gold and similar things. And if the sign, in which the significator is, is feminine and the star signifies something fearful, then he sees a high, elevated place or a high cliff overlooking rocks, or it is as if he falls from a height or is being raised up against a place and being overthrown or a stormy wind.

And if the star that signifies fear is in an earth sign, then he is like one stoned or besieged or who has fallen into a pit, or is in a dark place, and, having been in a tight place, he has nevertheless found an exit. And if it is in a fire sign, then he sees hanging or burning or flame or fire or smokiness or blackness. And if it is in a water sign, then he sees submersion or a flood or reflux or the sea or experimentation.

Then look [to see] with which star the ruler of the ASC and the significator of the vision is conjoined; for if both of them or [even] one is with a benefic, then there will not come any harm to him from what he sees; and if it is conjoined with a malefic, then harm will come to him from that vision according to the kind of house of the conjunction.

---

[1] Coins.

For if it is the ruler of his property,[2] harm will come to him in connection with his property. And if it is the ruler of the seventh, harm comes to him in connection with women. And if it is the ruler of the fifth, then in children; and it is done similarly in the rest of the houses. And similarly, if the house is appropriate, then look at the kind of house connected with the significator, and similarly with its houses, and judge the assistance from the kind of its house.

---

[2] The Latin has *dominus census*, which I take to mean 'ruler of his property'.

Index of Persons

Abraham Ibn Ezra, *astrologer* xi,21n.1,32n.1-2,88n.1

Albohazen Haly (See ͨAlî ibn abî al-Rijâl.)

ͨAlî ibn abî al-Rijâl, *astrologer* xvn.1,100n.1

Bonatti, Guido, *astrologer* xii,xiii,xv,xx,12n.1,21n.1,32n.1-2, 37n.2-3,39n.2,53n.1,68n.1,73n.1,84n.1,88n.1,89n.1-4,111, 149n.1,151n.1,153n.3,157n.1-2,160n.1,169n.1,110n.1-2, 173n.2,176n.1,177n.1,178n.1,179n.1

Cantera, Francisco, *editor* xiii n.1

Carmody, Francis J., *bibliographer* xi n.2

Coley, Henry, *astrologer* xx n.3,xiii,39n.2

Dodge, Bayard, *translator* xi n.1

Dorotheus of Sidon, *astrologer* xiv,154,156,157,170,172,179

Harris, B., *publisher* xiii n.3

Haly (See ͨAlî ibn abî al-Rijâl.)

Haly Abenragel (See ͨAlî ibn abî al-Rijâl.)

al-Hasan ibn Sahl, *Vizier* xi

Hephaestio of Thebes, *astrologer* xiv

Levy, Raphael, translator xiii n.1

Lilly, William, *astrologer* xiii n.3,xx

Locatellus, Bonatus, *publisher* xii n.1,xix

al-Mahdî, Caliph xiv

al-Maʾm n, Caliph xi,88n.1

Mâshâʾallâh, *astrologer* xv,xvii,14n.1,49,166,188,193,197,198

al-Nadîm, Muḥammad ibn Isḥaq, *bibliographer* xi n.1

Partridge & Blunden, *publishers* xiii n.2

Pingree, David, *scholar* xiv n.1-2

Ratdolt, Erhard, *publisher* xvi n.1, xii n.3

Sahl ibn Bishr, *astrologer passim*

Santos, Demetrio, *astrologer* xii n.2
Stegemann, Viktor, *scholar* xx
Teubner, B. G., *publisher* xiv n.1
Theophilus of Edessa, *astrologer* xiv
Tunis, Prince of xv n.1
Varâhamihira, *astrologer* 88n.1
Zael (See Sahl ibn Bishr.)
Zahel (See Sahl ibn Bishr.)

Bibliography

Abû ʿAlî al-Khayyat
The Judgments of Nativities.
trans. from the Latin by James H. Holden
Tempe, Az.: A.F.A., Inc., 1988.

al-Bîrûnî
The Book of Instruction in the Elements
of the Art of Astrology.
trans. by R. Ramsay Wright
London: Luzac & Co., 1934.

Bonatti, Guido
Liber astronomicus.
Augsburg: Erhard Ratdolt, 1491.

Carmody, Francis J.
Arabic Astronomical and Astrological
Sciences in Latin Tanslation.
Berkeley and Los Angeles: California University Press, 1956.

Catalogus Codicum Astrologorum Graecoru,
(various editors)
Brussels: (Various Publishers), 1898-1953. 12 vols.

Dorotheus of Sidon
Carmen Astrologicum.
ed. and trans. from the Arabic by David Pingree
Leipzig: B. G. Teubner, 1976.

Hephaestio of ThebesApotelesmatica.
ed. by David Pingree
Leipzig: B. G. Teubner, 1973-1974. 2 vols.

Holden, James Herschel
A History of Horoscopic Astrology,
Tempe, Az.: A.F.A., Inc., 1996. 1st ed.
Tempe, Az.: A.F.A., Inc., 2006. 2nd ed. rev.

Ibn Ezra, Abraham ben Meîr
The Beginning of Wisdom.
trans. from the Hebrew by Raphael Levy
Baltimore: The Johns Hopkins Press, 1939.

Lilly, William
Christian Astrology Modestly Treated of
in three Books.
London: John Partridge and Humphrey Blunden, 1647.
Exeter: Regulus Publishing Co., 1985. facs. repr. of 1647

A Guide for Astrologers.
[actually by Henry Coley]
London: B. Harris, 1676
Tempe, Az.: A.F.A., Inc., 2005. repr.

Mâshâ'allâh
The Reception of the Planets
and other tracts
trans. from the Latin by James Herschel Holden
Tempe, Az.: A.F.A., Inc, 2008.

al-Nadîm
The Fihrist of al-Nadîm.
ed. & trans. by Bayard Dodge
New York: Columbia University Press, 1970. 2 vols.

Paul of Alexandria
Introduction to Astrology.
trans. from the Greek by James Herschel Holden
Tempe, Az.: A.F.A., Inc., 2008.

Quadripartitum Ptolemaei, et al.
[an omnibus edition of astrological authors
including Sahl ibn Bishr]
Venice: Bonatus Locatellus, 1493/1494.

al-Rijâl, ʿAlî ibn abî (Haly Abenragel)
Praeclarissimus liber completus
in judiciis astrorun.
[The Very Famous Complete Book
on the Judgments of the Stars]
Venice: Erhard Ratdolt, 1485.

Santos, Demetrio, translator
Textos astrológicos Zahel-Hermes-Bethen-Almanzor.
Spain: Teorema, 1996.

Stegemann, Viktor
Dorotheos von Sidon und das sogennante
Introductorium des Sahl ibn Bishr.
[Dorotheus Sidonius and the so-called Introduction
of Sahl ibn Bishr]
Prague: Archiv Orientální, 1942.

Theophilus of Edessa
A Book on Elections.
[in Greek, not yet edited.]
Baghdad: The Author, 8th century

www.ingramcontent.com/pod-product-compliance
Ingram Content Group UK Ltd.
Pitfield, Milton Keynes, MK11 3LW, UK
UKHW041422180426
11947UKWH00007B/241